UNDERSTANDING PHILOSOPHY

TOM REGAN

North Carolina State University

DICKENSON PUBLISHING COMPANY

Encino, California, and Belmont, California

ISBN-0-8221-0122-X
Library of Congress Catalog Card Number: 73-88123
Printed in the United States of America

TO MY PARENTS

Acknowledgements

Many people help to make a book possible. This book is no exception. I have profited from the critical suggestions of the following persons, each of whom read the whole or part of my work: Monroe C. Beardsley, Donald R. Burrill, Hal Levin, J. Thomas Johnson, Charles L. Reid, Donald VanDeVeer, and Brian Williams.

Less specific, but no less real, are my debts to my past teachers at the University of Virginia. These gentlemen can, I think, take responsibility for what I do understand about philosophy, and claim innocence for what I do not. Each in his own way has helped me make progress in a discipline that never has come easy to me. And for this I am grateful.

I am also grateful to Mrs. Ruth Boone and Mrs. Winnie Bolton for help in the material preparation of this book. Each has had to deal with my less than expert typing and the mysteries of my handwriting. And each has done so in unflagging good spirit.

To many of my former students, of course, I owe a special debt. I have learned much from them. In particular, they have helped me understand the seriousness with which philosophy must be taken, even in that most unlikely of places—the classroom! But they have never let me forget that even philosophy has a place for humor in it.

Finally, my wife, Nancy, has assisted me in those intangible ways that love and companionship make possible, and for this I am more than grateful.

Contents

Introduction

The discipline called philosophy is not the easiest thing to understand. It is even harder to practice. Part of the reason why it is difficult to understand is because philosophers too often assume their readers already know something about their discipline, thus making the study of philosophy even more difficult than it should be.

To help remedy this, the first half of this book tries to clearly state some important ideas philosophers regularly assume their readers understand. The second half tries to show how these ideas can illuminate three philosophical problems: the problems of God's existence, human freedom, and life after death. It is my judgment that a firm grasp of the ideas covered in the first half will make it easier for you to understand philosophy, and I believe the manner in which this understanding can be gained is illustrated by the discussions in the second half. Needless to say, I very much hope that these judgments of mine are correct.

One thing this book does not do is present ideas or techniques that can make you think carefully and patiently. But then, *no* book can do this. The person himself must freely decide to do this. And the decision must be made and remade until thinking carefully and patiently becomes part of his character. Now, to think this way is hard. And though we all applaud "thinking for ourselves," most of us find the challenge to think carefully and patiently surprisingly difficult. Well, it is hard to meet this challenge, and that, in part, is why it is hard to practice the discipline called philosophy. For whatever else philosophy is, it challenges us, not simply to think, but to do so with care and patience.

When we think about what is involved in this challenge, we see that philosophy demands what most students admire—a willingness to be open-minded, to follow the truth wherever it leads, to get rid of prejudice whenever one finds it. You would think, then, that large numbers of students would be drawn to it. Yet just the reverse is true: most who take the first course in philosophy do so because it is required, and few take a course beyond the introductory level.

Why this disparity? The answer here is quite complex. It involves considerations about our customary approach to education; and it involves a recognition of the fact that philosophy is not a marketable skill, while many students are career orientated. To get a full explanation here would be very helpful. It also would be very difficult.

One partial explanation we might overlook, and one that relates to the challenge of philosophy itself, deserves mention here. This is the popular student belief that truth is a matter of individual opinion, that what is true is relative or subjective. Why do so many people, especially young people, accept this idea? Once again, this is a difficult question, and I do not pretend to have the complete answer. But part of it seems to lie in the reaction many young people have to the apparently highhanded way their elders operate, especially in the area of individual morality, where older people seem to be so insecure about what is valuable or the right way to live that they seem to want everyone else to believe and act as they do. For the young, it is their elders who are most clearly prejudiced, because it is they who cannot tolerate a difference of opinion or life-style; and it is their elders who are so "set in their ways," as we say, that they are either unwilling or unable to become aware of their prejudices or to think them through critically. To proclaim, in the face of these clear prejudices, that "truth is a matter of individual opinion" seems to be the most tolerant and least prejudicial of things to say.

Yet none of this, however natural it may appear, can alter the fact of what this subjective account of truth very often is—namely, a prejudice, and one whose effects are especially lethal because it masks as just the reverse. A prejudice is any belief a person forms without due consideration or examination of the facts. It is a premature opinion, though not necessarily a *false* one, since an opinion formed on inadequate grounds sometimes turns out to be true. What is at stake, then, when the prejudicial character of a belief is in question, is not whether the belief is true or not; it is whether the person who accepts it has fulfilled the appropriate conditions for the making of a rational judgment of its truth. And it is in this sense that the subjective account of truth just mentioned very often deserves the name, "prejudice." For the decision to accept this belief very often is made on inadequate grounds. And the effects of this prejudice are lethal, indeed, especially when it runs headlong into the challenge of philosophy. For philosophy, we have said, requires that we be open-minded, willing to follow the truth, and committed to removing all prejudice from our thinking. If, however, we think we are *already* open-minded, and the like, how will we react to philosophy's challenge? Probably we will think it has little to offer. And how could it, if we think we already possess what it has to offer us?

How often students react to philosophy in this way, for this reason, it is, of course, impossible to say. My guess is, however, that it happens far more often than we might like to think. And that's a great pity, not only because it works against philosophy's making a contribution to such a person's life, but also because the belief in question might very well be true. The Greek philosopher Protagoras stated that "man is the measure of all things," a view that implies that truth is just a matter of individual opinion. But this belief is not self-evidently true or false—which implies that claims concerning its truth or falsity should be supported by an argument of one kind or another. And, of course, these supporting arguments might be good or bad, enlightened or unenlightened. But how are we to determine which they are? We cannot say, before examining them, that this determination, too, is "all a matter of opinion," without begging the very question at issue—namely: *Is it true* that truth is all a matter of individual opinion? Thus, if we are prepared seriously to examine this question, and not close our minds to the point and rigors of a careful examination, we must ask whether there can be an acceptable basis for evaluating arguments as good and bad. And we must do this, then, without prejudging the outcome of our investigation by saying that "your basis is true for you, and mine is true for me." For *that* attitude works against taking any step in the direction of thinking. *That* attitude is a prejudice of the worst kind: it is prejudicial to thinking itself.

Even to begin to practice philosophy, therefore, requires that we first take stock of our real prejudices. Otherwise, we shall not "follow truth" very far. Now, to take stock of our real prejudices is a difficult challenge, for a prejudice always carries with it a certain amount of security, and its investigation always entails a certain amount of anxiety. More difficult is the attempt to meet the challenge to think about our prejudices carefully and patiently. Most of us would rather get our thinking over with quickly, and so it is natural to construct defenses against having to think about them in this way. This is how I understand the view that "truth is a matter of individual opinion," when it has the status of a prejudice. Fundamentally, it is a defense against having to do hard thinking. And the irony is that the people who voice this prejudice most strongly also celebrate the value of "thinking" and repudiate the false comfort prejudice affords.

Clearly, nothing that I say in this book, and nothing that is said in any other book, can force such a person to become aware of his prejudices or to think them through carefully. As mentioned earlier, the decision to undertake this examination must come freely from the person himself. Thus, while what I have to say in this book may help you understand philosophy, it cannot in any way compel you to practice it. For to attempt to do this is to attempt to think through your prejudices carefully and patiently.

If we bear in mind, however, that what is at stake is the reasonableness of our most fundamental beliefs; and if we are mindful of the fact that how we live is influenced by what we believe, then we can realize that, fundamentally, what is at stake in philosophy is the reasonableness of our whole way of life. And this is an issue that deserves our most careful and most patient thought—doesn't it?

PART *I* UNDERSTANDING PHILOSOPHICAL ARGUMENTS

1 What Is Philosophy?

The word *philosophy* has two meanings. Sometimes we use it to refer to a person's general beliefs about and attitudes toward life, his "philosophy of life" or, borrowing from the German, his *Weltanschauung,* which literally means his *world-view*. But the word philosophy also is used to refer to an academic subject or discipline. Philosophy is taught in college, usually in a department of philosophy, just as, say, biology and psychology are taught as disciplines. Let us begin by reflecting on these two meanings of the word.

PHILOSOPHY AS "WORLD-VIEW" AND AS A DISCIPLINE

Every person has a world-view, general beliefs about and attitudes toward life, even if he has never articulated them or examined them critically. Even the much-maligned cracker-barrel philosopher has title to the name "philosopher" because of his seemingly inexhaustible interest in recommending attitudes toward life. Fortunately for us all, this interest sometimes finds a more stylistic form, and yet it is in this same sense of "philosophy" that many of the best poets and novelists are said to be "philosophical." Through their work they make their beliefs and attitudes known, and often help shape ours.

A person's total world-view is often divided into various "philosophies" —political, moral, economic, religious, and so on. One's political philosophy, for instance, consists of his beliefs about and attitudes toward, not life in general, but such things as the proper role of government and the place of the individual within the state. Again, a person's moral philosophy consists of his beliefs about and attitudes toward, not life in general, but those more specific matters that pertain to what are his obligations and what things are valuable. And a similar account could be given of a person's economic philosophy, legal philosophy, religious philosophy, and so on. But to speak of, say, a person's political philosophy does not mean he has had the opportunity to examine his beliefs and attitudes. It is merely to attribute such beliefs and attitudes to him.

As a subject or discipline, on the other hand, philosophy, like other academic subjects, has its origins in the past, its periods of innovation and stagnation, its geniuses and frauds. In a word, it has a history. It also has more or less clearly defined purposes, interests, and methods. Yet to *define* the subject called philosophy is very difficult. Even philosophers themselves do not agree on what, precisely, philosophy is. In fact, one of the problems of philosophy *is* what philosophy is. Why do philosophers disagree? Before we try to explain, let us note that philosophers are not unique in this. Historians, for example, have disagreed over what history is, and psychologists and sociologists still are not of one voice on what is the nature and function of their disciplines. So, while it is difficult to find a definition of philosophy acceptable to all philosophers, it is equally difficult to find a definition of many other disciplines that would satisfy all their practitioners.

TWO CONCEPTIONS OF THE DISCIPLINE:
THE TRADITIONAL VERSUS THE POSITIVIST

There are many competing conceptions of philosophy, but for the moment we will sketch only two. What we will call the *traditional* conception is accepted by those we will call traditional philosophers and rejected by those who are nontraditional. Of course, two nontraditional philosophers might have different conceptions of what philosophy is (they agree only in rejecting the traditional conception). Thus, as a contrast with the traditional, we will pick *one* kind of nontraditional conception—namely, what is known as the *positivistic* conception. Once we have sketched these two conceptions we will see why it is so hard to find a definition of philosophy acceptable to all philosophers. Then we will offer a provisional definition of our own.

THE TRADITIONAL CONCEPTION

The history of philosophy is largely the history of man's effort to develop a systematic, complete *Weltanschauung*. Such a world-view would include ideas about all of life's concerns—art, law, science, morality, economics, politics, and so on—and would embrace and organize these ideas in a systematic way. As civilization has changed and man's knowledge has grown, each new generation of thinkers has had to explore the merits of different *Weltanschauungen* (world-views). They have reopened questions not only about the nature of art, science, religion, and the like, but also of the very nature of reality itself, of human nature, and of our capacity to comprehend this reality and ourselves. This is the traditional conception of philosophy, then: to view philosophy as the search for the true or most enlightened *Weltanschauung*. This conception of philosophy has been accepted by perhaps most of the philosophers of the past and is still shared by many today.

Obviously, to construct and defend such a total world-view is an overwhelming undertaking, and the greatness of a traditional philosopher often is a result of the breadth of his vision rather than its exactness. It is the sheer magnitude of the task the traditional philosopher sets before himself which often most excites and impresses us, and it is in this respect that the completed *Weltanschauung* of a great philosopher is to the history of reflective thought what the great cathedral paintings of the past are to the history of art: both have a magnitude of grand dimensions.

Actually, these dimensions can be better appreciated if we understand some of the types of questions the traditional philosopher takes upon himself to ask and answer. Clarifying these types of questions gives rise to what are known as the *branches of philosophy*. These branches are not exhaustive, and often the same question will come up in more than one branch. Again, however, this is not peculiar to philosophy: it seems to be shared by all academic disciplines. No discipline has hard and fast internal divisions.

There are five branches of traditional philosophy, and they are concerned, roughly speaking, with what is reality (*metaphysics*), what is knowledge (*epistemology*), what is beauty (*aesthetics*), what is good (*ethics*), and what is correct reasoning (*logic*). We will describe them in more detail below.

METAPHYSICS

In this branch the philosopher is concerned with determining what is *real* or what *exists*. Examples of metaphysical questions are: Does God exist? Does man have a soul? Is there life after death? Does man have free will? Do the properties of things, such as their color and shape, exist independently of the things of which they are properties? Is everything that is real in space and time? Are space and time real? Is everything real material? Is everything real spiritual? Do abstract entities, such as numbers, exist?

It is much easier to give examples of metaphysical questions than to say, precisely, what makes a question metaphysical. Certainly it is possible to inquire about the existence of something without engaging in metaphysics. Asking whether the Loch Ness monster or the Abominable Snowman exist is not practicing metaphysics. Why not? Because the answers can be tested *empirically*—that is, by making relevant observations by means of our senses. Once we understand the question, we know what observations would count as confirming that there is a monster in Loch Ness, and what observations would count as disconfirming this. Such questions are said to be *empirically* decidable, a concept we will clarify further in Chapter 3. Metaphysical questions, on the other hand, do not appear to be empirically decidable: No amount of sensory observation appears to be adequate to decide what is the correct answer to a metaphysical question. Rather, then, than say that metaphysics asks what is real, we should add that the questions it poses about reality seem not to be empirically decidable.

EPISTEMOLOGY

This branch is concerned with the nature and limits of human knowledge. Examples of epistemological questions: What, precisely, are we aware of? Are we aware of *things* such as tables and chairs or instead of *ideas* or *images* (of tables and chairs), which it is our habit to assume are faithful copies of the things they represent? Does all our knowledge of reality come from what we experience through our five senses? Or can we know some things about reality without relying on our senses? On what basis, if any, can we know that a conscious being or other mind exists? How can we know that a world outside our own consciousness continues to exist when we are not aware of it? Indeed, just what kind of claim are we making when we claim to *know* anything?

Epistemological questions, as these examples suggest, often challenge us to rethink certain of our assumptions—for example, our assumption that we know there is a world outside our consciousness or that we know there are other human minds. But a glance at these questions suggests that the concepts in them—"same person," "the past," "other minds," and so on—need to be clarified before potential answers can be gauged intelligently. In fact, this need for conceptual clarification is not peculiar to epistemological questions; all interesting philosophical questions stand in need of preliminary elucidation. Now, since what this elucidation attempts to determine is what we must know in order to operate with the concepts in question, whether they are difficult ones like "identity" or "causality" or simple ones like "chair" and "red," the philosophical elucidation of any concept is itself part of the division of philosophy called epistemology.

AESTHETICS

This term refers to the philosophical investigation of art and art criticism; it also examines many of our evaluative appraisals of nature—for example, the idea that a sunset can be beautiful. The philosopher doing aesthetics does not engage in art or art criticism but tries to understand them. Examples of aesthetic questions: What is art? What is art criticism? Are works of art good in proportion to how they influence people to behave well? Are there any objective criteria for evaluating the beauty of natural objects such as meadows and sunsets? What makes a work of art or natural object beautiful or a work of art great? Is beauty in the eye of the beholder? Is beauty or greatness anything at all?

Some philosophers assume that aesthetics can exist as a distinct branch of philosophy only if there is a uniquely identifiable "aesthetic experience." The exact nature of this experience, and even if there is one, is, like the other questions just mentioned, a matter of controversy. Incidentally, it is worth noting here how the questions of one branch of philosophy naturally spill over into the others. To inquire seriously into art, for example, leads us naturally to inquire into its relation to morality.

ETHICS

This branch of philosophy, also known as moral philosophy, is concerned with value in general and moral value in particular. Examples of ethical questions: What kinds of values are there? What makes something valuable? What things are valuable? What, if any, are the principles by which we can determine our obligations? What are our obligations, if any? Should art serve morality or morality serve art? Can the social and behavioral sciences discover what is valuable or obligatory? Is it possible to have a morality without religion?

The great philosopher Socrates (470–399 B.C.) first turned to philosophy in hopes of finding answers to ethical questions. This is an important fact, not only about Socrates, but about traditional philosophers in general. For one of the things the traditional philosopher thinks philosophy can provide is knowledge of how we ought to live. What Socrates discovered in his pursuit of this knowledge also is important—namely, that in order to answer ethical questions, one must answer other kinds of philosophical questions as well. Still, Socrates never lost sight of the initial motive for his commitment to philosophy, nor, it seems, have other traditional philosophers.

LOGIC

This branch is concerned with the properties of good and bad reasoning. Examples of the logician's questions: Are all uses of reasoning the same?

What makes an argument good or bad? What is the connection between the truth of what is believed and the logic of arguments based on this truth? What, if any, are the principles underlying our concept of good reasoning? Are these principles, if they exist, necessarily true or merely accepted as true by most people? Are there different kinds of logic?

The need for asking logical questions should be fairly apparent. We ask questions, both philosophical and otherwise, because we find something puzzling. Not surprisingly, those things we find *most* puzzling often call forth different answers—from different people at the same time and from the same person at different times—and these conflicting answers often are backed by arguments. In choosing between these conflicting answers, then, we must evaluate the arguments given to support them. But we cannot evaluate the logic of a particular argument without knowing the standards for evaluating the logic of *all* arguments of that type. Thus, it is to logic we must turn for the means of evaluating an argument.

This description of the branches of philosophy should help us understand traditional philosophy, for we can see that when the traditional philosopher seeks to find and defend the true *Weltanschauung,* he commits himself to an inquiry into all these five branches of philosophy and thus tries to answer all the questions we listed—and many more. And when we pause to consider that, in doing so, he sets himself the task of weaving a systematic, coherent tapestry of ideas rather than recording a series of unrelated, loosely sewn impressions, we can see why only a few men have been engaged in such an undertaking and why, of those engaged, only very few have made lasting contributions.

THE POSITIVIST CONCEPTION

That few people have sought the traditional philosopher's goal may be testimony to these philosophers' special wisdom—or their special brand of foolishness. Positivists would seem to believe the latter. For they believe that the traditional philosopher sets out to do what he cannot do because it is impossible. And it is impossible, the positivist believes, because it demands of the traditional philosopher knowledge of certain things he cannot even pretend to have.

Traditional and positivist philosophers principally disagree about metaphysics, aesthetics, and ethics. The positivist denies two very important assumptions of the traditional philosopher. First, he believes that all intelligent questions about what is real must be empirically decidable— we must be able to answer them by appealing to what we do or could observe by our senses. Thus, since a metaphysical question, by its very nature, seems to deal with what is *not* empirically decidable, it follows, the positivist thinks, that the traditional philosopher cannot even begin to carry on his investigations in metaphysics. In other words, traditional metaphysics, the positivist thinks, is not a genuine category of human knowledge.

Second, the positivist denies the traditional philosopher's assumption that he can tell mankind what is beautiful, good, and how men ought to live. What the positivist denies here is not the traditional philosopher's right to hold certain things valuable or to accept one or another life-style, but rather that he is in a position to have discovered important truths about values or life. And the reason, the positivist says, is that there is no moral or aesthetic knowledge to be had in the first place, by a philosopher or anybody else. Thus, according to the positivist, to the extent that any philosopher presumes to be imparting knowledge, it cannot be knowledge of what is good, beautiful, or obligatory.

Now, if either or both of these beliefs of the positivist are true, then traditional philosophy is dealt a decisive blow. If you accept the traditional philosopher's conception of his subject, then you are committed to asking and answering questions in metaphysics, aesthetics, and ethics. Besides clarifying such concepts as "real" and "unreal," "good" and "bad," "beautiful" and "ugly," the traditional philosopher also seeks *knowledge* about what things are (metaphysically speaking) real, what things are good, and what makes things beautiful. Thus, if knowledge of the kind he seeks is found to be impossible, then, because such knowledge is necessary for his goal of a complete *Weltanschauung,* his goal becomes impossible as well.

The scope of philosophy, given the positivist's conception, is considerably less than the scope of the discipline, given the traditional philosopher's conception. Still, much remains open to philosophical investigation, even given the positivist's view. All those metaphysical, aesthetic, and ethical concepts that the traditional philosopher believes need to be clarified—such as reality, goodness, beauty—still call for attention. Of course, the positivist does not think he can tell us what things are metaphysically real, good, or beautiful, but that does not prevent him from trying to clarify these concepts if he wants to. And the positivist can consistently urge a close scrutiny of these concepts while at the same time denouncing metaphysics, aesthetics, and ethics. For the positivist does not denounce *epistemology,* the question of what is knowledge. And, since, as noted, part of epistemological inquiry consists in elucidating concepts, it is not contradictory to denounce, say, traditional metaphysics yet simultaneously urge that the concepts of "reality" and "unreality" be clarified.

Epistemological inquiry of this kind is often called *meta-philosophy,* so that, for example, *meta-ethics* designates the inquiry into the meaning of such terms as 'good' and 'right', while the term *ethics* is reserved for the inquiry into what things are good and what actions are right. Each of the various branches of philosophy lends itself to "meta" or epistemological inquiry of this type. As such, each contains within it something of potential interest to the positivist.

Much else that is of interest to the traditional philosopher remains as a proper object of study, given the positivist's conception. The concepts that play a role in such concerns as politics and religion or science and mathematics stand in need of careful elucidation. Moreover, the assumptions of thinkers in these areas need to be stated, examined for possible relationships, and appraised as justified or not. Thus, we have the philosophy of politics, the philosophy of religion, and so on. But, again, the positivist believes that philosophical investigation into these activities should be exclusively epistemological or "meta." The philosopher himself, says the positivist, can discover no scientific or political truth; he can provide no knowledge of reality or of aesthetic or ethical values. His inquiry is or should be exclusively conceptual.

Why doesn't the positivist denounce epistemology? Because he commits himself to certain quite definite views about the limits of human knowledge. He denies there is metaphysical knowledge of reality or knowledge of what is beautiful or good, and such denials have no weight if he cannot muster some arguments that purport to show why such knowledge is impossible. That is, these arguments must make a case for why knowledge is limited by certain factors and why these factors make metaphysical, aesthetic, and ethical knowledge impossible. Thus, there is no escaping the need to conduct epistemological inquiry, given the positivist's conception of philosophy. Indeed, to him, that is all philosophy is—epistemological inquiry, whose goal is to acquire knowledge by correctly analyzing concepts and resolving the problems concerned with what we can know and how we can know it. In Chapter 3 we will examine the positivist's position in more detail.

WHAT PHILOSOPHY IS: THE SEARCH FOR GOOD ARGUMENTS

Immanuel Kant (1724–1802), one of the greatest philosophers, thought definitions should come at the end, rather than at the beginning, of philosophical investigation. Definitions could not be understood, he believed, before the terms that figured in them were understood, and it took the whole investigation to come to understand these terms. Perhaps we should take Kant's advice, at least in trying to define *philosophy* itself. The split between traditional and positivistic philosophers over the nature and goals of their discipline is so deep and so sharp that to define philosophy here at the beginning would seem to require us to distort one or both views. To say philosophers "seek truth" is no doubt safe enough, but to say what the truth they seek is *truth about* would seem to force us to choose sides.

There is, however, one way we can define philosophy that does not compel us to make this choice, a way that emphasizes what is common to both the conceptions discussed. What is common to them? It is this: Both emphasize the need for rational argument; that is, both involve the belief that a claim made, say, in or about metaphysics needs to be defended—needs to be argued for in a rational way. Accordingly, one way we might define philosophy is as follows: *Philosophy is the search for good arguments that support claims to knowledge made in or about metaphysics, epistemology, ethics, aesthetics, logic,* and so on. This definition, it bears repeating, is neutral in the traditional-positivist dispute, since it does not say what claims to knowledge *are* supported by good arguments. And notice, too, that its accuracy cannot be settled before we examine what philosophers actually do. At this point, in other words, we must regard it as a hypothesis, to be tested by our future experience.

Have we heeded Kant's advice? Not to the letter. But Kant surely was right in believing that a definition cannot be understood before the terms used in it are understood. In the present case this means we must come to grips with the concept of a *good argument*. Now, earlier we said that logic is the branch of philosophy that investigates what makes an argument a good argument. Before we can test our definition, then, we need to acquaint ourselves with what logicians say about the nature of a good argument as well as some of their techniques for determining what makes one good. As we shall see, however, an argument can be a good argument, from the standpoint of logic, yet fail to prove that anything is true, because the argument is not itself based on what is true. To present a good argument, all considered, you must not only make it good from the point of view of logic, but you must also base your reasoning on what is true.

Thus, to get back to our definition of philosophy, before we can understand or assess it, we must learn some method for testing the logic of an argument and we must acquaint ourselves with some of the different ideas about knowing what is true. We will take up the logic in the next chapter, various concepts of knowledge in Chapter 3, and, in an Interlude, we will return to our definition of philosophy to see if what we have learned helps us understand the definition and the discipline itself. Then we shall apply what we have learned to three problems of deep philosophical significance —God's existence, human freedom, and life after death.

FOR FURTHER READING

Broad, C. D., *Scientific Thought*. London: Routledge and Kegan Paul, 1923, Chap. 1. A good, spirited discussion of the nature of philosophy as a discipline.

EXERCISES

1. Give brief characterizations of each of the following branches of philosophy:
   a) metaphysics
   b) ethics
   c) epistemology
   d) aesthetics
   e) logic

2. In what branch or branches of philosophy would you classify each of the following questions:
   a) Is space real?
   b) How do we know what happened in the past?
   c) Was the world created by God?
   d) What are the criteria for assessing the probability that something is the case?
   e) What is a work of art?
   f) Can a good man knowingly do what is wrong?
   g) Is pleasure the only good?
   h) Do spiritual beings exist?
   i) How can we know what will happen in the future?
   j) Is it always wrong to kill another person?

3. Compare and contrast the traditional philosopher's and the positivist's view of philosophy.

4. How do you think a philosopher's investigation of memory might differ from that of a psychologist or a neurologist?

5. Compile a list of questions that you think might be asked by someone engaged in these areas.
   a) philosophy of language
   b) philosophy of science
   c) philosophy of law
   d) philosophy of mathematics
   e) philosophy of mind

6. Try to explain what philosophy is to a friend who has never read or thought about it. Where do you experience the greatest difficulty in your explanation? What questions does your attempt bring to light?

2 Elements of Logic

The logic we will discuss is called *truth functional logic* or *propositional logic*. It is not the only logic logicians have developed, and we will not explore all its techniques or ramifications. What we will explore, however, will be sufficient to give a clear meaning to the concept of a good argument, judged from the point of view of logic. It also will enable us to clarify certain very important technical concepts that enjoy a wide usage in philosophy, ones, in fact, that we will use in our own discussions of philosophical problems in the second half of this book. In addition to familiarizing ourselves with these points, moreover, we also need to acquaint ourselves with various ways in which arguments can commit what are called *informal fallacies*. Coming to understand and recognize some of these fallacies is important because an argument can be good in some respects but not a good argument, all considered. We will postpone our discussion of informal fallacies until after we have completed our examination of propositional logic.

TRUTH FUNCTIONAL LOGIC

Truth functional logic is an example of a two-valued logic, the two values being *true* and *false*. A *proposition* may be defined as what is either true or false, and thus truth functional logic is called *propositional logic*. Techniques have been devised within truth functional logic to determine which propositions are always true and which always false, and which forms of argument are always good, and which are not, judged from the point of view of logic.

PROPOSITIONS

The concept of a proposition is one philosophers have had as much trouble living with as without. We cannot go into all the debates about its use, but if we consider that there is something to which the concepts of truth and falsity apply, we must ask what that "something" is. A common-sense answer is that it is *sentences*.

Suppose someone says, "It is raining," and suppose what he says is true. Then can we say, "What is true is the sentence 'It is raining.' "—or can't we? This answer encounters some formidable difficulties. To begin with, it surely could not be the sentence "It is raining" that is true, but this sentence as used by a particular person speaking at a particular time about a particular state of affairs. To understand this better, suppose we find the sentence "It is raining" written on a blackboard. How could we determine what place the sentence refers to (for example, to Zanzibar or Memphis) or when it refers to either (in the morning or the afternoon)? What makes the reference of a sentence clear is its setting or context—for example, who says it, when, with what intonation and gestures. And we cannot reasonably determine whether what someone has said is true or not without taking the context into account, a fact that supports the contention that it is not sentences, considered all by themselves, that are true or false.

A more serious problem is that sentences are made up of particular words from particular languages. Accordingly, if we say that it is sentences that are true, we seem to be claiming that what is true is this or that string of words in this or that particular language. But consider what you know of the connections between different languages. If it is true to say, in English, "It is raining" of a particular happening at a particular time, then it is also true to say, in German, *"Es regnet"* of this same happening at this same time. But how can we do this if truth applies *only* to sentences? In other words, how can we say that it would be true to speak the *German* sentence *"Es regnet"* if all we know is that the *English* sentence "It is raining" is true? Thus, if we ascribe truth to sentences, we do not seem to have any reasonable way of explaining something that we all know perfectly well is true—namely, that when it is true to say, of a particular state of affairs, at a particular time, "It is raining," it is also true to say *"Es regnet."* It is against this backdrop that the introduction of the concept of a proposition can best be understood. For this concept is supposed to make it possible to account for this knowledge.

A proposition may be defined in part as *what is expressed by the use of any sentence in the indicative mood* (this definition can be challenged, as we shall see in Chapter 3). Notice that a proposition is *not* itself a sentence; it is what is *expressed by* the use of certain sentences—namely, those in the indicative mood. Thus, the sentence "It is raining" is not a proposition, although it can be used to express one. A proposition, therefore, is not something that exists in any particular language; there are not English propositions and German propositions, as there are English and German sentences. Propositions are what certain sentences may be used to express, whether these sentences are in English, German, Spanish, or whatever. The important point is that *different sentences in the same or different languages can be used to express the same proposition.* For example, the English sentence "It is raining" and the German sentence *"Es regnet"* may be used to express the same proposition. This is why the idea of a proposition may help solve the problem above, for if the proposition expressed by someone's use of "It is raining" is true, then what would be expressed by this same person's use of *"Es regnet,"* given the same context of utterance, would be true also.

Philosophers have wondered whether propositions exist—especially whether they exist independently of the use of any natural language such as English or German—but we will not pursue this question here. The important thing to understand is that there has been a tradition in philosophy according to which it is *what is expressed* by the use of a sentence in the indicative mood that is either true or false, not the sentence itself, and that the name given to this "something" is proposition.

One final point. As we said, a proposition is what is expressed by the use of certain sentences; it is not itself a sentence in any language. Still, we sometimes will want to talk about a particular proposition—say, the one expressed by someone's use of the sentence "It is raining." Now, to do this we will sometimes have to suppose that this proposition can be written in a language, such as English. To make it clear when we are talking about a proposition, rather than a sentence, we will use the following device. When we are talking about a *sentence*, we will enclose the words in *double quotation marks*—for example, "It is raining." When we are talking about the *proposition* expressed by someone's use of that sentence, we will enclose the words in single quotation marks—for example, 'It is raining'.

SYMBOLIZATION

The logic we want to examine, then, is truth functional or propositional logic. It is a logic that investigates the connection between propositions— between what is expressed by the use of sentences in the indicative mood. Such sentences may be of two kinds, simple and compound. The sentence "It is raining" is a *simple* sentence and so may be used to express a simple proposition. The sentence "If it is raining, then the game will be called off" is a *compound* sentence and thus may be used to express a compound proposition. In the logic of propositions, individual letters, such as p, q, and r, are used to stand for or *symbolize* individual simple propositions. For example, we could let *p* stand for the proposition 'It is raining'. What letter we use to symbolize any given proposition is completely up to us; there are no "right" or "wrong" letters. The only restriction we must observe is not to let the same letter stand for two or more different propositions at the same time.

It should be noticed that, strictly speaking, letters such as *p*, *q*, and *r* are used to symbolize individual simple propositions; they are not, themselves, propositions. Nevertheless, it will be convenient to speak at times as though they were. That way we can avoid the tiresome repetition of such phrases as "the proposition symbolized by *p*" or "the proposition *q* stands for." To refer to these letters, then, as propositions, will be merely a shorthand way of referring to the propositions they symbolize.

Now, within the framework of propositional logic a simple proposition is sometimes true and sometimes false; that is, no simple proposition is always true or always false. We can present this idea graphically by means of what is called a *truth table*. For example, suppose we let *p* symbolize the proposition 'It is raining'. Then the truth table for this proposition would be as follows:

	p
Line 1	T
Line 2	F

This table presents the possible values of any simple proposition, *p*: That *p* could be true is indicated by the T in line 1; that *p* could be false is indicated by the F in line 2. We see, then, that the proposition symbolized by *p* (in this case, the proposition 'It is raining') is not always true and not always false, and we should see that, since *p* could symbolize *any* simple proposition, and not just 'It is raining', no simple proposition is always true or always false, judged truth functionally.

To detect whether propositions are always true or always false, the techniques of truth functional logic must be applied to *compound* propositions–those propositions that we express by means of compound sentences in the indicative mood. Now, a compound sentence is any grammatically correct combination of simple sentences. Thus, a compound proposition is any proposition expressed by our use of any grammatically correct combination of simple sentences in the indicative mood. The combinations dealt with in propositional logic are (1) *conjunction*, (2) *disjunction*, (3) *implication*, and (4) *co-implication*. These concepts are referred to as the *logical* or *sentential connectives*. Before we see how these connectives are to be understood, however, it will be useful to make a few further comments about the construction and use of a truth table.

CONSTRUCTING A TRUTH TABLE (I)

A truth table consists of columns and lines. Lines are read from left to right, columns from top to bottom. A column is written under every simple proposition and under every distinct compound proposition. Thus, how many columns a given table has depends on how many simple and compound propositions we are examining. If there is just one simple proposition, then it will have just one column; if two, two; and so on. How many lines a table contains depends on how many simple propositions are being considered. If there is just one simple proposition, then the table will have 2 x 1 or two lines; if two, then 2 x 2 or four lines; if three, 2 x 2 x 2 or eight lines; and so on.

The reason the number of lines increases as the number of simple propositions is increased is that the purpose of a truth table is to exhaust the possible combinations of truth and falsity between the simple propositions being considered. Thus, the greater the number of simple propositions, the greater the number of possible combinations of truth and falsity and, therefore, the greater the number of lines on which to represent these possibilities. For example, if the only proposition in question were p, then only two lines would be necessary, one on which to indicate the possibility that p is true and the other on which to indicate the possibility that p is false:

	p
Line 1	T
Line 2	F

Notice also that, since p is the only proposition being considered, the table has only one column.

If we had to construct a table for some combination of two simple propositions, p and q, the table would require four lines, because there are four possible combinations of truth and falsity: (1) p and q are both true; (2) p is false and q is true; (3) p is true and q is false; (4) p and q are both false. We can present these same combinations in more digestible form by constructing a table for p and q consisting of four lines and two columns:

	p	q
Line 1	T	T
Line 2	F	T
Line 3	T	F
Line 4	F	F

Notice that, in the column under p, we have alternated T and F every other line, while in the column under q, we have alternated T's and F's in pairs. We need not construct every truth table in just this way, but it is desirable to have a uniform construction that exhausts every possible combination of truth and falsity.

As noted earlier, if we increase the number of simple propositions considered by a table to three, the table will contain eight lines; increased to four, it will contain sixteen lines; and so on. Fortunately for us, tables of just four lines will be sufficient to clarify the ideas we need to understand.

THE LOGICAL CONNECTIVES

The logical connective called *conjunction* is associated with the English word 'and' and its equivalents, such as 'but' and 'yet'. The conjunction of two propositions is expressed, in other words, whenever we use two sentences in the indicative mood that are joined by the word 'and' or its equivalents. To illustrate this idea, consider the sentence "Plato was a student of Socrates' " and the sentence "Aristotle was a student of Plato's." Both are simple sentences in the indicative mood, and thus both may be used to express a simple proposition. Accordingly, in order to express the conjunction of these two propositions, all we need do is join these two sentences by the word 'and' or one of its equivalents: "Plato was a student of Socrates', and Aristotle was a student of Plato's." Thus conjoined this sentence may be used to express the conjunction of the two propositions 'Plato was a student of Socrates' ' and 'Aristotle was a student of Plato's'. And a similar explanation could be given of how the following sentences could be used to express the conjunction of their constituent propositions.

> "Logic is helpful, and chemistry is helpful."
> "He said he'd come, but he didn't."
> "He tried very hard, yet he failed again and again."

Now, recall that we already have explained how to symbolize simple propositions. This we do by means of individual letters, such as p, q, and r. Suppose we let p symbolize the proposition 'Plato was a student of Socrates' and q symbolize the proposition 'Aristotle was a student of Plato's'. To symbolize the idea that these two propositions are conjoined, we use the symbol called the *ampersand* (&). Thus, the way we will symbolize the conjunction of any two propositions, p and q, is as follows: $(p \& q)$.

The conjunction of any two propositions, like any other proposition in truth functional logic, must have a truth value. Accordingly, what we now need to indicate is when the conjunction of any two propositions is true and when it is false. To do this let us first define a *conjunct* as any proposition that is conjoined to another proposition. In the example we have given, then, the proposition 'Plato was a student of Socrates' ' is a conjunct, and so is the proposition 'Aristotle was a student of Plato's'. Then we can define conjunction, truth functionally, as follows: *a conjunction is truth functionally true only when both conjuncts are true; in every other case, a conjunction is false.*

This definition can be presented in a truth table for conjunction, as follows:

	p	q	$(p \,\&\, q)$
Line 1	T	T	T
Line 2	F	T	F
Line 3	T	F	F
Line 4	F	F	F

This table represents all the possible combinations of truth and falsity for p and q, but only in line 1 do we find a T under p and a T under q; only in line 1, therefore, do we find a T under the conjunction, $(p \,\&\, q)$. To return to our example, what this definition of conjunction implies is that the conjunction 'Plato was a student of Socrates', and Aristotle was a student of Plato's' is true only if the proposition 'Plato was a student of Socrates' ' is true, *and* if the proposition 'Aristotle was a student of Plato's' also is true.

Disjunction, another logical connective, is expressed by using the words 'either' and 'or' (or their equivalents) to disjoin sentences in the indicative mood. The following sentences may be used to express the disjunction of two propositions:

> "Either Bill did it, or Suzy did it."
> "Either John will win, or Don will win."
> "Either we'll go to the show, or we'll study."

Notice, however, that we can assert the disjunction of two propositions without using the words 'either' and 'or'. For example, if someone says "Unless you study logic, you won't do well in it," one way of clarifying what is meant is by translating this to read "Either you will study logic, or you will not do well in it."

Now, suppose we let p and q symbolize any two simple propositions. The symbol we shall use to represent the idea that two propositions are disjoined is a small 'v'. Thus, we can symbolize the disjunction of any two simple propositions, p and q, as follows: $(p \,v\, q)$.

Of course, like any other proposition in truth functional logic, the proposition $(p \,v\, q)$ has a truth value. What remains for us to do, then, is to define when a disjunction is true and when it is false. To do this, let us first define a *disjunct* as any proposition that is disjoined from another proposition. Thus, *p* in (*p* v *q*) is a disjunct, and so is *q*. Then we can define disjunction, truth functionally, as follows: *a disjunction is truth functionally false only when both disjuncts are false; in every other case, a disjunction is true.* This definition, like the one for conjunction, can be represented in a truth table for disjunction. Thus:

	p	*q*	(*p* v *q*)
Line 1	T	T	T
Line 2	F	T	T
Line 3	T	F	T
Line 4	F	F	F

Only in line 4 do we find an F under both *p* and *q*; only in line 4, therefore, is it correct to put an F under the disjunction (*p* v *q*). In every other case, the disjunction is true. Thus, for example, if someone were to say "Either Bill did it, or Suzy did it," the disjunctive proposition expressed would be truth functionally true if Bill did it, or if Suzy did it, or if both Bill and Suzy did it. Only if neither of them did it–that is, only if it is false that Bill did it and also false that Suzy did it— would the disjunctive proposition be false.

A third logical connective is *implication*. This connective is associated with conditional sentences—that is, sentences of the form, "*If* so and so, *then* such and such." The following conditional sentences could be used to express the idea that one proposition truth functionally implies another proposition:

"If it rains, then the voter turnout will be small."
"If McGovern had won, then the POW's would be home."
"If the Cubs win the pennant, then I'll eat my hat."

As in other cases, we can express the idea that one proposition implies another without using the words 'if' and 'then'. For example, the statement "Unless you study logic, you won't do well in it" might be translated as "If you don't study logic, then you won't do well in it."

The symbol we will use for the idea of implication is the arrow: →. Thus, we can symbolize the relationship of implication between any two simple propositions, *p* and *q*, as follows: (*p* → *q*). What remains to be explained is how this relationship is defined truth functionally.

To understand this definition we first need to explain what is meant by the words 'antecedent' and 'consequent'. The *antecedent* of an implication is the proposition expressed by the if-clause; it is the proposition that comes first, the one that is said to imply the other. The *consequent* is the proposition expressed by the then-clause; it is the proposition that comes last, what is said to be implied by the other (the antecedent). For example, in the proposition 'If it rains, then the voter turnout will be small', the proposition 'It rains' is the antecedent and the proposition 'the voter turnout will be small' is the consequent.

With these concepts before us, we can define implication, truth functionally, as follows: *an implication is truth functionally false only when the antecedent is true and the consequent is false; in every other case, it is true.* The truth table for this definition reads as follows:

	p	q	$(p \rightarrow q)$
Line 1	T	T	T
Line 2	F	T	T
Line 3	T	F	F
Line 4	F	F	T

In line 3 we find a T under the antedecent and an F under the consequent; therefore, there is an F under the implication, $(p \rightarrow q)$, in line 3. Since this is the only time we find the antedecent true while the consequent is false, this is the only time the implication is false, considered truth functionally. With respect to our example, then, the only time it would be false to say "If it rains, then the voter turnout will be small" is if it is true that it rains but false that the voter turnout is small. In every other case this sentence could be used to express a proposition that is truth functionally true. This is an idea that many people have found very puzzling. We will return to it in a moment, after we have defined the fourth and final logical connective.

The final logical connective is called *co-implication*. It is associated with *bi-conditional* sentences, or sentences of the form "This *if and only if* that." The following bi-conditional sentences could be used to express the idea that two propositions co-imply one another.

> "Laws are just if and only if they treat all people fairly."
> "A plane, closed figure is a triangle if and only if it has three sides and three interior angles."
> "Actions are right if and only if they accord with God's will."

The symbol we will use for co-implication is the double arrow: ($\leftrightarrow$). Thus, we can symbolize the relationship of co-implication between any two propositions, p and q, as follows: $(p \leftrightarrow q)$.

The truth functional definition of co-implication is straightforward: *The co-implication between any two propositions is truth functionally true when both the propositions are alike as regards truth and falsity; in every other case, the co-implication is false.* Thus, if both propositions are true, their co-implication is true, and if both are false, their co-implication is true; it is only when they have opposite truth values that it is false to assert that they co-imply one another. These points are exemplified in the truth table for co-implication.

	p	q	$(p \leftrightarrow q)$
Line 1	T	T	T
Line 2	F	T	F
Line 3	T	F	F
Line 4	F	F	T

In lines 1 and 4, p and q have the same truth values; in lines 2 and 3 they do not; therefore, the truth value of their co-implication is true in the former cases but false in the latter ones. Thus, the proposition 'Laws are just if and only if they treat all people fairly' would be truth functionally true if the proposition 'Laws are just' is true *and* if the proposition '(These) laws treat all people fairly' also is true; and this co-implication also would be true if both of these propositions are false.

SOME DIFFICULTIES WITH THE CONNECTIVES

Serious questions can be raised about how adequately the truth functional definitions of the logical connectives reflect our ordinary understanding of the ideas of conjunction, disjunction, implication, and co-implication. Take conjunction, for example. The truth value of the proposition $(p \ \& \ q)$ is precisely the same as the truth value of the proposition $(q \ \& \ p)$, a fact that illustrates the idea that, considered truth functionally, the positions of the conjuncts makes no difference to the truth value of the conjunction of which they are a part. Yet in our ordinary thought and language the position of a conjunct sometimes *does* make a difference to the truth of what we say. If someone says, "I went for a run and took a shower," we ordinarily understand him to mean that *first* he went for a run and *then* he took a shower. Thus, his remark would be false or at least misleading if the position of the conjuncts were turned around as: "I took a shower and went for a run."

This aspect of conjunction is ignored in propositional logic, and so we should be aware that the nuances of our ordinary concept are not adequately translated into the artificial language of the logic. At the same time, however, a fundamentally important feature of our ordinary concept is preserved—namely, that the conjunction of any two propositions is true only when both the conjoined propositions are true.

More controversial still is how we ordinarily conceive of implication and how it is dealt with in truth functional logic. In ordinary language, we usually think of implication as involving a causal element; that is, we sometimes think of the antecedent (the if-clause) and consequent (the then-clause) as being causally related, the antecedent referring to the cause, and the consequent referring to the effect. This is nicely illustrated in the example, 'If it rains, then the voter turnout will be small'. Here, surely, what the speaker is claiming is that there is a causal connection between the antecedent and the consequent, that rain *will cause* people to stay home rather than vote. Now, the truth functional definition does not define implication in this way. To make this clearer, suppose that it does not rain. Suppose, that is, that the antecedent of the implication is false. And suppose that the voter turnout is small (the consequent is true). What would we say about the implication, 'If it rains, then the voter turnout will be small'? Wouldn't we be reluctant to say *either* that it is true *or* that it is false? After all, even though it didn't rain, and even though the voter turnout was small, it might have rained, and if it had, the voter turnout might have been smaller than it was. Then again, it might not have been any different; or it might have been larger. It seems, in short, as though we just do not know enough to say whether the implication is true or false—whether, that is, rain really would have caused the voter turnout to be small.

However, if we treat this implication truth functionally, we have no difficulty at all in determining when it is true and when it is false. In particular, if it is the case, as we are supposing, that the antecedent ('if it rains') is false and the consequent ('then the voter turnout will be small') is true, then the implication is most certainly truth functionally true also. For this is part of the very definition of implication, considered truth functionally. Thus, it seems clear that the truth functional definition of implication differs from how we usually understand the concept—that is, that it involves causality.

The truth functional account of implication, then, sometimes fails to agree with our ordinary understanding of this concept, but it is important to realize that there is no one way in which we ordinarily understand it, and that the truth functional definition does accord with how we sometimes understand it. Consider first the idea that, truth functionally considered, a false can truly imply a false. This perplexing idea seems very strange, especially if we think of implication exclusively in terms of causality. But consider the example "If the Cubs win the pennant, then I'll eat my hat." You might use this sentence in ordinary life to say something you regard as true. Yet what you intend to convey is that you think it is true the Cubs *will not* win the pennant. In other words, you think it is false that the Cubs will win the pennant (that is, you think the antecedent is false), which is why you think you will *not* eat your hat (that is, you think the consequent is false also). Thus, we have a case where a false antecedent and a false consequent can be used to affirm something that is thought to be true. There seem, then, to be at least some cases where the truth functional definition of implication is borne out by our ordinary thought and language.

Consider next cases where a false antecedent might truly imply a true consequent. An example is the sentence, "If McGovern had won, then the POW's would be home." Now, it is false that McGovern won, and it is true that the POW's are home. But does that show that the implication is false? Hardly. Each of us recognizes that the implication might very well be true under these circumstances. Once again, therefore, the truth functional definition of implication does not seem to be totally at odds with how we sometimes understand this concept outside the confines of propositional logic.

NEGATION

The final idea we need to be able to symbolize is *negation*. Negation signifies that something *is not the case*. The sentence "Johnny won't come" can be interpreted to mean "It is not the case that Johnny will come." It expresses the negation of the proposition expressed by the use of the sentence "Johnny will come." The symbol we will use for negation is $\sim$. Thus, if we let p symbolize the proposition 'Johnny will come' then $(\sim p)$ would symbolize its negation—that is, the proposition 'It is not the case that Johnny will come'.

As for the truth table for the negation of any proposition, this is what we might expect it to be: *the truth table for the negation of any proposition is just the opposite of the truth table for its affirmation.* Thus, if the truth table for p is

$$\frac{p}{\begin{array}{c} T \\ F \end{array}}$$

then the truth table for $\sim p$ would be

$$\frac{\sim p}{\begin{array}{c} F \\ T \end{array}}$$

Notice that the negation of the negation of any proposition yields a proposition that has the same truth values as the original proposition. Thus, for instance, $\sim \sim p$ has the same truth value as p.

BRACKETING

As the definitions of the logical connectives illustrate, the truth or falsity of any compound proposition depends on the truth or falsity of the propositions that comprise it—hence the aptness of the name "truth functional logic" to designate the logic we are considering. Now, inasmuch as compound propositions may be comprised of propositions that are themselves compound, and these, in turn, comprised of still other compound propositions, and so on, some symbolic device is needed to make clear with what other proposition(s) any given proposition is connected and by what connective. The device used here is called *bracketing* or *grouping*.

To illustrate the need for this device, let us consider the following proposition:

p & q v r

This proposition is ambiguous. It is unclear whether it asserts (1) the *conjunction* of p and $(q$ v $r)$, that is, whether p is a conjunct and $(q$ v $r)$ is a conjunct, or (2) the *disjunction* of $(p$ & $q)$ and r, that is, whether $(p$ & $q)$ is a disjunct and r is a disjunct. Introducing parentheses into our symbolism, and thereby bracketing those propositions that go together, removes this ambiguity. Thus, if we want to make it clear that it is (1) that we are asserting, we can write this proposition as

p & $(q$ v $r)$

If it is (2) that we wish to assert, we can write the proposition this way:

$(p$ & $q)$ v r

The parentheses in each case make it clear which of the two connectives, & or v, is the *central connective*. The central connective is that connective which determines what *kind* of proposition is asserted—for example, a conjunction or a disjunction. The central connective in (1) is &, and the central connective in (2) is v. The truth values we find in the column under the central connective tell us whether and when the proposition asserted is truth functionally true or false.

Propositions may be very complex, and to find the central connective may require both care and patience. There are three general rules to rely on.

First, parentheses always go in pairs; for every left parenthesis, (, there is a right parenthesis,). Second, the symbols enclosed by any pair of parentheses are to be treated as expressing one compound proposition. Third, the central connective never itself is enclosed by a pair of parentheses. The examples we have considered so far illustrate these three rules, and so do the propositions that follow. Try finding the central connective.

$$(p \ \& \ (r \rightarrow \sim q)) \ v \ (p \leftrightarrow q)$$
$$(p \rightarrow (s \rightarrow (r \rightarrow q))) \ v \sim p$$
$$(p \ \textrm{r} \ (r \ v \ s)) \leftrightarrow ((s \ v \ r) \ v \ p)$$

CONSTRUCTING A TRUTH TABLE (II)

How a truth table is constructed is a natural consequence of the nature of truth functional logic itself. Since we cannot determine the truth or falsity of complex propositions before we have determined the truth or falsity of the less complex of propositions and, ultimately, of simple propositions, we should begin with what is simplest. The first columns in any truth table, therefore, are those for the relevant simple propositions. For example, if the proposition whose table we are trying to construct is

$$((p \rightarrow q) \ \& \ (p)) \rightarrow q$$

then the first columns that should be written are those for p and q.

Which column should be constructed next? In view of what we know about the nature of truth functional logic, the answer is clear enough—the *next least complex* proposition. How can we determine which proposition that is? Once again, the answer should be clear enough: that proposition having the fewest propositions bracketed by parentheses. Since we already have dealt with the simple propositions, the next least complex proposition could only be one that consisted of two simple propositions joined by one logical connective, and it is for a proposition of this type that we should next look. In this case, it is $(p \rightarrow q)$.

Exactly the same line of reasoning underlies our choice of all additional columns. Thus, in our example, the proposition $((p \rightarrow q) \ \& \ (p))$ is the next least complex proposition, and a column should be written under it before we write our column under the whole proposition. The structure of the columns in our truth table, therefore, should be as follows:

Column 1	Column 2	Column 3	Column 4	Column 5
p	q	$(p{\rightarrow}q)$	$((p{\rightarrow}q) \ \& \ (p))$	$((p{\rightarrow}q) \ \& \ (p)){\rightarrow}q$

Recall, finally, that how many *lines* a truth table should contain is a direct result of the number of simple propositions we need to consider: if 2, 2 × 2, or 4 lines; if 3, 2 × 2 × 2, or 8 lines; and so on. As mentioned earlier, however, tables of just four lines will be sufficient to illustrate the ideas we need to understand.

EVALUATING PROPOSITIONS

We are now in a position to begin to apply the ideas we have been discussing. The first thing we will do is apply them to individual propositions.

TAUTOLOGY

When we construct a truth table for a given proposition, sometimes we find a T in every line under its central connective. This tells us that the proposition is *always* true, not because of what the proposition is about, but simply because of the logical structure of the proposition; it is true, that is, because of how its constituent simple propositions are put together by the logical connectives. *Whenever a proposition is always true because of its logical structure or form, it is said to be logically true, and whenever a proposition is said to be logically true it also can be said to be a tautology.* A proposition of the form $(p \lor \sim p)$, for example, is a tautology, as its truth table confirms:

p	$\sim p$	$(p \lor \sim p)$
T	F	T
F	T	T

The reverse also can occur. Sometimes when we write a truth table for a given proposition, we find all Fs under its central connective. This tells us that the proposition is *always* false, not because of what it is about, but simply because of its logical structure. It is false because of the way its simple propositions are put together by the logical connectives. *Whenever a proposition is always false because of its logical structure or form, it is said to be logically false, and whenever a proposition is logically false it is said to be a contradiction.* A proposition of the form $(p \ \& \ \sim p)$, for example, is a contradiction, as its truth table confirms:

p	$\sim p$	$(p \ \& \ \sim p)$
T	F	F
F	T	F

Notice that, in these cases, it is the form or structure of a proposition that makes it a contradiction or a tautology, not what it is about. For example, both the proposition 'Today is Monday and today is not Monday' and the proposition 'Socrates was alive in the fifth century B.C. and Socrates was not alive in the fifth century B.C.' are contradictions, but neither is logically false because of what it is about—a day of the week, on the one hand, and an ancient philosopher, on the other. They are false because of their form or structure. The conjunction of any proposition and its denial never can be true. And this is true whether the proposition that is both asserted and denied is simple, as in the examples above, or compound. To affirm the conjunction of a compound proposition and its negation is just as much a contradiction—and for the same reason—as to affirm the conjunction of a simple proposition and its negation.

LOGICAL EQUIVALENCE

In addition to being able to determine when individual propositions are truth functionally true or false, we also can use our logic to determine a variety of ways in which propositions are *logically related* to one another. Logical equivalence is one such relation. *Two propositions are said to be logically equivalent if they have the same truth values on each line under their central connective.* Thus, since all tautologies must, by definition, have Ts on every line under their central connective, and since all contradictions must, by definition, have all Fs on all the lines under their central connective, it follows that all tautologies are logically equivalent to one another, as are all contradictions.

Now, sometimes the column under a proposition's central connective contains both Ts and Fs. This tells us that the proposition is neither a tautology nor a contradiction, considered truth functionally; its form alone is insufficient to determine its truth or falsity. Such propositions often are called *contingent* propositions. Such propositions are still of interest to the logician, however; in particular, we may wish to determine what other propositions the contingent proposition is equivalent to. To find this out, we must find out what other propositions have an arrangement of Ts and Fs under their central connective that is the same as the given proposition has under its central connective. As we said earlier, p and $\sim\sim p$ have the same truth values. We now can see that this makes them logically equivalent. Similarly, by making use of this test for equivalence, we discover that $\sim(p\ \&\ q)$, for example, is equivalent to $(\sim p \vee \sim q)$, and that $\sim(p \vee q)$ is equivalent to $(\sim p\ \&\ \sim q)$. These equivalences are referred to as *DeMorgan's Laws,* after the nineteenth-century logician Augustus DeMorgan. Their tables are as follows:

p	q	$p \& q$	$\sim(p \& q)$
T	T	T	F
F	T	F	T
T	F	F	T
F	F	F	T

p	q	$\sim p$	$\sim q$	$\sim p \vee \sim q$
T	T	F	F	F
F	T	T	F	T
T	F	F	T	T
F	F	T	T	T

p	q	$p \vee q$	$\sim(p \vee q)$
T	T	T	F
F	T	T	F
T	F	T	F
F	F	F	T

p	q	$\sim p$	$\sim q$	$\sim p \& \sim q$
T	T	F	F	F
F	T	T	F	F
T	F	F	T	F
F	F	T	T	T

Since every proposition must have a particular connective as its central connective, it is possible to find a logically equivalent way of expressing any proposition, using each of the other logical connectives. It is often important to discover what these equivalences are. For example, if we know that any given proposition is true (or false), then we can be assured that those propositions that are logically equivalent to it are also true (or false).

CONSISTENCY AND INCONSISTENCY

Consistency and inconsistency are concepts that apply to sets or groups of propositions. Propositions are said to be (or constitute) consistent or inconsistent sets. *A consistent set of propositions consists of two or more propositions all of which can be true at the same time.* On the other hand, *a set of propositions is said to be inconsistent if the propositions comprising it cannot all be true at the same time.* To determine, in any given case, whether a set of propositions is consistent or inconsistent, one need only to construct a truth table for the *conjunction* of all the propositions in question. *If the conjunction comes out true in at least one case, the set is consistent.* Example 1 below shows a set of propositions that is consistent; example 2 shows a set that is inconsistent.

Example 1

p	q	$p \to q$	$p \& (p \to q)$
T	T	T	T
F	T	T	F
T	F	F	F
F	F	T	F

Example 2

p	q	$\sim q$	$p \& q$	$p \& \sim q$	$(p \& q) \& (p \& \sim q)$
T	T	F	T	F	F
F	T	F	F	F	F
T	F	T	F	T	F
F	F	T	F	F	F

EVALUATING ARGUMENTS

The concepts and techniques of truth functional logic can be applied to arguments as well as propositions. *An argument consists of at least one proposition, called the premise, which is alleged to support another proposition, called the conclusion.* Of course, arguments can be constructed that have many more than one premise, and most arguments of philosophical interest are like this. Nevertheless, we can acquire the understanding required to examine some arguments of considerable complexity by mastering ones that contain just two premises and a conclusion. For some complex arguments, as we shall see, consist of a series of these simpler ones.

Notice that in our definition of an argument we have not specified *how* the premises are thought to support the conclusion. Two important different types of arguments need to be distinguished here—inductive and deductive arguments.

Let us consider the inductive argument first. To say that a premise provides *inductive support* for a conclusion means that, if the premise is true, then it increases the *likelihood* or *probability* that the conclusion is true also. The premise, that is, is not thought to establish the truth of the conclusion conclusively or (to use the technical term) *necessarily*. To illustrate the inductive argument, let us consider the following example:

> *Premise:* The sun has risen every day in the past.
> *Conclusion:* Therefore, the sun will rise tomorrow.

A moment's reflection will show that the conclusion does not follow necessarily from the premise; that is, it is *possible* for the premise to be true and the conclusion to be false, that indeed the sun might *not* rise tomrorow. Of course, this is very unlikely, and we have no good reason to believe it won't. But it might not, and just because it always has done so doesn't show that it must do so tomorrow. Yet this fact does not challenge this argument since, as an inductive argument, it is not intended to show that the sun *must* rise tomorrow but, instead, that it probably will—indeed, in this case, that it *very* probably will do so.

When does a premise in an inductive argument provide good support for the conclusion? This is a very complex question which, were we to pursue it, would take us into technical fields such as probability theory. Fortunately for us, this is not a question we need to pursue at this juncture. Our principal interest lies in understanding the other variety of argument listed above—namely, deductive argument. Later on, however, both in this chapter and in Chapter 3, we will have some additional comments to make about the idea of an inductive argument.

In the second type of argument, the *deductive argument,* the truth of the premises is thought to make the truth of the conclusion not merely probable but *certain*—and certain not in a psychological but in a logical sense. What is this logical sense of certainty? *To say that the conclusion of an argument follows deductively from the premises means that the conclusion of the argument cannot be false if the premises are true.* It means, in other words, that it would be a *contradiction* to affirm the premises and deny the conclusion, for it would be asserting something that *could not possibly* be true. Thus, if the premises are true, then it is a logical certainty that the conclusion is true also, if the conclusion follows deductively from the premises.

We can make this idea clearer by means of an example:

> *Premise:* John loves Mary, and Bill loves Sue.
> *Conclusion:* Therefore, John loves Mary.

Now, suppose we let p symbolize the proposition 'John loves Mary' and q the proposition 'Bill loves Sue'. Then we can symbolize this argument as follows, where "$\therefore$" symbolizes "therefore."

> *Premise:* $(p \ \& \ q)$
> *Conclusion:* $\therefore \ p$

The question we now want to raise is whether this premise does make the truth of the conclusion certain, in the sense explained. In other words, we want to ask whether the conclusion could be false, if the premise were true, or, alternatively, whether it would be a contradiction to affirm the premise and deny the conclusion. To determine whether this is so or not, all we need do is write a truth table for the conjunction of the premise and the negation of the conclusion and see whether or not this conjunction is or is not a contradiction. And this is all that we need do because, if it *is* a contradiction to affirm the premise and the negation of the conclusion, then the *conjunction* of the two will be just that—a contradiction. Thus, in order for us to answer our question, let us construct a truth table for the conjunction of the premise $(p \ \& \ q)$ and the denial of the conclusion $(\sim p)$; that is, for the proposition $(p \ \& \ q) \ \& \ \sim p$:

p	q	$\sim p$	$p \,\&\, q$	$(p \,\&\, q) \,\&\sim p$
T	T	F	T	F
F	T	T	F	F
T	F	F	F	F
F	F	T	F	F

This table tells us that it *is* a contradiction to affirm the premise and to deny the conclusion. Thus, it tells us that the premise does deductively establish the conclusion, so that the conclusion is certain in the sense explained—namely, *if* the premise is true, then the conclusion *must* be true.

Now, this is precisely what we said is not the case in an inductive argument (even a good one), for there the conclusion *could* be false even if the premise is true. We are now in a position to clarify this idea further. Consider our earlier inductive argument:

> *Premise:* The sun has risen every day in the past.
> *Conclusion:* Therefore, the sun will rise tomorrow.

Let us symbolize the premise p and the conclusion q. Then we can ask whether the premise could make the conclusion certain, in the sense explained. And to answer this question all we need do is construct a truth table for the conjunction of the premise and the negation of the conclusion—that is, for the proposition $(p \,\&\, \sim q)$—and see whether or not this proposition is a contradiction:

p	q	$\sim q$	$(p \,\&\, \sim q)$
T	T	F	F
F	T	F	F
T	F	T	T
F	F	T	F

This table tells us that it is *not* a contradiction to affirm the premise and deny the conclusion; in other words, the conclusion can be false even though the premise is true. Thus, the premise does not deductively establish the conclusion. And the same is true of every other argument that is intended to be inductive: the conclusion of an inductive argument never follows necessarily from the premise or premises; that is, to affirm the premises of an inductive argument and to deny the conclusion never is to assert something that is necessarily false.

An important lesson follows from these considerations: it is very important to determine *how* the proponent of an argument intends his argument to be taken—that is, whether inductively or deductively. This is important because a damaging criticism we might be able to launch against his argument, when it is interpreted in one way, would not count as a criticism at all, if it is interpreted in another way. Suppose he intends his argument as an inductive one. Then it would be no criticism of his argument to show that the conclusion does not follow necessarily from the premises, for the conclusion of an inductive argument *never* follows necessarily from the premises. Of course, if the premises are thought to deductively establish the conclusion, and it can be shown they do not, this would be a very serious criticism of the argument. But what all this should make clear is that, before we try to criticize an argument on the grounds that the conclusion does not follow necessarily from the premises, we first have to make sure what kind of argument the argument is supposed to be—inductive or deductive.

How can we be sure of this? All we can do is try to understand the proponent of an argument, to be fair to him and not thrust intentions upon him he does not have. This means we must listen carefully to what he says as well as what he assumes and implies by what he says, and then we must ask what is the fairest, most reasonable way to interpret his argument. In philosophy, at least, the difficulties inherent in resolving a question of this type are reduced somewhat. For philosophers almost always are in search of a kind of knowledge that is not knowledge of what is *probably* the case. Accordingly, when they present arguments, they are almost never intended as inductive ones.

FORMAL VALIDITY AND INVALIDITY

Let us now define two important ideas, formally valid and formally invalid deductive arguments. *A deductive argument is formally valid if and only if it would be a contradiction to affirm the premises and deny the conclusion.* On the other hand, *a deductive argument is formally invalid if and only if it would not be a contradiction to affirm the premises and deny the conclusion.* Thus, if we were to concede the truth of the premises in a formally valid deductive argument, we would have to concede the truth of the conclusion as well. In a formally invalid deductive argument, on the other hand, even if we concede the truth of the premises, we would not have to concede the truth of the conclusion. This is because the conclusion of a formally invalid deductive argument *can* be false, even if the premises are true.

A formally valid deductive argument is one where the premise or premises *do* deductively establish the conclusion, and we have already said a good deal about this idea. What we need to illustrate is how we can detect that a deductive argument is formally *invalid*. Not surprisingly, the method is the same one used to determine whether a deductive argument is formally *valid*—namely, a truth table. For what is definitive of every formally invalid deductive argument is that it is *not* a contradiction to affirm the premises and deny the conclusion, and whether or not it would be a contradiction to do this is, in any given case, something we can discover by means of a truth table. Consider the following argument.

> *Premise 1:* If the devil exists, then man does what is wrong.
>
> *Premise 2:* Man does what is wrong.
>
> *Conclusion:* Therefore, the devil exists.

Let us symbolize the first premise $(p \rightarrow q)$. Then the second premise would be symbolized q and the conclusion p. Thus, the conjunction of the premises would read $((p \rightarrow q) \,\&\, (q))$, so that the conjunction of the premises and the *negation* of the conclusion would read $((p \rightarrow p) \,\&\, (q))$ $\&\, \sim p$. Thus, in order to determine whether this argument is valid or invalid, all we need do is construct a truth table for this last proposition. If it is a contradiction, then the argument is valid. If it is not, then the argument is invalid. The truth table is as follows:

p	$\sim p$	q	$p \rightarrow q$	$(p \rightarrow q) \,\&\, q$	$((p \rightarrow q) \,\&\, q) \,\&\, \sim p$
T	F	T	T	T	F
F	T	T	T	T	T
T	F	F	F	F	F
F	T	F	T	F	F

The table tells us that it is *not* a contradiction to affirm the premises and deny the conclusion of the argument at hand. Thus, the argument is *not* formally valid, or, in other words, it *is* formally invalid. And this is precisely what we would find in the truth table for *any* formally invalid deductive argument: the conjunction of the premises and the negation of the conclusion is not a contradiction. Thus, it would show us that there is no necessary connection between the premises and the conclusion, which would show us that we could grant that the premises are true and not be rationally obliged to grant that the conclusion must be true also.

SOME VALID FORMS OF ARGUMENT

Some formally valid forms of argument are so basic and occur so frequently that they have been singled out and given names. It is desirable to familiarize yourself with these argument forms, since we will make use of many of them in this chapter and later in the book. Those that follow are presented schematically—that is, they are presented in terms of premises and conclusion—but each of them can be rewritten so that its validity can be checked by means of a truth table. To do this all we need do is, first, to conjoin the premises and, second, to conjoin them with the negation of the conclusion. For example, the argument form called *modus ponens* is written schematically as follows:

$$p \rightarrow q \quad \text{Premise}$$
$$p \quad \text{Premise}$$
$$\therefore q \quad \text{Conclusion}$$

To reformulate this argument so we can check its validity with a truth table, we should first conjoin the premises, which yields the proposition $((p \rightarrow q)$ & $p)$; and then conjoin this proposition with the negation of the conclusion, which yields the proposition $((p \rightarrow q)$ & $p)$ & $\sim q$. As the truth table will show, this proposition is a contradiction. Thus, *modus ponens* is a formally valid form of deductive argument.

Reformulate each of the following forms of argument in this way and verify their formal validity by means of a truth table.

Modus ponens:

$$p \rightarrow q \quad \text{Premise}$$
$$p \quad \text{Premise}$$
$$\therefore q \quad \text{Conclusion}$$

Modus tollens:

$$p \rightarrow q$$
$$\sim q$$
$$\therefore \sim p$$

Chain argument:

$$p \rightarrow q$$
$$q \rightarrow r$$
$$\therefore p \rightarrow r$$

Valid disjunctive argument:

$$p \vee q$$
$$\sim q$$
$$\therefore p$$

$$p \vee q$$
$$\sim p$$
$$\therefore q$$

Conjunctive arguments:

$\sim (p\ \&\ q)$
p
$\therefore \sim q$

$\sim (p\ \&\ q)$
q
$\therefore \sim p$

Reductio ad absurdum:

$p \rightarrow q$
$p \rightarrow \sim q$
$\therefore \sim p$

SOME INVALID FORMS OF ARGUMENT

Some formally invalid forms of argument occur so frequently that a recognition of them also is desirable. Construct truth tables to verify the invalidity of the following arguments.

Fallacy of affirming the consequent:

$p \rightarrow q$
q
$\therefore p$

Fallacy of denying the antecedent:

$p \rightarrow q$
$\sim p$
$\therefore \sim q$

Fallacy of affirming a disjunct:

$p\ \lor\ q$
p
$\therefore \sim q$
$p\ \lor\ q$
q
$\therefore \sim p$

LOGICAL FORM

A valid form of argument, such as *modus ponens*, is valid for any argument of that form—in this case, for any argument that has the form, "If antecedent, then consequent. Antecedent. Therefore, consequent." The following arguments all have the same logical form:

$$p \rightarrow q \qquad (r \ \& \ s) \rightarrow t \qquad (w \lor (x \rightarrow z)) \rightarrow a$$
$$p \qquad\qquad (r \ \& \ s) \qquad\quad (w \lor (x \rightarrow z))$$
$$\therefore q \qquad\quad \therefore t \qquad\qquad\quad \therefore a$$

What is true of *modus ponens* is true of all other valid forms of argument. Thus, it is the *logical form* of an argument that determines its formal validity and not what the propositions comprising it are about. To the extent that logic can be understood as the inquiry into valid reasoning, it can be regarded as the inquiry into the logical form of valid arguments.

TRUTH AND VALIDITY

We can now distinguish between two concepts that often are treated as the same—namely, *truth* and *validity*. As we have seen, validity is a property that certain arguments have because of their form. Any argument having the form of, say, *modus ponens* is a valid argument. Arguments that do not have a valid form, on the other hand, are said to be invalid. Thus, validity and invalidity are concepts that apply to *arguments*, or, since an argument is the form our thinking takes when we are reasoning, we may speak of valid or invalid forms of reasoning.

The point that needs to be emphasized is that arguments are *not* true or false. The conclusion of an argument either does or does not follow from the argument's premises. When it does follow, the argument is valid, and when it does not, the argument is invalid. But no argument is true or false. Truth and falsity are concepts that apply to *propositions*, not to arguments. From the point of view of propositional logic, given any proposition it is either (1) necessarily true (*a tautology*), (2) necessarily false (*a contradiction*), or (3) neither necessarily true nor necessarily false (*a contingent proposition*). In no case, given our usage, is a proposition valid or invalid.

Let us bear in mind, therefore, that the concepts of truth and validity are distinct and should not be treated as the same. Then we can minimize the effects of some apparent paradoxes involving these concepts. For example, many people find it puzzling that a person can reason validly using premises that are known to be false. The following argument, for example, is a formally valid deductive argument:

Premise 1: If Napoleon was President of the United States, then at least one of the American Presidents was a Frenchman.

Premise 2: Napoleon was President of the United States.

Conclusion: Therefore, at least one of the American Presidents was a Frenchman.

This argument has the form of *modus ponens,* and any argument having this form is, as we know, formally valid. Thus, this argument is formally valid. But at least one of its premises is false—namely, the second one. So it clearly is possible to reason validly using premises known to be false.

However, this fact should not be as puzzling as some people find it. All we maintain, when we say an argument is formally valid, is that the conclusion follows necessarily from the premises. We do *not* maintain that the premises are true, or that the conclusion is. Instead, we are saying that they stand to one another in a fundamentally important relationship— namely, that the one follows necessarily from the other. Thus, if it happens that a premise or the conclusion is false, that does not in the least affect whether this relationship of necessity holds between them. For whether or not this relationship holds or not does not depend at all on whether the premises and the conclusion actually are true or false. Indeed, recall the method we have used to test for validity: we have constructed truth tables to do so. And what we should recognize is that nowhere in the truth table do we have to answer the question, "Are the premises and the conclusion actually true?" That is a question that is entirely immaterial to assessing the validity of an argument.

Of course, the concepts of truth and validity are *related* to one another in a very important way. For *if* the premises of a formally valid argument happen to be true, then the conclusion *must* be true also. But notice, once again, that this does not mean that we cannot reason validly using false premises. All that this commits us to is the view that what is false cannot follow necessarily from what is true. Indeed, if it could, philosophy, as well as every other discipline that sets out to add to our knowledge of what is true by using what we already know is true, would necessarily be as empty as it would be frivolous.

EXTENDED ARGUMENTS

As we mentioned, arguments frequently are longer than the ones we have considered so far, but these extended arguments often are nothing more than a series of basic arguments, such as *modus ponens* and *reductio ad absurdum.* If we can recognize these basic arguments, we should be able to assess the logic of an extended argument and do so without having to construct elaborate truth tables. How can we do this?

Let us begin by reminding ourselves that every deductive argument will contain, first, a *conclusion,* a proposition that the argument is supposed to prove, and, second, a *premise* or *premises,* propositions that are supposed to prove the conclusion. Let us refer to the premise of any argument as an *assumption,* meaning that *the premise itself is not derived from any other proposition in the argument* in which it occurs. And let us refer to any proposition that is supposed to validly follow from some other propositions as a *consequence.* Then what we can say is that every argument will consist of at least one assumption and one consequence, and that the more complex an argument becomes, the more assumptions or consequences it will contain.

This idea can be made clearer by example. Consider the following argument.

If racism leads to violence, then racism is wrong.

Racism leads to violence.

Therefore, racism is wrong.

This argument has the valid form called *modus ponens,* as is seen if we let p symbolize 'Racism leads to violence' and q symbolize 'Racism is wrong'. Then we see that the form of the argument is

$$p \rightarrow q$$
$$p$$
$$\therefore q$$

Now, one thing we could do to make the status of each of these three propositions clearer is to make use of the concepts of assumption and consequence. In other words, we could identify which is which, as follows:

1. $p \rightarrow q$ Assumption
2. p Assumption
3. $\therefore q$ Consequence, from (1) and (2), by *modus ponens*

Writing the argument in this way makes it very clear that propositions (1) and (2) are not supposed to be proven by the argument, whereas proposition (3) is. Notice, moreover, that when we say that one proposition is the consequence of others, as we do in the case of q in step (3) above, that we should say *how* it is a consequence—that is, we should give the name of the argument form the argument has—for example, *modus ponens.*

Of course, the symbols in (1), (2), and (3) *stand for* something—namely, the propositions that comprise the original argument about racism and violence. Accordingly, if we were to give a complete presentation of this argument, it would look like this:

Steps	Symbolization	Status
1. If racism leads to violence, then racism is wrong.	$p \rightarrow q$	Assumption
2. Racism does lead to violence.	p	Assumption
3. Therefore, racism is wrong.	$\therefore q$	Consequence, from (1) and (2), by *modus ponens*

In other words, a full or complete presentation of any argument would consist of three columns—first, one headed "steps," in which are written the propositions that comprise the argument; second, one headed "symbolization," in which these propositions are symbolized; and, third, one headed "status," in which the logical status of each proposition is identified as being either an assumption or a consequence, and, if the latter, *how* it is related to the other propositions. Whenever we present an argument in this fashion we will say that we have given it a *formal presentation* or a *formal statement*. Theoretically, therefore, given any extended argument, it should be possible to give it a formal statement. What we now want to do is see how this can be done.

Consider as our first example the following argument:

If men have souls, then men are not destructible. Men do have souls. Therefore, men are not destructible. If men are mortal, then they are destructible. Therefore, men are not mortal.

To give a formal presentation of this argument, we need, first, to identify each of the steps that occur in it; second, to symbolize each of the propositions that occur in each of these steps; and, third, to indicate whether each is an assumption or a consequence, and, if the latter, how it is logically related to other propositions. For this argument, we end up with the following:

Steps	Symbolization	Status
1. If men have souls, then men are not destructible.	$p \rightarrow\, \sim q$	Assumption
2. Men do have souls.	p	Assumption
3. Therefore, men are not destructible.	$\therefore \sim q$	Consequence, from (1) and (2), by *modus ponens*
4. If men are mortal, then men are destructible.	$r \rightarrow q$	Assumption
5. Therefore, men are not mortal.	$\therefore \sim r$	Consequence, from (3) and (4), by *modus tollens*

Consider next this lengthier extended argument:

Either there is life on other planets or the earth is unique in supporting life. If the earth is unique in supporting life, then it would be mysterious why life is present only on the earth. If it were mysterious why life is present only on the earth, then there could be no scientific explanation of why there is life on the earth. Therefore, if the earth is unique in supporting life, then there could be no scientific explanation of why there is life on the earth. But there is a scientific explanation of why there is life on the earth. Therefore, the earth is not unique in supporting life. Therefore, there is life on other planets.

A formal statement of this argument would read as follows:

Steps	*Symbolization*	*Status*
1. Either there is life on other planets or the earth is unique in supporting life.	$p \lor q$	Assumption
2. If the earth is unique in supporting life, then it would be mysterious why life is present only on the earth.	$q \rightarrow r$	Assumption
3. If it were mysterious why life is present only on the earth, then there could be no scientific explanation of why there is life on the earth.	$r \rightarrow \sim s$	Assumption
4. Therefore, if the earth is unique in supporting life, then there could be no scientific explanation of why there is life on earth.	$\therefore q \rightarrow \sim s$	Consequence, from (2) and (3), by chain argument
5. But there is a scientific explanation of why there is life on earth.	s	Assumption
6. Therefore, the earth is not unique in supporting life.	$\therefore \sim q$	Consequence, from (4) and (5), by *modus tollens*
7. Therefore, there is life on other planets.	$\therefore p$	Consequence, from (1) and (6), by disjunctive argument

Some extended arguments can be even lengthier than the ones just given, but they can still be presented in the same way, and all we need to know in order to understand them are the valid and invalid forms of argument listed earlier. Presenting them in this fashion also yields certain benefits. First, it enables us to discuss the validity of extended arguments without having to construct elaborate, tedious, and time-consuming truth tables. Second, it helps us keep certain important questions distinct—in particular, questions about the validity of an argument versus questions about the truth of the argument's premises or assumptions. This is because, given a formal statement of an argument, the assumptions are explicitly identified as just that—assumptions. In fact, it is because of these immediate benefits of a formal presentation that we will give formal presentations of many of the arguments we will be examining in the second half of this book.

Just two more points should be mentioned here. First, people do not always set forth their arguments in a way that corresponds perfectly with a formal statement of them. Not even philosophers do this. Therefore, when- ever we do set forth an argument in this fashion, we no doubt are guilty of leaving out some of their nuances and stylistic devices. This is not neces- sarily bad. What we are trying to do is to strip the argument of whatever conceals its logical structure so that we may assess its validity or lack of it. And this is not unfair, either to the argument or to its proponents, for whether a deductive argument is a good one or not depends in part on whether it is formally valid.

Second, when we consider extended arguments in detail, we shall see that an argument can *appear* to be formally valid when it is not; that is, the consequences deduced in an extended argument often can appear to follow validly when in fact they do not. To determine whether a conse- quence actually does validly follow is far from easy, and we will have to be on our guard not to let shoddy thinking pass for something it is not. Indeed, a deductive argument can be formally valid and its premises can be true and still it may fail to prove the truth of its conclusion. This can happen if the argument commits what is called an informal fallacy. Let us consider what this idea means.

INFORMAL FALLACIES

Any time a conclusion does not follow from its premise or premises, we say that the argument contains a *nonsequitur*, which is Latin for "it does not follow." Any time an argument contains a nonsequitur, it commits a *fallacy*. If the logical form of an argument is unambiguous, and if the argument is formally invalid, then the argument is said to commit a *formal fallacy*. To illustrate this, let us consider the following argument:

If wars are fought, then capitalists make money. Capitalists make money. Therefore, wars are fought.

The logical form of this argument is clearly

$$p \rightarrow q$$
$$q$$
$$\therefore p$$

The argument is an example of that invalid form of reasoning we described above as the fallacy of affirming the consequent, and so, like all the invalid forms of reasoning we have distinguished thus far, is an example of a formal fallacy.

Not all arguments that contain nonsequiturs are formally fallacious. In some, the conclusions do not follow for reasons other than those that deal exclusively with the argument's logical form. These are said to commit an *informal fallacy*. Examples of such fallacies follow.

FALLACIES OF EQUIVOCATION

AMBIGUOUS TERM OR EXPRESSION

Sometimes arguments appear to be valid when they are not because an ambiguous term or expression is present in the argument; that is, an expression that has two or more different meanings. The word *bank*, for example, is ambiguous; it can mean either "the side of a river, stream, etc." or "a financial institution." Such popular words as *square* and *grass* are other examples. Sometimes whole sentences can be ambiguous—for example, "She wore his favorite dress" and "She broke down in the car." When an argument uses a term or expression that is ambiguous, and when the argument is formally valid only if we suppose that the word or expression has just one meaning, then the argument is said to commit a *fallacy of equivocation*. The following argument illustrates this fallacy:

If you can keep money dry in a bank, then you can't fish from a bank. You can keep money dry in a bank. Therefore, you can't fish from a bank.

If we disregard the ambiguity of the word *bank*, the argument is formally valid (it has the form of *modus ponens*). Still, we would hardly be satisfied that this argument proves that you cannot fish from a bank (in the sense of the side of a stream). And if someone were to suppose that this argument did prove this, we should surely want to object on the grounds of equivocation.

THE FALLACY OF COMPOSITION

This kind of fallacy occurs whenever anyone reasons fallaciously from a fact about the individual members of a group to a conclusion about the group considered as a whole. An example is the following:

> No man can lift a ton. All the members of the weight-lifting team are men. Therefore, the weightlifting team can't lift a ton.

THE FALLACY OF DIVISION

This fallacy occurs whenever anyone fallaciously reasons from a fact about a group, considered as a whole, to a conclusion about each of the individual members of the group. Example:

> Students are late for classes every day. Phyllis and Don are students. Therefore, Phyllis and Don are late for classes every day.

FALLACIES OF IRRELEVANCE

Fallacies of irrelevance (or *ignoratio elenchi*) occur in arguments when the premise or premises set forth to support the truth of the conclusion are altogether irrelevant to establishing its truth. Detecting such fallacies would seem easy, yet it is distressing how often we are persuaded by arguments that commit fallacies of this type.

AD HOMINEM ARGUMENTS

Ad hominem arguments are examples of arguments that commit a fallacy of irrelevance. There are various forms of *ad hominem* argument. One important variety is that in which the argument is directed against the person whose belief the argument purports to criticize rather than at the belief itself. These arguments thus aim at "abusing the man." Example:

> That man is a known racist. Therefore, when he says Martin Luther King was a Communist, we know that what he says is false.

This argument clearly is fallacious. The fact that a man is a racist, even if he is, is logically irrelevant to any question we might have about the political outlook or sympathies of a black leader.

APPEALS TO ILLICIT AUTHORITY, FORCE, PITY

Other irrelevant and hence informally fallacious arguments are those that purport to support their conclusion by appeals to illicit authority ("Einstein knew so much, and still he believed in God; therefore, there must be a God"); by appeals to force ("If you don't agree with me, I'll tell your mother about the other night"); and by appeals to pity ("The boy is so unloved and forlorn, he can't be guilty"). One or another of these arguments might persuade a given individual to agree to do or believe something; but none of the reasons given for believing or doing the things in question is a logically relevant reason for believing or doing them.

BEGGING THE QUESTION

A frequent charge raised against arguments is that they commit the fallacy of *begging the question* (or *petitio principi*). Arguments that commit this fallacy are formally valid, so they are quite unlike the fallacies of equivocation and of irrelevance. (Indeed, some logicians are reluctant to classify begging the question as an informal fallacy, but the general consensus would seem to be that it is.) An argument begs the question if it *assumes* the truth of what it is trying to prove. A classical example is this one:

All men are mortal. Socrates is a man. Therefore, Socrates is mortal.

What this argument is supposed to show is that Socrates is mortal. However, the premises clearly assume that this is true since they assume that *all* men (including Socrates) are mortal. Hence, the argument begs the question.

An argument that begs the question rarely does it so conspicuously. More often than not the begging is more subtle, and the power of the argument to convince us is proportionately greater. For example, many people are convinced that what the Bible says is true because the Bible itself declares that it contains the truth. Many people are also convinced that nondemocratic forms of government are bad simply on the grounds that they believe democratic forms of government are the only good ones. Both these arguments are question begging, but that does not alter the fact that they exercise the power they do over the people they do.

SOUND OR CONCLUSIVE ARGUMENTS

A *sound deductive argument* (or a *conclusive proof*) may be defined as a fomally valid argument that commits no informal fallacy and consists of premises that are true and are known to be so. Any deductive argument that does not satisfy all three of these conditions is *unsound*. Thus, any formally valid deductive argument whose premises are tautological and known to be so would constitute a conclusive proof of its conclusion. Sound arguments or proofs are not necessarily limited, however, to arguments whose premises are tautological. It is possible to construct valid arguments whose premises are not logical truths but are nonetheless true and known to be so. As we shall see in later chapters, issues of philosophical interest turn out most often to involve arguments whose premises are not tautological.

One thing the concept of a sound deductive argument helps us do is give a definite meaning to the idea of a good argument, the kind of argument we have said philosophers search for to support claims to knowledge made in or about such things as metaphysics and ethics. What we can now say is that, if the philosopher is looking for a good *deductive* argument to support his claims, then he is looking for a *sound* deductive argument—that is, one that is formally valid, commits no informal fallacy, and contains premises known to be true. The techniques we have developed in connection with propositional logic enable us to determine whether an argument is formally valid; our discussion of some types of informal fallacy should help us to see whether an argument does or does not commit such a fallacy. But as to whether the premises in an argument are known to be true, that is a question we cannot answer by logic alone. To answer it we must reflect on the nature and possible varieties of knowledge. And this is a subject that must be taken up in epistemology, not in logic. In the next chapter, we will take our first steps in that direction.

FOR FURTHER READING

There are literally scores of logic texts available, most of equivalent quality. Here are two modestly priced paperbacks, each containing sections on propositional logic:

Gorovitz, Samuel, and Ron G. Williams, *Philosophical Analysis: An Introduction to Its Language and Techniques.* New York: Random House, 1963, Chap. 1.

Salmon, Wesley, *Logic.* Englewood Cliffs, N.J.: Prentice-Hall, 1963.

A complete examination of informal fallacies is provided in these paperbacks:

Kahane, Howard, *Logic and Contemporary Rhetoric.* Belmont, Calif.: Wadsworth, 1971.

Michalos, Alex C., *Improving Your Reasoning.* Englewood Cliffs, N. J.: Prentice-Hall, 1970.

EXERCISES

1. Define and give examples of each of the following:
   a) tautology
   b) contradiction
   c) logical equivalence
   d) consistency
   e) inconsistency
   f) valid deductive argument
   g) invalid deductive argument
   h) inductive argument
   i) *modus ponens*
   j) *modus tollens*
   k) fallacy of affirming the consequent
   l) fallacy of denying the antecedent
   m) *reductio ad absurdum*
   n) formal fallacy
   o) informal fallacy
   p) fallacy of equivocation
   q) fallacy of division
   r) fallacy of composition
   s) fallacy of irrelevance
   t) begging the question
   u) sound argument

2. Construct truth tables to determine whether each of the following propositions is a tautology, a contradiction, or neither.
   a) $p \rightarrow (q \vee \sim q)$
   b) $p \rightarrow ((q \vee \sim q) \rightarrow p)$
   c) $p \rightarrow ((q \vee \sim q) \vee (\sim q \& q))$
   d) $(q \vee \sim q) \rightarrow p$
   e) $((q \vee \sim q) \rightarrow p) \rightarrow p$
   f) $((p \rightarrow (q \rightarrow p)) \& \sim (q \& \sim p)) \vee (\sim p \rightarrow (p \vee \sim p))$
   g) $((p \leftrightarrow (q \vee p)) \& (\sim p)) \rightarrow p$

3. Construct truth tables to determine whether each of the following pairs of propositions are logically equivalent.
   a) $p \rightarrow (p \& q)$ and $\sim p \vee (p \& q)$
   b) $p \rightarrow (p \vee q)$ and $\sim (p \& \sim (p \vee q))$
   c) $\sim (p \& q) \rightarrow \sim p$ and $\sim (p \vee q) \rightarrow \sim p$

4. Construct truth tables to determine whether each of the following sets of propositions is consistent or inconsistent.
   a) $p \vee (q \vee p)$
      $(p \vee q) \vee p$
      $\sim p$
      $\sim (q \vee p)$
   b) $p \sim (q \rightarrow q)$
      $\sim q$
      $\sim p$

5. Translate the following arguments into symbolic form and test for their formal validity. In those cases in which an argument is valid, give the name of the valid form it has; for example, "modus tollens." In those cases where an argument is invalid, give the name of the invalid form it has; for example, "the fallacy of affirming the consequent."
   a) If John is industrious, then he does not loaf. John does loaf. Therefore, John is not industrious.
   b) If marijuana is illegal, then those who get caught with it are sent to jail. Those who get caught with it are sent to jail. Therefore, marijuana is illegal.

c) Either logic is dull or logic is educational. Logic is educational. Therefore, logic is not dull.

d) It is not the case both that Jim will win and that Bill will win. Jim won't win. Therefore, Bill will win.

e) If man is by nature aggressive, then man is by nature violent. If man is by nature violent, then wars are unavoidable. Therefore, if man is by nature aggressive, then wars are unavoidable.

f) Either the world had a beginning or it did not. It is not the case that the world did not have a beginning. Therefore, the world had a beginning.

g) If Jane is shrewd, then she tells the truth. If Jane is shrewd, she doesn't tell the truth. Therefore, Jane isn't shrewd.

h) If the Cubs win, I'll have to eat my hat. The Cubs won't win. Therefore, I won't eat my hat.

i) If beauty is in the eyes of the beholder, then beauty is not a quality in things. Beauty is not in the eyes of the beholder. Therefore, beauty is a quality in things.

j) It is not the case both that vitamin C is good for your health and that vitamin C is not good for your health. Vitamin C is good for your health. Therefore, it is not the case that vitamin C is not good for your health.

6. Present a formal statement of each of the following extended arguments.

a) If the fetus is a human being, then abortion involves the taking of an innocent human life. If abortion involves the taking of an innocent human life, then abortion is wrong. Therefore, if the fetus is a human being, then abortion is wrong. The fetus is a human being. Therefore, abortion is wrong.

b) It is not the case both that people are totally selfish and that people sometimes act for the sake of another person's happiness. If people never act for the sake of another person's happiness, then no person loves another. But people do love other people. Therefore, people sometimes act for the sake of another's happiness. Therefore, people are not totally selfish.

c) If the truth is relative, then people would not mean the same thing by the word "truth." If people did not mean the same thing by the word "truth," then they could not understand the same thing by the words "The truth is relative." But people do understand the same thing by words "The truth is relative." Therefore, people do mean the same thing by the word "truth." Therefore, the truth is not relative.

d) Either what is truly right and wrong varies from culture to culture or there are some moral principles that apply to all men, at all times and in all places. If to cause unnecessary pain is absolutely wrong, then no man can be justified in causing unnecessary pain. To cause unnecessary pain is absolutely wrong. Therefore, no man can be justified in causing unnecessary pain. If no man can be justified in causing unnecessary pain, then there are some moral principles that apply to all men, at all times and in all places. Therefore there are some moral principles that apply to all men, at all times and in all places. Therefore, what is truly right and wrong does not vary from culture to culture.

e) It is not the case both that the theory of evolution and the creation story in the myth of Genesis are true. Now, if the creation story in the book of Genesis is in the Bible, then, if the Bible contains the truth, then the creation story in the book of Genesis is true. The creation story in the book of Genesis is in the Bible. Therefore, if the Bible contains the truth, then the creation story in the book of Genesis is true. But if the Bible contains the theory of evolution, then, if the Bible contains the truth, then it is not the case that the creation story in the book of Genesis is true. The Bible does contain the theory of evolution. Therefore, if the Bible contains the truth, then it is not the case that the creation story in the book of Genesis is true. Therefore, it is not the case that the Bible contains the truth.

f) Either philosophy yields knowledge or it does not. If philosophy does not yield knowledge, then either philosophers are all foolish or they are to be pitied. If philosophers are all foolish or they are to be pitied, then wisdom is impossible. Therefore, if philosophy does not yield knowledge, then wisdom is impossible. If wisdom is impossible, then the search for truth is in vain. Either the search for truth is not in vain or there is no reason to exist. It is not the case that there is no reason to exist. Therefore, the search for truth is not in vain. Thus, it is not the case that wisdom is impossible. Therefore, it is not the case that philosphers are all foolish or they are to be pitied. Hence, it is not the case that philosophy does not yield knowledge. It follows, therefore, that philosophy does yield knowledge.

3   Concepts of Knowledge

Roughly speaking, epistemological questions deal with what we know or can know or with the nature and limits of human knowledge. As we saw in Chapter 1, traditional and positivistic philosophers agree that epistimological questions must be asked, but they do not agree either among themselves or with each other on how they should be answered. It is largely because of such disagreements in epistemology that philosophers have conflicting beliefs about the feasibility of metaphysical, ethical, and aesthetic inquiry. In this chapter we will describe some of the technical concepts philosophers have developed in their epistemological investigations. Although few in number, these concepts are widely used. Thus, understanding them will enable us to represent some of the most basic outlooks concerning the nature of knowledge. Moreover, these same concepts, together with the logical concepts developed in Chapter 2, will provide a framework for understanding the substantive issues discussed later.

THE ANALYTIC–SYNTHETIC DISTINCTION

We agreed to use the technical term 'proposition' to designate whatever is true or false. We also characterized a proposition as what is expressed by the use of any complete sentence in the indicative mood. Whether propositions exist, or whether, more generally, it makes sense to speak of them at all, are, we know, questions that have been much debated by philosophers. Later on in this chapter, in fact, we will see how it is possible to challenge the view that a proposition is expressed by the use of *every* sentence in the indicative mood.

Propositions have been divided into two major classes—*analytic* and *synthetic*. These classes have been thought of as *mutually exclusive* (that is, no proposition can be both analytic and synthetic) and *jointly exhaustive* (that is, every proposition is either analytic or synthetic). Philosophers do not all agree on this distinction or on how, precisely, these two types of propositions can be characterized, but we will postpone examining this problem until the Afterword at the end of this book.

ANALYTIC PROPOSITIONS

Analytic propositions may be defined as those propositions that are true or false by virtue of their meaning or of their logical form. Such propositions are said to be logically true or logically false. A *synthetic* proposition is a proposition that is *not* analytic, and we will discuss the nature of such propositions after we complete our discussion of analytic propositions.

We already are familiar with two kinds of analytic proposition—those that are truth functionally tautological [for example, $(p \ v \sim p)$] or truth functionally contradictory [for example, $(p \ \& \sim p)$]. Those propositions that are truth functional tautologies are true by virtue of their logical form, and thus are analytically or necessarily true. Those propositions that are truth functional contradictions are false by virtue of their logical form, and thus are analytically or necessarily false.

But not all analytically true or false propositions are true or false because of their logical form. Some are necessarily true or false because of their meaning or content. To make this clear, let us consider the English sentence, "A triangle must have three interior angles." If we let p symbolize the proposition expressed by our use of this sentence and write a truth table for it, we get:

$$\frac{p}{\begin{array}{c} \hline T \\ \hline F \\ \hline \end{array}}$$

Judged solely on the table, the proposition expressed by our use of the sentence "A triangle must have three interior angles" is neither tautological nor contradictory—that is, it is not analytic. But this result is mistaken. Let us ask whether the proposition could ever actually be false. Could that geometric figure we understand to be a triangle ever have more or fewer than three interior angles? Wouldn't we say of any figure that had more or fewer than three interior angles that it not only was not, but *could not* be, a triangle? And wouldn't we say this precisely because a triangle, as we understand it, *must necessarily* have no more or less than three interior angles? So much seems obvious, but it illustrates an important point—namely, there are propositions that are necessarily true but not truth functionally tautological. Or, to put it another way, there are *two* different ways in which propositions can be tautological or contradictory: (1) because of their logical form and (2) because of their content or meaning.

Now, propositional logic, by itself, is incapable of distinguishing those propositions that are tautological or contradictory for this latter reason. Yet it seems obvious that some propositions are tautological or contradictory not because of their logical form, but because of their meaning. And to say that they are true because of their *meaning* should be intelligible. For suppose someone drew a figure that had, say, six interior angles and called it a triangle, and suppose this were no slip of the tongue. Then we would quite correctly say he did not understand the meaning of 'triangle'; for part of the meaning of 'triangle' *is* that it is "a figure with three interior angles."

As our discussion of the triangle example suggests, there is no mechanical test, comparable to truth tables, for detecting propositions that are analytically true or false by virtue of their meaning alone. Instead, we must rely on our insight, ingenuity, and imagination to detect the logical ties that bind our language. In general we must inquire into the *conceivability* or *logical possibility* of certain states of affairs—for instance, the conceivability or logical possibility of a four-sided triangle or a round square. If we cannot conceive of something being otherwise than what it is said to be—if it is logically impossible for it to be otherwise, as in the triangle example—then we must classify the proposition in question as analytically or tautologically true. If we cannot conceive of something being what it is said to be—if it is logically impossible for it to be what it is said to be, as, say, in the case of a round square—then we must classify the proposition in question as logically or analytically false (a contradiction).

NECESSARY AND SUFFICIENT CONDITIONS

When we inquire into the conceivability of states of affairs we are inquiring into the logic of the concepts we apply to these states of affairs, trying to understand the logical connections that bind the concepts together. Such inquiry is the very stuff of which philosophy is made, according to the positivist's conception we discussed in Chapter 1. It is an investigation into the *necessary and sufficient conditions* for the correct application of our concepts.

This investigation may be explained as follows. To say that x is a *necessary condition* of y means that x and y are related in this general way: if x is *not* the case, then y is *not* the case. Thus, x is required by y, but x's being the case does not guarantee that y is the case.

Two varieties of necessary condition need to be distinguished: (1) factually or empirically necessary conditions, and (2) logically or conceptually necessary conditions. If *x is* an *empirically necessary condition* of *y,* then *x* is related to *y* in the following way: *as a matter of fact, y* will not be the case if *x* is not the case. For example, oxygen is a factually necessary condition of combustion. This means that, if oxygen is not present, then, as a matter of fact, given the world in which we live, combustion will not take place. Or, again, oxygen is also a factually necessary condition of life, as we know it; that is, if there is no oxygen present, then, as a matter of fact, no living being will be present either. To say that one thing is a factually necessary condition of another, therefore, is to make a very general factual claim to the effect that the world is so constituted and regulated that, if the former is not the case, then the latter will not be the case either.

A *logically necessary condition* differs from a factually necessary one in a fundamental way. As we have seen, a proposition that truly sets forth a factually necessary condition of something is conceivably false; for example, it is conceivable that combustion *might* take place without oxygen. A condition that is logically necessary for something else, however, is very different. For, in general, to say that *x* is a logically necessary condition of *y* means that, if *x* is not the case then *y cannot possibly be* the case. Recall our example of the proposition, 'A triangle must have three interior angles'. We might reformulate this as follows: 'A logically necessary condition of any figure's being a triangle is that it have three interior angles'. And once we reformulate the proposition in this way, we see what we commit ourselves to: if we agree this proposition is true, then when a figure does not have three interior angles, it is logically impossible for it to be a triangle—it *cannot* be a triangle.

Whenever we say, therefore, that one thing is a necessary condition of something else, we need to be sure that we are clear whether it is supposed to be factually or logically necessary, for the two ideas are very different. Since a failure to distinguish clearly between them can lead to serious misunderstanding, let us summarize them. Necessary conditions may be of two kinds, factual and logical. If *x* is factually a necessary condition of *y,* then, as a matter of fact, *y* never is the case unless *x* is the case, although we can conceive of *y* being the case without *x* being the case. If, however, *x* is a logically necessary condition of *y,* then not only is *y* never the case unless *x* is the case, but it also is impossible to conceive of *y* being the case without *x* being the case.

The concept of a sufficient condition may be defined as follows. To say that *x* is a *sufficient condition* of *y* means that, if *x* is the case, *y* must be the case. In other words, *x* being the case guarantees that *y* will be the case also, but not vice versa; that is, *y* being the case does not guarantee that *x* is also the case. As might be expected, sufficient conditions, like necessary conditions, may be of two kinds: empirical (or factual) and logical (or conceptual). If x is a *factually sufficient condition* of y, then, as a matter of fact, whenever x is the case, y will always be the case, despite the fact that we can conceive of y not being the case when x is.

Consider, for example, Charles's Law, which states that if the pressure remains constant, the rise in temperature in all gases is equivalent to their increase in volume. Given that all gases observe this law, we can say that the law embodies a condition that is factually sufficient for the volume of any given gas to increase a given amount. In other words, if the pressure of a given gas remains constant, and if the temperature is raised n degrees, then the volume of the gas *will* increase n amount. However, no logical necessity is involved here; we can conceive of a world in which Charles' Law does not apply. So, although this law does apply and is, it seems, always true as a matter of fact, it is not necessarily so.

How, then, should we define a logically sufficient condition? If we take our clue from our discussion of necessary conditions, the answer is straightforward: If x is a *logically sufficient condition* of y, then, if x is the case, y *must* be the case; indeed, it is inconceivable to suppose that x is and y is not the case. To illustrate this, let us suppose we are given the following information: A plane, closed figure has three sides and three interior angles. And suppose we are asked what figure this is. Our answer would be that it *must* be a triangle, since the conditions we are given are logically sufficient for a figure's being a triangle. And we would want to say the figure *must* be a triangle, not just because triangles always have three interior angles, but because it is inconceivable that a figure might have these properties and not be a triangle, given the meaning we attach to the word 'triangle'.

We said that this discussion of necessary and sufficient conditions could be of help when we turn to ask whether any given proposition is or is not analytic because of its meaning. Let us consider how. Suppose we have a proposition of the form 'All x's are y's'—for example, 'All triangles are plane closed figures', 'All rainy days are wet days', 'All sons are offspring'. Then we can ask whether x is a logically necessary or sufficient condition of y—whether, for example, being a son is a logically necessary or sufficient condition of being an offspring. If it is, then we can say that the proposition in question is analytically or necessarily true, not because of its logical form (which, when symbolized, is just p) but rather because of its meaning. In other words, we are suggesting that at least *part* of what we mean by "the meaning of a word" can be brought out by exploring the logically necessary and sufficient conditions of the concept that we use the word to apply. When we find that a true proposition does set forth a logically necessary or sufficient condition of a given concept, we will say the proposition is necessarily true because of its meaning and that the proposition is analytic. If a proposition fails to do this, we shall say that it is not analytically true just because of its meaning. In other words, even those propositions of the form 'All *x*'s are *y*'s', where *x* is a *factually* necessary or sufficient condition of *y*, are not analytic, nor are they true just because of their meaning.

To illustrate how we can discover whether a proposition is analytically true or false because of its meaning, consider the following example. Additional examples are presented in the exercises at the end of this chapter.

Example 1: 'All dogs bark'.

The question we must ask is, "Can we conceive of an animal that is a dog but does not bark? Is barking either a logically necessary or a sufficient condition of being a dog?" Surely not. If we have a pet dog that loses its capacity to bark, or if a puppy is born that lacks this capacity, we would not stop calling either of them a dog. Moreover, we can easily conceive of animals other than dogs barking. So barking is neither a logically necessary nor a logically sufficient condition of being a dog. The proposition 'All dogs bark' is, therefore, not an analytic proposition. It is an example of what is called an inductive generalization, a concept we will discuss shortly, and, as it turns out, it is false. A breed of dogs known as Basenji actually lack the ability to bark.

Example 2: 'All dogs are animals'.

Once again our question is, "Is being an animal a logically necessary or sufficient condition of being a dog?" It is not logically sufficient, surely, for otherwise every animal would be a dog! But is it logically necessary? Here we must take care to specify what, precisely, is the extension of the term 'dogs.' By the *extension* of a term we mean the class of objects to which the term can be correctly applied. (By its *intension* we mean those properties of the objects by virtue of which the term applies to them). Does the extension of "all dogs" include stuffed dogs, mechanical dogs, cardboard dogs, and rubber dogs? If so, then the proposition 'All dogs are animals' clearly is not analytically true. A cardboard dog, for example, is not an animal. Presumably, however, the intended extension of "all dogs" is "all *living* dogs," so that cardboard dogs are excluded. Then our question becomes, "Is being an animal a logically necessary condition of being a living dog? Can we conceive of a living dog that is not an animal?" The answer here, clearly, is that we cannot. For part of the intension of the terms "living dog" is 'animality'; that is, nothing can be a living dog if it is not also an animal. The proposition 'All (living) dogs are animals', therefore, is analytically true.

Questions about how to classify a proposition, about whether it is analytic or not, are not always as clear-cut as these examples. Philosophers often think a proposition is analytic when it is not, and perhaps we should not be surprised, in view of the subtle, variegated concepts they have tried to analyze, such as 'causality', 'freedom', 'punishment', and 'person'. Although it is easy to use these words correctly, it is difficult to say what they mean, and certainly a good deal and perhaps the whole of what the philosopher can contribute to our intellectual life is just this kind of analytic insight.

SYNTHETIC PROPOSITIONS

As we said, *synthetic propostions* may be characterized negatively as propositions that are *not* analytic. That is, they are not true or false by virtue of their logical form or of their meaning; they are not tautologies or contradictions. Thus, in order to know whether a given synthetic proposition is true or false, we must know more than what it means or what its logical form is, since it is not true or false just because of either. Examples of synthetic propositions are propositions about the past (for example, 'Alexander was a pupil of Aristotle's'), the future ('The *U.N.* will disband by the year 2000'), and presently observed states of affairs ('The words on this page are printed in black letters'). None of these propositions is analytically true. We need only to consider how much more than their logical form or meaning we need to understand, before we can know that they are true or false, to understand how much these synthetic propositions differ from those that are analytic.

A final difference between synthetic and analytic propositions is this: Synthetic propositions, when true and when known to be so, are said to add to our knowledge of reality, whereas analytic propositions, when true and when known to be so, are not said to do so. Analytic propositions, when true and when known to be so, are said to add to our knowledge of the logical form of propositions or the meanings of words, and we never can validly infer anything about reality from truths about form or meaning. Synthetic propositions, on the other hand, have what sometimes is called an extralinguistic content; they point beyond themselves, so to speak, to a reality to which they refer and which, when true, they correctly describe. When true and known to be so, therefore, they add to our knowledge of this reality.

What is this 'reality' to which all synthetic propositions refer? We cannot answer this question at this point, because we have to answer other questions we have yet to ask. For the present, then, let us say that, while all philosophers would seem to agree both that synthetic propositions are "about reality" and that all propositions "about reality" are synthetic, they are not all agreed on just how this "reality" is known or should be described.

THE A POSTERIORI–A PRIORI DISTINCTION

In discussing the analytic-synthetic distinction, we referred to "what we need to know" in order to know whether a given proposition is true or false. For any given analytic proposition, to know and understand its meaning or logical form is sufficient to know whether it is true or false; for any given synthetic proposition, however, something more is required. To clarify this we shall make use of another important distinction philosophers have developed, that between *a posteriori* and *a priori* knowledge. These two categories of knowledge have been conceived to be mutually exclusive and jointly exhaustive. It has been supposed, that is, that all knowledge must be either a posteriori or a priori and that no knowledge can be both.

A POSTERIORI KNOWLEDGE

A posteriori knowledge (literally, "knowledge from the latter") may be defined as that knowledge we gain and test by observation—that is, by the use of our senses, whether aided or unaided by instruments. Knowledge of this type sometimes is referred to as *empirical* knowledge—knowledge of fact or factual knowledge. Such knowledge can be knowledge of some *particular* fact, such as the name of the planet furthest from the sun or the location of the Taj Mahal, or it can be knowledge of some *general* truth, such as what happens whenever anyone touches a red-hot coal with his bare hand or what happens to various gases under pressure. Such general truths are said to be *inductive generalizations*, and we may suppose that we both discover and confirm the truth of such generalizations by observing an indefinitely large but finite number of similar cases. For example, the generalization that heavy, non–self-propelling objects fall, when support is removed from them, is based on the observation of what happens when support is taken away from such objects as pencils and rocks. If just one case is found where the generalization does not hold true— where, for example, a heavy, non–self-propelling object does not fall, when support is taken from it—then the generalization is shown to be false. Such a case is called a *counter instance* and the generalization is said to be *disconfirmed* or *falsified* by its occurrence. Of course, if the generalization merely asserts that something *usually* happens or *probably* will happen, then the occurrence of just one counter instance will not falsify it. Propositions of this type, which involve the notion of probability, present special problems that we will not deal with here.

A posteriori knowledge is a mongrel category. At its most unsystematic level, it often is thought to include that knowledge we have of the existence and obvious characteristics of our immediate environment—that, say, there are tables and chairs of specific colors, shapes, and sizes. At its most systematic level it is thought to consist of that knowledge the scientist acquires of the less obvious characteristics of this environment—for example, its atomic structure or a mathematical description of the behavior of falling objects. Notice that a scientist is not limited to speaking about only what he can actually observe. No scientist has yet to observe an electron, but there have been countless observations of what scientists construe to be the effects of electrons. An electron is identified not as what is itself observed, but as what has the properties capable of *causing* what is observed. However, even in those numerous cases in which the scientist talks about something he cannot observe directly, he must still make reference to what can be observed directly, and the knowledge he has of the unobserved entity he theorizes about (if it is knowledge) still should be classified as a posteriori.

What is true of the knowledge acquired by the natural sciences, such as physics, also is true of any knowledge acquired by the behavioral or social sciences, including history. No contemporary historian can now directly observe, say, Aristotle tutoring Alexander. Nevertheless, the historian's knowledge that this occurred is based on the other observations he can make, including his observations of the records of Aristotle's and Alexander's contemporaries.

When are inferences from the "observed" to the "unobserved" valid? A full-scale investigation of epistemological issues, especially as they arise in the natural and social sciences, could not avoid an in-depth examination of this question, and the makings of one answer will become evident as we proceed. For now, however, let us simply repeat that all a posteriori knowledge is knowledge confirmed by observation, and the knowledge provided by the sciences is presumed to be of this type.

How might the concept of a posteriori knowledge be connected with synthetic and analytic propositions? Consider the possibility of our having a posteriori knowledge of the truth of an analytic proposition (p). If we thought that the knowledge of p's truth was a posteriori, we would think that it was found to be true as a result of observation. If we thought that p was analytically true, however, we would think that it was true by virtue of its logical form or meaning alone. But if we think p is true by virtue of its logical form or meaning *alone*, then why should we suppose we need to make any observations to confirm its truth? Surely all we would need to know is what p's meaning or logical form was. The conviction begins to arise that our knowledge of analytic propositions is not a posteriori.

In fact, a stronger argument than this can be developed to support this conviction. If p is analytically true, then it is a *necessary* truth; what it expresses is something that cannot conceivably be otherwise than it is. Now, no single observation or series of observations can be sufficient to show that a proposition is necessarily true, and anyone who thinks otherwise betrays his misunderstanding of the concepts involved. Observation can inform us only of how things happen to be as a matter of fact, never of how things must be. Whatever state of affairs it is that we observe, it is always *conceivable* that it should be otherwise than as it is or that it should not be at all. No logical or necessary truth, therefore, can be known to be true by means of observation. Assuming, therefore, that we have some knowledge based on observation, it should be apparent that it must be knowledge of the truth of synthetic propositions. In summary, *all a posteriori knowledge must be knowledge of synthetic truths.*

A PRIORI KNOWLEDGE

A priori knowledge (literally, "knowledge from the former") is knowledge that is independent of observation, knowledge that is *not* a posteriori. In saying it is independent of observation, we do not mean that it must be innate, in the sense that we are born possessing it, before we have had the opportunity to observe anything. Rather, a priori knowledge is of propositions whose truth is *logically* independent of what we observe to be the case—whose truth or falsity cannot be verified or falsified by observation and do not follow from any one or more propositions whose truth can be verified or falsified by observation. For a priori knowledge always is claimed to be knowledge of *necessary* truths. Thus, since no observation or series of observations can confirm the necessary truth of any given proposition, what we observe to be the case is logically irrelevant to the assessment of any a priori claim to knowledge we might make.

This can be illustrated most clearly, perhaps, in the area of mathematics. Our knowledge of mathematical truths is a clear example of a priori knowledge. Suppose mathematician Jones claims to have discovered that 2 and 2 do not equal 4. When we ask how he discovered this, he replies that first he put two apples in an empty sack, and then he put two more in—and every time he did this he got a total of five apples. What would we say of such a case? Surely we would say he must have made a mistake, either in believing the sack was empty to begin with or in believing that he twice put just two apples into it. We would not for a moment seriously believe that, for all we know, Jones might really have discovered that '2 + 2 = 4' is false. Rather, we would seek out some explanation of why what appears to be evidence that conflicts with this proposition's truth actually is no evidence against its truth at all.

Prior to any observation we might make of Jones' sack, we would be absolutely certain that 2 + 2 = 4. And it is because we would be certain of this, *prior* to any observation we might make, that explains why what we know, when we know that 2 + 2 = 4, is not knowledge based on favorable evidence gained by observation. Once we recognize that no evidence from observation can falsify it, we also should recognize that no evidence from observation can verify or confirm it either. For what it and all other true mathematical propositions assert is true independent of what we observe, so that such truths would be true even if there had never been a physical universe, which makes them quite unlike such truths as 'Columbus discovered America in 1492' or 'Saturn is a planet in our solar system'. For these latter propositions would not be true, if the physical universe had never existed. This is why mathematical propositions are said to have the property of being true in all conceivable worlds or in any conceivable universe, whereas propositions that describe persons, places, or things in this universe, even when true, are conceivably false.

The concept of a priori knowledge is not easy to grasp, and its difficulty is compounded by the distinction between two possible kinds of a priori knowledge—*synthetic* and *analytic*. Fundamental disputes have arisen over whether there can be synthetic a priori knowledge; how we answer the question about the possibility of there being such knowledge is a pivotal decision in the development of our philosophical outlook. We will postpone this matter, however, and discuss first the category of analytic a priori knowledge.

What would a given instance of knowledge that is both analytic and a priori be like? As knowledge of an analytic truth, such knowledge would be knowledge of a proposition that is necessarily true because of its meaning or logical form; as a priori knowledge, this knowledge would not be based on evidence gathered by the senses. Now, precisely these two features seem to characterize our knowledge of mathematical truths—for example, $2 + 2 = 4$. Our knowledge of this truth is not based on observation, and it also seems clear that what we know, when we know that this proposition is true, is what these symbols *mean*. Or consider, for another variety of such knowledge, our knowledge of logical truths—for example, $(p \lor \sim p)$. Once again, this knowledge is not derived from evidence gained by observation; so once again this knowledge is a priori, the difference being that, in this case, we apprehend that the proposition is true because of its logical form, and not, as in the case of $2 + 2 = 4$, because of its meaning alone. We do not have to look very long or hard, therefore, to find what appear to be clear examples of a priori knowledge of analytic truths.

Knowledge of this kind is not necessarily confined to knowledge of mathematical or strict logical truths. Recall our earlier example, 'All dogs are animals'. Earlier we agreed that this proposition is analytically true. Moreover, it certainly is one whose truth we seem to be entitled to claim to know. How shall we classify this knowledge? Not as a posteriori, surely, since that would fail to account for the proposition's necessity. Shall we classify it as a priori? We must, if all knowledge is either a posteriori or a priori. And so it seems reasonable to do in this case. For it would be as silly to try to verify the truth of this proposition by observation as it would be to try to falsify it by this means. Once we understand the meaning of the proposition, we understand, in advance of any observation, that anything that could count as a dog would *necessarily* be an animal, and, with this, we understand the pointlessness of trying to test it by observation.

Now, these examples may be taken to illustrate an important truth about analytic propositions—namely, that our knowledge of their truth is always a priori. On this all philosophers are agreed (though not all agree *that* we have such knowledge or *what* truths are analytic). The question that causes profound division is whether the converse is true; that is, is a priori knowledge exclusively or necessarily knowledge of analytic truths? Those who believe in the existence of synthetic a priori knowledge would deny this, and we must now try to clarify what it is they believe and why.

It is easy enough to say what the concept of synthetic a priori knowledge is, but far from easy to determine whether we have any. As synthetic, such knowledge would be knowledge of propositions that are not true by virtue of their meaning or form alone, and, as synthetic, our knowledge of the truth of any one such proposition would add to our total knowledge of reality. Moreover, as a priori, such knowledge would be knowledge of a necessary truth whose truth is logically independent of any information we might gather via observation. Since such knowledge is not based on observation, one main reason for denying its possibility is removed—we are not trying to verify a necessary truth by means of observation of how things happen to be. But notice, nonetheless, that it *is* a necessary truth that such knowledge would be knowledge of. For synthetic a priori knowledge, if there is any, would be knowledge of a necessary truth that is, in some sense, about reality but that is known to be true without relying on any knowledge of reality gained from observation.

Many philosophers have recoiled at the idea of our having knowledge of reality that is not based on observation, and many have denied that there can be necessary truths about reality. Whether they are right is perhaps the most fundamental question in epistemology, and we will explore some aspects of it in the next section. For the present, however, we should make it clear that though synthetic a priori knowledge would be knowledge of necessary truths, these truths would not be necessary truths in the same sense that logical truths or other analytically true propositions are. The denial of a synthetic a priori truth, in other words, would not be a contradiction, so that the state of affairs described by its denial would be conceivable. Synthetic a priori truths, if there are any, must be another variety of "necessary truths," ones that are not necessarily true just because of their meaning or form.

Consider one example of what some philosophers claim is a case of synthetic *a priori* knowledge. (It deserves mention here that, just because two philosophers happen to agree *that* synthetic a priori knowledge is possible, it does not follow that they agree on *what* synthetic truths are known a priori.) Consider, then, the proposition 'Every event has a cause', a proposition that expresses what we shall refer to as the *principle of caus-ality* or the *causal principle* (an idea we will discuss in detail when we take up the problem of free will in Chapter 5). Roughly speaking, the principle declares that everything that happens is related to something else and that this "something else" is the cause of what happens. The principle implies, in other words, that nothing in the world occurs "all by itself," so to speak. It implies that the events that happen in the world are connected with other things that happen in the world, and that these "other things" make it possible for the event to occur that does occur; these "other things" are the event's factually sufficient condition—its cause. Thus, it implies that, given that some causally sufficient condition has been fulfilled, the event for which it is causally sufficient *will occur*.

Clearly, the causal principle is very general in scope: it applies to *all* events. Also clearly, it is a very important claim to make about all events, one that, if true, certainly would seem to add to our knowledge of the real world. The principle, that is, does not appear to be analytic. Indeed, if it expresses a proposition, it expresses a *synthetic* proposition. On this there appears to be complete unanimity. Where the unanimity is lacking is over the questions, "*How* is this principle known— a posteriori or a priori?" and "*Is* this principle known?" We cannot hope to answer either question here, but it is worth noting that we do constantly seem to assume this principle and think ourselves reasonable in doing so. Whenever something happens—a building collapses, a person falls ill, an armed conflict breaks out, or darkness descends upon the earth at midday—we think it reason-able to ask why or how these things have happened; we recognize the point of inquiring into the cause or causes of the phenomenon in question.

Now, suppose we assume the causal principle is known to be true. Obviously, this is an important assumption, and it would be quite inappro-priate to make it in some circumstances—for example, if we were trying to decide whether the priniciple *is* true! It is appropriate here, however, since we are interested in determining not whether we know that it is true but how we should classify our knowledge of its truth, *if* we know it. In particular, we want to understand why some philosophers think this knowl-edge of ours, assuming we have it, must be classified as synthetic a priori. So let us assume that the principle is known to be true and see if we can grasp the thought of these philosophers. The logic of their argument is really very simple. It consists in arguing that we cannot account for our knowledge of the causal principle if we suppose that this knowledge is a posteriori; therefore, it follows that it must be a priori. This argument assumes, once again, that we do know that the principle is true *and* that all knowledge is either a posteriori or a priori—both assumptions that might be challenged. But we will assume them anyway because our interest here lies not so much in determining the truth about these matters as simply trying to understand them.

Suppose, then, that someone maintains we know the causal principle a posteriori. If this were so, then the principle could be, at most, what we have termed an inductive generalization, arrived at by means of observing a more or less large number of similar cases. In the present instance, the similarity would have to consist in the fact that each of the events we have observed has had a cause. In other words, given the view that we know the causal principle a posteriori, what we must suppose is that we observe one event (say, the collapse of a building) and find out by observation that this event had a cause (for example, a faulty beam); then we observe another event (say, the darkness descending upon the earth at midday) and find out by observation that it had a cause (say, a solar eclipse); and so on. Then, having observed an indefinitely large number of cases in which events occur and are caused to do so, and no cases in which events occur in the absence of some cause, we are supposed to arrive at the inductive generalization, 'Every event has a cause', a principle whose truth is supposed to be grounded in observation and hence is alleged to be known a posteriori.

Now, if the causal principle were an inductive generalization, it would be possible to show that it is false by finding just one genuine counter instance; that is, just one case in which an event occurred but was not caused. But in order even to begin to try to falsify or disconfirm a proposition, we need to know what to look for as a counter instance; we need to know *what would count* as such an instance and *how to recognize one*. Without such understanding, our 'search' for a counter instance would be an exercise in futility; we would not know where to begin or how to end. For example, if someone said that all swans are white, we would have a clear grasp of what would count as, and how to recognize, a counter instance. All we would need to do is find a swan whose color was something other than white. And this is why we regard the existence of black swans as genuine counter instances to the claim that all swans are white, which, in turn, is why we regard this claim as false. As for the claim that every event has a cause, when this is interpreted as an inductive generalization, we must ask what would count as a counter instance and how we could recognize it. What would count as a counter instance is straightforward enough. A counter instance to the inductive generalization that every event has a cause would be a case of an event that occurs without a cause or, more simply, an *uncaused event*. Accordingly, if we could find just one case of an uncaused event, then we could show that it is false to say that *every* event has a cause.

But to find such a counter instance presupposes that we know what we are looking for. In the present case, it presupposes that we could recognize an uncaused event if we saw one, that we would know how to tell if any event were caused or uncaused. It is this necessity of one's having to distinguish between caused and uncaused events that inspires some of those philosophers who think that the causal principle is synthetic and known a priori to dispute the claim that it is synthetic and known a posteriori. For, they argue, there simply is no intelligible way for us to distinguish between (1) events that occur that *lack* a cause and (2) events that occur that *have* a cause but whose cause is unknown.

To make this clearer, suppose that an event, E, occurs and suppose that the question arises as to whether E was caused or not. Suppose, further, that after considerable research, it is announced that no cause of E has been discovered. Would this show that E was uncaused? Not at all, these philosophers argue. For the proposition 'E was caused' is logically consistent with the proposition 'The cause of E has yet to be discovered'. This is because, in saying that E was caused, we do not commit ourselves to the claim that we know what caused it. Our ignorance of what caused E, therefore, is perfectly compatible with the fact that E was caused. Similarly compatible, therefore, are the claims, (1) 'We have not been able to find E's cause' and (2) 'E has a cause'.

What follows from this? Something very important, these philosophers think. What follows, they think, is that in some crucial cases, no matter how much observational research might go into looking for the cause of E, there is *no way* for us to determine, *by observation*, which of two contradictory propositions is true—either 'E was caused' or 'E was uncaused'. And this is an important consequence for those who maintain that the causal principle is known a posteriori and is, therefore, an inductive generalization. For to accept this view does seem to commit one to the position that this principle could be shown to be false a posteriori by discovering, *by observation*, that at least one event was uncaused.

What the argument just given purports to show, however, is that we never could discover, by observation, that an event was uncaused. For no matter how often or long we might fail to discover that E had a cause, it would not follow that it lacks one. It is just as possible that it has one that we have yet to discover. Accordingly—and this is the nub of the matter —if a proposition can be an inductive generalization if and only if we can conceive of its having a genuine counter instance discoverable by observation, then, from what we have said above, it appears to follow that the proposition 'Every event has a cause' is not an inductive generalization. For it does not seem possible for us to conceive of discovering, by observation, a genuine counter instance to this principle.

Something important is thought to follow from this also, at least according to some of those philosophers who believe that the causal principle is synthetic a priori. What they think follows from all of the above is precisely the view they espouse—namely, that the causal principle is synthetic and is known a priori. The grounds for their thinking so are now before us and can be summarized as follows. Recall, first, what we have agreed to assume, for the sake of argument—(1) that all knowledge is either a posteriori or a priori and (2) that we do know that the casual principle is true. And from this it evidently follows that if we do not know the causal principle a posteriori—if, for example, as the above argument has it, we cannot give a satisfactory account of our knowledge of this principle, when it is thought to be known a posteriori—then our knowledge of this principle must be a priori. And to understand this is to understand half of the position under discussion. All that remains to observe is that the causal principle is *not* analytic, which implies that it must be synthetic, if it is either. And clearly it is not analytic since its denial is not self-contradictory. (Even if it is false as a matter of fact that some events are uncaused, the proposition 'Some events are uncaused' is not false just because of its meaning or just because of its form.) Thus, if the causal principle expresses a proposition, it expresses a synthetic proposition, and our knowledge of it does add to our knowledge of reality. And thus it is that we can see how, by using a particular line of reasoning, a philosopher might argue that we do have genuine knowledge of reality that is not based on observation or, to put the same point more technically, we do know at least one synthetic proposition a priori.

Yet another point is thought to follow from this—namely, that the causal principle is a *necessary* truth. This follows, it is alleged, because our knowledge of this principle is supposed to be a priori. For all a priori knowledge, as we have seen, is knowledge of truths that are necessary. However, we have just seen that the causal principle is not analytic; that is, it is not necessarily true just because of its meaning. And we observed earlier that it is not necessarily true because of its form. Accordingly, the kind of necessity that this principle has, if it is necessary, is not the kind of necessity that characterizes tautologies. For it is not a contradiction to deny that the causal principle is true. How we are to understand this idea of necessity is a difficult problem we cannot resolve here. For our purposes, however, let us note that some philosophers have maintained that this principle is necessary (because it is known a priori) but is not necessary in the way that a tautology is (because its denial is not a contradiction).

There are options to this view, of course. Following the English philosopher David Hume (1711–1776), we could deny that the principle of causality is known to be true in the first place. Or we could deny that it is either true or false but is, instead, a rule that directs certain kinds of activity such as scientific ones. But the truth of the principle is not the issue presently before us. The issue is: assuming that this principle is true, and assuming that we know that it is, why have some philosophers maintained that 'Every event has a cause' is a synthetic a priori truth? Enough has been said, it seems, to provide a partial answer to this question. And enough has been said, perhaps, to suggest how philosophers who accept the idea of synthetic a priori knowledge might argue for their position in general. This they do often, though not exclusively, by attempting to show that the classification of some item of knowledge as a posteriori runs into difficulties not unlike those we have just discussed in the example of the causal principle.

EPISTEMOLOGICAL OUTLOOKS

Perhaps the most important general division that can be drawn in epistemology is that between the *rationalists* and the *empiricists*. These terms and their cognates, *rationalism* and *empiricism*, are not names affixed to some settled body of knowledge. Not all rationalists agree with one another concerning what is known, and neither do all empiricists. Rather, these terms are convenient labels we use to refer to a philosopher's most fundamental epistemological outlook.

RATIONALISM AND EMPIRICISM

At first glance, the primary difference between the rationalist's and empiricist's outlook may seem negligible: rationalists hold that our knowledge of reality, if we have any, must be synthetic a priori; empiricists believe that our knowledge of reality, if we have any, must be synthetic a posteriori. But what might seem a small difference of opinion has consequences that are as far reaching as they are profound. For consider what this difference amounts to in practice. An empiricist would maintain that the data from which we build and test our knowledge of reality is the content of those observations we make by means of our senses: all knowledge of reality must be authenticated by sense experience, just as all knowledge of reality must likewise have its origin in sense experience. A rationalist, on the other hand, would maintain that our knowledge of what is real must be acquired, tested, and authenticated independently of the senses: our reason, or some other nonsensory way of knowing, is the source and arbiter of knowledge claims about reality.

No two outlooks could be more unlike, more pervasively in conflict. Imagine how rationalists and empiricists would approach any particular question concerning our knowledge of the existence of something. In the case of the existence of God, say, or of an allegedly transcendent being meeting a certain description, empiricists would hold that we would know that such a being exists if we either directly observed him by means of our senses or could validly infer his existence from what we do directly observe. In a word, they would hold that, if we must argue at all for God's existence, we must do so a posteriori: at least one of the premises in our proof would have to be claimed to be known by observation. Rationalists, on the other hand, would maintain that, if a proof of God's existence is possible, it must be carried out wholly a priori: no premise whose truth is claimed to be a posteriori could be permitted in the proof. Thus, as our future discussions will confirm, rationalists and empiricists differ not necessarily over *whether* we can prove that something is real (some agree, for example, that God's existence can be proven), but always and necessarily they will disagree over *how we know* what is real. It is, perhaps, a frustrating fact about philosophy that philosophers cannot themselves agree on a "method," comparable in its role to the "scientific method" of the scientists, in terms of which to carry on their investigations. But this very absence of agreement is one of philosophy's most invigorating features as well.

One point about the rationalist-empiricist controversy we have not clarified adequately is why it is that rationalists disparage sense experience as a source of knowledge and why empiricists return the charge by insisting that rationalists trespass the limitations of reason's power to know. A common rationalist maneuver here is to introduce considerations about the illusoriness of certain sensory experiences, as well as other related considerations that, both individually and cumulatively, are intended to cast doubt on the reliability of our senses. For example, each one of us has had experiences where the "testimony of our senses" has misled us. For example, which of the two lines below appears to be the longest?

The top line looks longest, but a careful measurement will reveal the lines are equivalent in length.

Related to these "illusions" are hallucinatory experiences, cases where we 'hear' noises or 'see' objects that are not there. Each of us, for example, has seen puddles in the road ahead of us, only to find no water in the place when we arrive. The philosopher Réné Descartes (1596–1650) provides a classic expression of these and other misgivings about the reliability of our senses in the first and second of his *Meditations*. We will consider

Descartes's argument in more detail in Chapter 6, but it will be useful to develop here one question he raises—namely "How do we know we are not now dreaming?" At first glance this seems easy to settle. We know we are not dreaming, we think, because everything we now see or touch or smell is sensed vividly. It's just not like the way we usually experience things when dreaming. Nevertheless, we must acknowledge that there have been occasions in the past when we have sensed things just as vividly as now only to find out that we were dreaming at the time. Such dreams, which we might call "realistic dreams," have this quality of convincing us of their veracity precisely because they are so vivid—so "lifelike," as we say. Thus, the question, "How do we know we are not now dreaming"? does not pose the question, "How do we know that we are not now having an imprecise, chaotic dream?" It asks, rather, "How do we know that we are not now having a *realistic* dream?" And in response to this question it will be idle to insist upon the vividness of our present sensory experiences. This would be idle because, by definition, the sensory appearances in a realistic dream are *just as vivid* as those sensory experiences we have in our waking life.

The difficulty here goes deeper still. For suppose that someone thinks he can test for whether he is dreaming or awake by, say, pinching himself. If awake, pinching oneself surely would produce a certain sensation. But would the occurrence of this sensation in any way support the contention that the person is awake and not dreaming? Not in the least. For it certainly is possible to be having a dream in which one pinches oneself and in which one experiences the sensation of pain caused by the pinch. Thus, since it is just as possible to have such an experience during the course of a realistic dream as to have one during our waking life, having such an experience could not provide any evidence that one was awake rather than asleep and dreaming. Moreover, once we understand why this is true in the special case of pinching oneself, we should be able to see that it also is true in the case of any sensation. Thus, given any sensation we might have during our waking life, it is logically possible to have a sensation of the same kind, intensity, vividness, and so on, while asleep and dreaming. It thus becomes impossible to provide evidence for the proposition 'I am awake' merely by appealing to anything we might experience by means of our senses. Thus, says Descartes, in effect, not only are the senses an unreliable, untrustworthy guide to the nature of reality; more than this, they cannot even be counted upon to provide an answer to so simple, so elementary a question as, "Am I awake or dreaming now?" The fact that we might nonetheless tend to rely on our senses for information about reality, Descartes thinks, merely displays how unenlightened we are and how much there is to overcome before we can make any headway in our search for a proper understanding of reality. And for Descartes, as for any rationalist, the first thing to learn is, so to speak, to *un*learn our dependence on our senses.

Now, rationalists are very much inclined to emphasize and dwell on cases like these in order to support their belief that our senses cannot be relied upon as a firm foundation for our knowledge of reality, and they are stern in their counsel that we look elsewhere than to the senses for such a reliable basis. But to what shall we look? Reason, we know, proves its dependability in other areas of knowledge, most notably in mathematics and logic where, independent of any evidence supplied by the senses, it is competent to discover analytic, necessary truths. It is a natural enough inference from this, finally, to the rationalist's belief that reason and reason alone can be counted upon as a reliable source of knowledge in general.

Perhaps we can make the rationalist's nomination of reason to the status of sole source of knowledge more intelligible if we view his procedure from a slightly different angle. For suppose we begin our search for knowledge, as the rationalist does, in the belief that all knowledge must be knowledge of some necessary truth and that only reason can apprehend what is necessarily true. Then it would follow that—short of philosophical skepticism, which is the denial that we have *any* knowledge of what is real—all knowledge, including that knowledge we have of reality, must be the work of reason and none the work of the senses. For observation, as we have seen, never can provide an adequate basis for necessary truth.

Empiricists have responses to the rationalist's criticisms that deserve to be studied closely. For the moment, however, we will look not at these responses, but at the empiricists' most fundamental charge against rationalism—namely, that reason is capable of discovering only those necessary truths that are analytic, not those that are synthetic. This charge and the contention that all knowledge of what is real must be synthetic constitute the empiricist's indictment of rationalism's pretensions. Notice that the empiricist does not deny that reason unaided by the senses is capable of discovering some truth; rather, he insists, it is that reason is *limited* in the kind of truth it can discover, namely, analytic truth.

Now, both the empiricist and the rationalist would agree that an apprehension of an analytic truth adds nothing to our knowledge of reality. Knowledge of analytically true propositions can only inform us about the meaning of *words* or the form of *propositions*; it cannot tell us whether anything real is named by the words or described by the proposition. As an illustration, consider the proposition 'A triangle must have three interior angles'. To know that this proposition is true is not to know either that triangles do or do not exist. It is simply to know part of the meaning of the word 'triangle'. Similarly, to know that the proposition 'If all leprechauns are Irish, then all leprechauns are Irish' is a tautology, is not to settle the question about the reality or otherwise of the wee folk. On this point, both rationalists and empiricists are agreed. Where they disagree is over the question, "Is all knowledge of necessary truth limited to knowledge of analytic truths?" Empiricists answer this question affirmatively and deny that rationalists succeed in demonstrating that there are necessary synthetic truths. Rationalists respond negatively and seek to clarify how it is that a proposition can be both synthetic and necessary. How adequate or inadequate these conflicting epistemological outlooks are, and how weak or strong are the arguments invoked to support them, are questions each of us will have to consider in the light of future experience.

POSITIVISM

As fundamental and pervasive as the division between rationalism and empiricism is, it is not exhaustive. Some philosophers do not fit comfortably into either category, while others, such as Immannel Kant (1724–1804), can be argued to fit in both. We must bear in mind, therefore, the limitations of this, as of our other, distinctions, without thereby denying their general accuracy or utility. However, one further epistemological outlook deserves to be dealt with here, namely positivism. Many philosophers regard it as a form of empiricism, and perhaps they are right. Still, not all empiricists are positivists, so in discussing positivism we will not be repeating what we just said about empiricism. Moreover, positivism, as we shall see later, adds a new dimension to the long-standing philosophical disputes between rationalists and empiricists. It also adds something of a contemporary flavor to such disputes since, as a movement in philosophy, positivism was by and large a twentieth-century phenomenon.

In our Chapter 1 discussion of the positivist's conception of philosophy we indicated some of the conclusions but few of the premises of his thinking—in particular, his epistemology. This needs to be remedied.

What is most distinctive about positivism is its emphasis on testing for the *meaningfulness* of expressions. By 'meaningfulness' here we do not mean "placing or finding value in," as when we speak of a "meaningful experience" or "a meaningful relationship." It is the meaningfulness of *expressions,* of *words,* into which the positivist characteristically inquires, and what he believes he discovers to be true, more often than we might suppose, is that what passes for the most profound truth or at least as an important falsehood lacks a meaning altogether.

Now, the suggestion that certain expressions or strings of words are meaningless is neither profound nor original with the positivist. The series of words, "John clotheslines under woke cellardoors," for example, fail to make sense—and thus may be said to be meaningless. And, in general, word constructions that violate the rules of grammar have been recognized as lacking a clear sense and sometimes as having none at all. We do not say that "John clotheslines under woke cellardoors" expresses a false proposition; we say, rather, that it fails to express a proposition at all. What is original with the positivist and, if true, what is profound as well, is the thesis that we can use sentences in the indicative mood that are in every respect grammatically in order and yet nevertheless can fail to express a proposition—can fail, that is, to assert something that is either true or false. It is such expressions as these that the positivist seeks to expose as nonsense and as expressing "pseudopropositions." And what is revolutionary about this investigation is that many of philosophy's most revered and respected contentions are, given positivism's tenets, fated to be found sputtering in a not very respectable heap of nonsense.

How does the positivist propose to distinguish what is meaningful from what is nonsense? The answer here lies in his appeal to the so-called *verification principle*. How, precisely, this principle should be formulated, is a controversy into which positivists recurrently plunged and about which there was no unanimity of opinion, but the most widely held view would seem to be as follows. When we use a sentence in the indicative mood we are said to express a synthetic proposition if and only if either (a) there is some observation or series of observations we now are able to carry out and as a result of which we can verify the truth of what is asserted or (b) there is some observation or series of observations that, although we now are not able to carry out, could *conceivably* be carried out by us and as a result of which we could verify the truth of what is asserted. If our use of a sentence meets condition (a), it is said to express a proposition that is *verifiable in practice*; if our use of a sentence satisfies condition (b), it is said to express a proposition that is *verifiable in principle*. If we use a sentence that satisfies either (a) or (b), the sentence is said to have *cognitive meaning*. Uses of sentences that do not satisfy either (a) or (b), and do not express an analytic proposition, are said to lack cognitive meaning; such sentences also are said not to express propositions or to express *pseudopropositions*. It is 'meaning' as understood within the network of these concepts–it is, that is to say, *cognitive* meaning—that the positivist denies many sentences have, despite the fact that they are grammatically sound.

Three nonphilosophical examples might help to make the foregoing clearer. Consider, first, our use of the sentence, "The words on this page are printed in black." To determine whether this sentence is cognitively meaningful, we need to ask whether our use of it expresses a proposition; that is, we need to ask whether there are any observations we are now able to carry out or could conceivably carry out to test for its truth or falsity. Here the answer is clear. In understanding the sentence, as used in the present context, we understand what to look for in order to determine whether what it expresses is true or not, and we now are able to look for it. In this case, therefore, the sentence expresses a proposition that is verifiable in practice. Notice that the same is true of our use of the sentence, "The words on this page are printed in red," except that the proposition expressed happens to be false.

Consider, next, the sentence, "There is water beneath the surface of Mars." Now, to date, the exploration of Mars has been insufficient as a test for the presence of water beneath its surface, though it has ruled out the presence of canals and other apparent features that helped foster the belief that there is water there. As a matter of fact, therefore, we lack the opportunity and knowledge, at present, to verify what is asserted. Thus, what is asserted, if anything is, is not verifiable in practice. However, we can *conceive* of what it would be like to verify what is asserted. This would amount to our being there and observing the planet at first hand, or otherwise gaining relevant knowledge of its environment, sufficient for us to observe or infer that it has water beneath its surface. This is conceivable; that is, the state of affairs hypothesized is logically possible. Thus, although we do not express a proposition that is verifiable in practice by our use of the sentence in question, we do express one that is verifiable in principle. Our use of this sentence, therefore, is cognitively meaningful, and any two persons who might disagree about the presence of water beneath Mars's outer crust, one affirming it and the other denying its existence, would be engaged in a genuine cognitive disagreement. That is, they would be disagreeing about something that is true or false and whose truth or falsity can be known, in principle.

Consider, finally, this last case. Suppose that Smith, a friend of ours, complains that there are people who enter and use his room when he is not there. We are sympathetic with his plight and ask him how he knows about them and what can be done to prevent their entrance. "I've never seen them or heard them," he tells us, "and, believe me, I've tried. Lots of times I've pretended to go out. You know, I've made a lot of noise and stuff. But then I've hidden in places. Under the bed sometimes, sometimes in the closet. But every time I've stayed around, they've failed to come."

We are even more sympathetic with his case, for we know how difficult it might be to catch such invaders, and we propose a more systematic procedure. We tell Smith that we will help him by standing guard along the hallway or spending the night in the next room, then, when he is gone, we will be able to see or hear his invaders and call the appropriate authorities. But Smith tells us that none of this will be to any avail. "You see," he says, "I've come to the conclusion that they're not your usual invader. I think they know if there's someone waiting, and it doesn't make any difference who it is. So long as there's someone around who might see them or hear them—or smell them, for that matter—they won't show up. So there's no point in any of you trying to set a trap for them."

We tell Smith that if they will not show up if we are around, perhaps they could be caught in some other way—say, by a camera or a tape recorder or some other machine or instrument that could detect their presence.

"I thought of that myself," Smith replies. "I've tried everything. Time-elapsed photography, closed-circuit TV, you name it, and I've tried it. It just doesn't do any good. I think they know when machines and such stuff have been left in order to detect them. And I think they will never come so long as some kind of detecting device is in my room. Like I said, these guys are not your usual invader. They're devilishly tricky."

We now are perplexed, though still sympathetic. For we can understand how people might have these extraordinary powers of perception, even though we have never met any. Poor Smith, we think, the victim of such devils. And no way to detect when they are there. We remark to Smith sympathetically that they must really make a mess of his room, rifling his drawers and ripping up his books and such stuff.

"Ah," says Smith, "If only they did such things! But these scoundrels are cleverer than that. The fact is they never disturb a single thing in my room. When I return after they've been there, everything in my room is exactly as I left it. Nothing is ever changed in the slightest degree. It's as though no one has been there at all!"

Now we are *really* perplexed, and we are beginning to wonder whether our sympathy has not been misplaced. "Look," we say, "you say they never do a thing to your room. And you say they never come if someone or something can detect their presence. We find this all very strange. There hardly seems to be any difference between what you call 'people who invade your room when you're not there' and no people at all. That is, it seems to be the case that everything you say about these people could equally well be the case if nobody entered your room when you left. We just find all this very perplexing."

"Boy, don't think I don't, too!" says Smith.

"But look here," we say, "even granting all you've said, it still remains to be asked whether it is *possible* or *conceivable* that someone might see or hear or smell your invaders, or whether it is *possible* or *conceivable* that some machine or instrument might detect their presence, or whether it is *conceivable or possible* that they might mess up your room or at least change it around to some noticeable degree. What do you say to these questions?"

"I've thought about them a lot," Smith says, "and I'll tell you what I think. I don't think any of these things are possible. I believe that even if someone *did* see or hear or smell someone in my room, or even if some machine *did* detect someone's presence there, or even if someone *did* mess up my room or change it in the slightest degree while I was out, that the person seen, heard, smelled, or the person mechanically detected, or the person responsible for the mess or change would *not* be one of the people I've been telling you about. The people I've been telling you about just aren't like that. Like I said, they're not your usual invader."

Now, given this imaginary situation, what are we to say? Certainly there are some things we can say with more than a fair degree of confidence. First, Smith clearly has ruled out verifying the existence of his 'invaders' in practice. No matter what we observe now, and no matter what presently existing instruments we might use, Smith has told us in no uncertain terms that we will not be able to verify their existence. Second, Smith also has ruled out verifying their existence in principle. For what he has said, in effect, is that it is simply impossible to see, hear, smell, or in any other way detect the existence of his 'invaders'. As he has said, if we *do* see, hear, smell, or in some other way detect someone's presence in his room, it follows that it *cannot* be one of the persons he is complaining about.

What more, then, can we say? The positivist has a clear answer. What we can and should say, he thinks, is that Smith is talking *nonsense,* that what he says fails altogether to have any cognitive meaning. Of course, that the positivist would maintain this is intelligible enough. For once we have seen of any alleged proposition that is not analytic (and, clearly, Smith's remarks about his invaders can hardly be construed as expressing an *analytic proposition*); and once we have seen that what is expressed is not verifiable, either in practice or in principle, then we know, from what has been said above, that the positivist will say just this.

But what may not be equally clear, and what deserves additional explanation, is what follows from what the positivist says. This is that it is *neither* true *nor* false that people, of the type supposed by Smith, enter his room. Of course, the suggestion that this is so cannot help but strike us as perplexing, especially if, as we have assumed up to now, we maintain that a proposition is expressed by the use of any sentence in the indicative mood. For when Smith says, "People use my room when I'm not there," the sentence he uses certainly is in the indicative mood.

To make the positivist's position more intelligible here, we need to distinguish between what we might term the ordinary meaning of this sentence, on the one hand, and the meaning that Smith gives it, on the other. Given the ordinary meaning of this sentence, what is expressed by its use certainly is verifiable. For, given its ordinary meaning, we can conceive of what would be necessary to verify the existence of people in Smith's room when Smith is absent. For example, we can conceive of sitting on his bed while he is gone and seeing a group of people enter the room. And it is because we can conceive of this that it would be reasonable to wait in his room and try thereby to detect their presence.

The sense that *Smith* gives to the sentence in question, however, is remarkably different. He thinks we cannot even *conceive* of how we might verify their presence. So, when we say that what Smith expresses by means of his use of the sentence "People visit my room when I'm not there" is, according to the positivist, neither true nor false, we must be careful to indicate that this is so in regard to Smith's conception of these "other people." Clearly, if Smith were to mean by 'people' what we ordinarily mean by 'people', then what he says would express something that is either true or false. Indeed, what he would express would be manifestly false, since there are no (ordinary) people who visit his room.

However, given Smith's *un*ordinary conception of the 'people' in question, there is no reason to regard what he expresses as true—or as false, for that matter, given positivism's tenets. For once we see that the existence of his alleged 'invaders' is supposed by him to be compatible with everything we do or conceivably could observe (for nothing that we either do or conceivably could observe could count as an observation of "them" or as evidence for "their" existence), we also see, the positivist thinks, that it would be as misleading to say that what Smith says is false as it would be to say that what he says is true. This is because, in saying either of these things, we imply, the positivist thinks, that what Smith says *makes sense,* and what this means is that we should at least be able to conceive of verifying the existence of his "invaders" by observation. Thus, since, as we have explained, Smith rules out the possibility of even conceiving of such verification, then it follows, given the positivist's verification principle, that what Smith expresses by means of the sentence in question not only is not true, it is not even false.

Now, no philosopher has set forth a view about persons who visit rooms but whose existence is not verifiable, in practice or in principle. What philosophers have done, however, at least according to positivists, is to set forth views that, in the relevant respects, are like Smith's view about his visitors. That is, philosophers have set forth views that are supposed to be about the real world but that are not verifiable, either in practice or in principle. Indeed, by definition, a rationalist does just this. For a rationalist believes that we gain insight into reality by apprehending a priori truths, and no a priori proposition can be verified by observation. For the positivist, therefore, rationalism is an empty epistemological outlook. There simply cannot be the kind of knowledge of reality that rationalists seek; and the kinds of problems rationalists raise, in their efforts to discredit the senses and thereby prepare the way for the celebration of reason, can be seen to be, according to the positivist, no problems at all. They are, he thinks, "pseudoproblems," or ones the correct answer to which is, "That problem cannot intelligibly arise."

To illustrate this, let us recall Descartes' question about how we know that we are not now dreaming. Recall that it is essential to this argument of his that we cannot verify that we are awake (or dreaming) merely by means of observation: for anything that we might observe when we are awake, we might also dream we are observing while we are asleep and having a realistic dream. It thus seems impossible to verify, either in practice or in principle, either the proposition 'We are awake' or the proposition 'We are asleep and having a realistic dream'. And recall, also, that Descartes believed that this inability to settle this issue by appealing to our observations bespoke an important limitation of the senses as a vehicle to knowledge of reality.

But this problem Descartes raises is, in one important respect, precisely like Smith's "problem" about his visitors: it cannot be settled by observation. Indeed, Descartes insists upon this fact. But if this "problem" cannot be settled by observation, either in practice or in principle, then how can any clear-headed person go on maintaining that it *is* a problem? That is the question the positivist wants us to ask, not only about Descartes' question about dreaming but about similar philosophical "problems" about reality. And what the positivist wants us to see is that, if the "problem" raised cannot be settled by observation, either in practice or in principle, then the "problem" is not a genuine problem at all. It is a pseudoproblem, one that can occur only to someone so long as he operates with a muddled conception of how reality is or can be known. Accordingly, the positivist thinks, the correct response to Descartes' question, "How do we know that we are not now having a realistic dream?", is not "We don't know" or "We don't know if all we rely on is what we know by our senses." The correct response, according to the positivist, is, "That question cannot intelligibly be asked."

Once we see how a positivist would argue in a particular case, like the preceding one, we can anticipate how he will argue in similar cases. Any time it becomes apparent to him that a supposed problem or a supposed proposition are such that they cannot be settled or verified in practice or in principle, he will attempt to discredit each by exposing them as pseudoproblems or pseudopropositions, respectively. It is characteristic of the positivist to do just this within the areas of moral and aesthetic judgment, as well as within the province of religious thought. Moral and aesthetic judgments, he argues, are not verifiable, in practice or in principle; therefore, such judgments are neither true nor false, and the meaning of such words as 'good', 'right', and 'duty' must be noncognitive. And the same is true of judgments about God, as we shall see in Chapter 4.

But however critical the positivist may be of attempts to construct theories of moral or aesthetic knowledge, he saves a special vehemence for those philosophers who attempt to construct theories of reality a priori—

namely, all those philosophers who are rationalists. These are the philosophers the positivist has in mind when he repudiates what he calls "metaphysics." Indeed, if we recall what we said in Chapter 1 about the nature of metaphysics, we can see why the positivist is opposed to it. There we said that to do metaphysics is to ask questions about reality that are not empirically decidable. We are now in a position to give a fuller explanation of this concept of empirical decidability. For to say that a question is empirically decidable is to say that its correct answer is verifiable in practice or in principle. Thus, since metaphysical questions are, by their very nature, not empirically decidable, it follows that the positivist must regard them as pseudoquestions. And this is why the term 'metaphysical', in the language of the positivist, takes on the negative implications of the term 'nonsense'. For nonsense, according to the positivist, just is what cannot be verified in practice or in principle; and metaphysical utterances are, it seems, necessarily incapable of such verification.

Thus it is that we can understand why the positivist rejects the traditional conception of philosophy. He does so because that conception of the discipline involves the belief that the philosopher can gain knowledge about what is good, what beauty is, and what is metaphysically real. However, claims about what is good, beautiful, and metaphysically real are, the posivitist believes, totally lacking in sense; that is, they make no sense. Thus, since a use of words must first make sense before it can express something that is either true or false (a proposition), it is clear, he thinks, that the traditional philosopher's claims about the good, the beautiful, and the real can be neither true nor false. It follows, therefore, given the positivist's premises, that a major portion of the traditional philosopher's area of inquiry—namely, ethics, aesthetics, and metaphysics—must be given up as devoid of intellectual interest. According to the positivist, there are no truths to be found here; neither are there any falsehoods.

The similarity between positivism and empiricism, and the antipathy between it and rationalism, should be obvious. Like the empiricist, the positivist denies that we have synthetic a priori knowledge: All nonanalytic propositions must be observationally verifiable, in practice or in principle, which entails that none can be known a priori. But, unlike the empiricist, the positivist makes a stronger and distinctive indictment against the a priori metaphysical speculation of the rationalists. Whereas the empiricist denies that there is such knowledge, the positivist denies that there *can* be. And whereas the empiricist is disposed to concede to the rationalist the possible intelligibility of what the rationalist struggles to discover—namely, truths that are both synthetic and necessary—and labors instead to show that the rationalist's effort fails, the positivist refuses to grant from the outset the possible intelligibility of synthetic a priori knowledge and does not accord to the rationalist's contentions the dignity of even being false.

From a strict positivistic point of view, therefore, the empiricist is as confused as the rationalist. For both assume that what the rationlist seeks is possible. Their disagreement centers on whether it is attained. It remains for the positivist to suggest that it cannot be. And it remains for us to investigate how these conflicting epistemological perspectives contribute to the discussion of some of philosophy's most difficult and urgent problems. This we will begin to do in the second part of this book. But first it will be worth our while to pause and collect together ideas we have discussed in this and in preceding chapters. This we shall do in the Interlude, which follows.

FOR FURTHER READING

Edwards. Paul, ed., *Encyclopedia of Philosophy*. New York: Macmillan Company and the Free Press, 1967. Contains good essays on rationalism, empiricism, and positivism. Available in reference room of most libraries.

Gorovitz, Samuel, and Ron G. Williams, *Philosophical Analysis: An Introduction to Its Language and Techniques*. New York: Random House, 1963. Devotes a chapter to the analytic-synthetic, a posterior-a priori distinctions.

EXERCISES

1. Define each of the following concepts.
   a) synthetic proposition
   b) analytic proposition
   c) a posteriori knowledge
   d) a priori knowledge
   e) a factually necessary condition
   f) a logically necessary condition
   g) a factually sufficient condition
   h) a logically sufficient condition
   i) an inductive generalization
   j) empiricism
   k) rationalizm
   l) synthetic a priori knowledge
   m) positivism
   n) the verification principle
   o) cognitive meaning

2. Indicate whether each of the following propositions is analytic or synthetic. If the latter, indicate whether you think knowledge of its truth is a posteriori or a priori. (In doing this, ask yourself whether you think the proposition is an inductive generalization or a necessary truth.) If you think the status of the proposition is controversial, indicate why.

 a) All birds fly.
 b) All birds have feathers.
 c) All birds are warm-blooded.
 d) Water contains oxygen.
 e) Either experience is the best teacher or it is not.
 f) All our observations are of objects in space and time.
 g) Kepler was an astronomer.
 h) The square upon the hypotenuse of a right triangle is equal to the sum of the squares upon the other two sides.
 i) All men are mortal.
 j) All men are homo sapiens.
 k) A basketball is round.
 l) Basketball is a game.
 m) A brother is a male sibling.
 n) Water is heavier than air.
 o) Whatever goes up must come down.
 p) Nothing is ever created or destroyed, only changed.

3. What is the connection between the idea of an inductive generalization, on the one hand, and the ideas of a factually necessary and a factually sufficient condition, on the other?

4. Explain how rationalists, empiricists, and positivists have conflicting points of view regarding the possibility of synthetic a priori knowledge.

5. Why does the positivist reject the traditional conception of philosophy?

Interlude:
Retrospect and Prospect

We closed the preceding chapter by saying it would be beneficial to review some of the ideas discussed earlier. This should help us get our bearings and prepare ourselves for the tasks ahead.

LOOKING BACK

In the first chapter we tentatively defined the discipline of philosophy as the search for good arguments to support claims to knowledge made in or about metaphysics, aesthetics, ethics, logic, epistemology, and so on. We said then that we could assess how adequate our definition was only after we had done considerable reading in the discipline, and that task still remains before us. But we also said that before we could assess our definition, we had to clarify and understand it. And that task would seem now to be behind us. For as we said, a good argument, in the sense of a sound deductive argument, is one that commits no formal or informal logical fallacy and one that contains premises that are known to be true. To understand what the philosopher seeks, accordingly, we have clarified the concepts of formal and informal fallacies, as well as alternative conceptions of how the truth of any given premise can be known and should be tested. With this understanding in mind we can now formulate those questions we need to ask any philosophical argument and to distinguish between types of disagreements that arise between philosophers.

PRINCIPAL QUESTIONS

The principal questions we should ask of any philosopher's argument are two: (1) Is his argument formally and informally valid? (2) Are his premises known to be true? According to our definition of philosophy, then, we will assume that any philosopher, whether traditional or positivist, sets himself the task of producing formally and informally valid arguments based on premises acknowledged by rational men to be true. And this is why we will suppose that if a philosopher fails to produce arguments free from formal and informal fallacies, or if he fails to convince rational men of the truth of his argument's premises, then it follows that he fails to achieve the goal that the discipline of philosophy has set for itself—namely, to find good arguments that support his position.

DO ALL KNOWLEDGE CLAIMS NEED TO BE SUPPORTED?

One objection that might be raised against our conception of philosophy is that it commits us to the belief that all knowledge claims need to be supported by valid arguments, a belief, it is objected, that is false. This objection is unfounded, but it does bring to light one long-standing debate of epistemology—namely, whether there is any knowledge of synthetic truths that is indubitable but indemonstrable. Some empiricist philosophers have maintained that some synthetic claims are *incorrigible*, meaning that no rational person can doubt their truth, but they neither can have nor need to be proven by an argument. For instance, to say "I am in pain" or "I feel faint" may be giving verbal expression to knowledge of this sort; so also descriptions of the data of immediate sensory experience such as "Red color patch here now."

On the other hand, some rationalist philosophers believe there are synthetic necessary truths that cannot be doubted by rational, mature men. These truths are said to be "intuited" to be so and thus are called *intuitive truths*. By "intuitive," these philosophers mean that the truths cannot be demonstrated, and do not need to be. In this connection, there has been considerable discussion of the so-called laws of logic—for example, '*A* is *A*' (the Law of Identity) and 'Either *A* or not-*A*' (the Law of Excluded Middle). Quite a few ethical philosophers, moreover, have maintained that there are moral truths of this same, intuitive kind.

Now, whether incorrigible or intuitive knowledge exists is an important question, but we are concerned here with whether our conception of philosophy commits us to the view that there is not or cannot be such knowledge. This is not the case. To claim that there *is* incorrigible or intuitive knowledge is to make a claim that stands in need of rational support, and those philosophers who make such claims have not been insensitive to the need to support them. Thus, we can expect and should demand that they set forth some supporting argument. And we should apply to this argument of theirs precisely the same standards of acceptability that we apply to any other philosophical argument.

DISTINGUISHING TYPES OF DISAGREEMENT

What we said earlier about how to distinguish between assessing an argument's validity and assessing the truth of an argument's premises can also help us here. It helps to make clear what is being debated and how deep the disagreement goes.

We can clarify this in the following way. Whenever a philosopher questions the truth of an argument's premises, we need to distinguish between criticism that denies or questions fundamental epistemological assumptions and criticism that does not deny or question such assumptions. Suppose, for example, that a philosopher sets out to prove the truth of p; and suppose that one of the premises he uses, or a proposition whose truth his premises assume, is k—'All knowledge of reality is derived from and must be authenticated by experience'.

Criticisms of this argument can take two different forms. First, they might deny the truth of k, k being a version of the empiricist's epistemological outlook. Now, *this* type of objection could not consistently be raised by an empiricist; it could be consistently raised only by a philosopher who does not share empiricist presuppositions. Such a denial of some fundamental epistemological belief shows the dispute itself is of a fundamental character, and the critic is obliged to show that the argument's proponent is committed to a false epistemology. Such debates are complex and subtle, and the verdict that competent philosophers pass upon them often is split.

The second form of criticism is to concede the truth of k, but challenge the truth of *some other premise* that occurs in the argument or question the argument's logic. Clearly, either objection can be made by a philosopher who agrees with the argument's proponent on fundamental epistemological beliefs. Thus, one empiricist can dispute the soundness of another empiricist's argument, and one rationalist can dispute the soundness of another rationalist's argument, and so on. We are saying nothing new here; earlier we tried to make clear that 'empiricism' and 'rationalism' do not describe settled bodies of knowledge but rather fundamental outlooks concerning how knowledge can be acquired and tested. This qualification deserves to be repeated because it is easy to forget that two philosophers sharing the same outlook do not necessarily agree on all points.

A critic who does not share the epistemological outlook of the proponent of an argument does not have to engage in a debate about whose assumptions are most adequate. A rationalist, for example, would not accept k as true, but he could simply assume it is for the sake of argument, and go on to argue that the empiricist advocate of the argument failed to prove the truth of some *other* premise or that the argument commits a formal or informal fallacy.

One final point: Two philosophers—an empiricist and a rationalist, for example—can agree that a given proposition, *p,* is true and yet disagree on how *p*'s truth is known or can be proven. And two rationalists or two empiricists might agree among themselves concerning the truth of *p* and still dispute each other's proofs. From the fact that a philosopher is critical of another philosopher's argument, in short, it does not follow that the two must differ in their judgment of the truth of the conclusion.

There are, then, logically distinct ways in which two philosophers might disagree in any given argument. They may agree or disagree on fundamental epistemological points; they may differ or concur on the truth of a conclusion; they may have conflicting judgments about the argument's validity. The fact that any two philosophers are at odds over the merits of a particular argument is insufficient by itself, therefore, to indicate how deep or fundamental is their disagreement. This can be understood only by a patient, informed investigation of the debate. It is understanding of this order and depth that we will seek to attain in what follows.

LOOKING AHEAD

Whether what we have said is true or useful cannot be tested in a vacuum. To test this, we must get into philosophy itself and stop talking about it. We already know, however, that philosophy has distinguishable branches of inquiry, so before we can satisfy the need to get into the discipline we first need to determine *where* to get into it—in ethics, aesthetics, metaphysics, or whatever. This choice is not easy, for no matter how much divisions of philosophy overlap, to choose from one branch means, because of time, we must ignore other branches. But perhaps if we remind ourselves that we cannot do everything at once, the limitations of the choice we will make will not seem unreasonable.

THE WELTANSCHAUUNG OF THE WESTERN WORLD

When a large percentage of an identifiable group share some general beliefs about and attitudes toward the world, it is appropriate to speak of the *Weltanschauung* of that group. Of course, this involves some oversimplification since it is unlikely that all its members will agree in all their beliefs. Still, this is a legitimate and, for our purposes, a useful way of thinking.

Now, there are certain beliefs that have been and continue to be accepted by so large a percentage of the people of the Western world that we may speak of the *Weltanschauung* of Western civilization. Among these beliefs, three in particular stand out: First, there is the belief that the natural universe stands in some relationship of dependence to a being, called God, who created and transcends it. Second, because of the activity of this God or for some other reasons, human beings are thought to have the unique capacity to make free choices and thus are responsible for the actions they choose to perform. Third, there is the belief that a human being does not cease but continues to exist after the death of his body. These three beliefs not only constitute the heart of the *Weltanschauung* of the Western world; they also comprise the core of traditional metaphysics. The problems of God, freedom, and immortality, as they are referred to, have occasioned a rich assortment of philosophical speculation, analysis, and debate. Thus, there is no dearth of philosophical literature inspired by these beliefs, and the problem of acquainting ourselves with it is mainly that of determining how much we can reasonably hope to cover, since not all of it can be.

Now, even if you do not accept any of these beliefs, you cannot have avoided being exposed to them, they are so much a part of our culture's *Weltanschauung* and, as a result, of our own education and upbringing. And since you are probably among either the believers or the nonbelievers, your position, whichever it is, stands in need of the clarification and close scrutiny the discipline of philosophy demands of it. One needs to ask, that is, what are the reasons he can bring forward to support his contentions, whether these reasons are known to be true, and whether they provide a firm logical basis for what he avers. The discipline of philosophy is nothing if it fails to make the same demands of our own thinking as it makes of the thinking of others.

It is a tribute to the seriousness with which man has taken the challenge to think clearly and believe truly that we have the rich philosophical heritage we do. Confronted with the possibility of being mistaken about the existence or nonexistence of God, free will, and immortality, philosophers have sought to distinguish fact from fiction, and they have bequeathed to us the results of this, their critical and creative reflection. Whether we can go beyond what they have discovered, their ideas are at least an appropriate place to begin. Often the ideas they set forth anticipate and correspond to our own, so that in examining them we are examining the credentials of our own beliefs. But we shall also find that the inventiveness of philosophers often exceeds what has occurred to us, and in examining these original ideas, we shall experience some of the distinctive pleasures philosophy affords. For to come face to face with an original, challenging idea affords a mind expansion as rare as it is invigorating.

THE TASKS BEFORE US

In the chapter that follows we will consider some of the more important arguments that have been put forth as proofs of God's existence, and we will also consider how the positivist's verification principle has added a new dimension to questions about the existence or nonexistence of God. In Chapter 5, we will take up the question of whether man is free and, hence, deserves to be held responsible for his behavior, or whether, as the view called hard determinism maintains, all our choices are unavoidable. The question of life after death will be taken up in Chapter 6, and there we will discuss both the question of how man must be conceived, if personal survival after death is to be realistically possible, as well as the question of how good the evidence for survival is. Finally, in a brief Afterword following Chapter 6, we will take another look back over the material and problems we have discussed, and we will take a final look forward to some of those questions and issues that we have been unable to discuss adequately or not at all.

PART *II* UNDERSTANDING PHILOSOPHICAL PROBLEMS

4 Does God Exist?

Belief in a God or gods has been so widespread, and the God or gods believed in so diverse, that, even if we limit our discussion to the religious beliefs of Western civilization, the question whether God exists is too vague to demand an unqualified yes or no answer. So that the question will pose a specific problem, let us try to give a definite sense to the term God by confining our attention to the God of Judaism and Christianity—the "Judeo-Christian God." Our principal object of inquiry, then, will be how or whether we can know that the Judeo-Christian God exists. Before turning to this, however, we will need to be certain that we understand how this God has been conceived. Only then can we examine representative proofs of his existence. And only after we have examined these proofs can we appreciate the debate over whether "God exists" can be used to express a genuine proposition.

Of course, Jews and Christians do not completely agree on all matters that pertain to their religious beliefs—especially the question of the divinity of Jesus Christ, although there are other differences, too. Still there is a substantial set of beliefs that both commonly accept, especially as these relate to the nature of God, so that we are entitled to speak of a God who is at once the God of both the Jews and the Christians. It is not our task to explain how Jews and Christians came to share a common conception of their God. No doubt this is due to a common understanding of what God is thought to have revealed about himself as recorded in the Bible, but we will leave the exact details of this revelation to biblical scholars. Here we need only recognize that a reasonably stable, rich, and apparently coherent conception of God evolved under Judaism and Christianity, and that the same God is worshiped by both Jews and Christians.

ATTRIBUTES OF THE JUDEO–CHRISTIAN GOD

The attributes of the Judeo-Christian God are those characteristics that distinguish him from everything else that exists. These attributes are commonly divided into two classes, the *moral attributes* and the *metaphysical attributes*. God's moral attributes characterize him as a *person*. They are attributes that God and other persons all possess in some degree. What distinguishes God from other persons, then, is not that he possesses these attributes but how or to what extent he does. God's metaphysical attributes are those that are not personal. Sometimes it is unclear whether a given attribute should be classified as personal or metaphysical. But classification is clear often enough so that all philosophers admit the distinction is useful. There are six principal metaphysical attributes of God. First, he is eternal: God always has and always will exist, and he has neither come into nor will he ever pass out of existence. Second, he is immutable or unchanging: what he is at any one moment of his existence is precisely the same as what he always has been and always will be. Third, God is wholly a spiritual or immaterial being and, as such, cannot be located as existing in or at some place in physical space. Fourth, God is that being upon which all other beings depend for their existence, whereas he depends on nothing else for his existence. Fifth, unlike all else that exists, God exists because of his very nature: God's nature is to exist and thus his nature is said to include aseity (self-existence). Sixth, God is utterly unique: there is one and only one being that is divine, and this is that one being who possesses the metaphysical and moral attributes of the Judeo-Christian God. In declaring that there is but one God, Jews and Christians commit themselves to a *monotheistic* conception of divinity, a conception that is at odds with all *polytheistic* conceptions, according to which there are many gods. In declaring that God is the creator of the physical universe and distinct from it, moreover, Jews and Christians commit themselves to rejecting a *pantheistic* conception of reality, according to which God and nature are one and the same.

It is conceivable that a being could have all the metaphysical attributes ascribed to the Judeo-Christian God and yet not be that God. This is because a being could have all these attributes and yet not be a *personal* deity. Some philosophers, including Aristotle (384–322 B.C.), have held that an impersonal deity exists, and some of the traditional proofs of the existence of a God fail to provide rational support for belief in the existence of the Judeo-Christian God because, in part, they fail to prove the existence of a personal deity. Thus it is important to note both of the Judeo-Christian God's sets of attributes, metaphysical and moral.

There are three principal moral attributes of God. First, he is omniscient: his knowledge has no limits. Second, he is omnipotent: his power has no limits. Third, he is omnibenevolent: his goodness has no limits. In other words, God is infinitely knowing, powerful, and good, and thus differs from other persons by the extent to which he possesses these attributes, not in simply possessing them. We humans have some power and knowledge, and display some inclination to do what is good, but we possess these as well as other attributes to a finite degree.

Often God's omnibenevolence is said to be manifested in more specific ways—for example, he is said to be just and understanding, merciful and forgiving. Since these traits are thought to be virtues when found in persons, they can be thought of as more or less specific manifestations of God's infinite goodness. Perhaps all these traits are summed up in the declaration that God is love. The Greek word we translate as 'love' in this declaration is *agape* (pronounced a-*gap*-pay), and our words 'caring' or 'concern' are perhaps less misleading ways to translate the meaning of the Greek. For to have *agape* or love for our neighbors, as the commandment enjoins, is not to have warm, heart-throbbing, romantic feelings toward them; it is not even necessarily to *like* them; it is, rather, to be concerned about their well-being and growth and to take an active interest in seeing that they do grow and do attain personal happiness and self-fulfillment. Thus, when God is said to *be* love, what he is said to be is unqualified concern for the well-being and personal growth of each of his children. To distinguish other ways in which God manifests his goodness, such as by his understanding and forgiveness, might be to distinguish more or less specific ways in which he manifests his love. For he *is agape*.

One final attribute of God is that he is a creator. But the way in which God is conceived to be a creator is quite different from the way in which other persons are said to create. A painter, for example, is said to create his painting, but he does not also create his brushes, easel, canvas, or the materials they are made of. When God is said to be a creator of the physical universe, however, he is not said to be merely an arranger of some already pre-existing matter; he is thought to be the creator of the matter *itself*. Thus, unlike the painter, God is credited with creating the very stuff out of which he created his creation. He thus is said to be a creator *ex nihilo* ("out of nothing").

Not all Jews and Christians agree on what God's relationship to his world has been since he created it; indeed, not all agree that he has *completed* creating it. *Deists* believe that a God, possibly even one having all the attributes of the Judeo-Christian God, created the world, established the laws by which it runs, set it in motion, and has since then had no further dealings with it. Such an "absentee God" is said not to intervene in the affairs of the world or men; he is not active in history and neither performs miracles nor answers prayers. *Theists,* on the other hand, believe that God not only created the universe *ex nihilo,* established the laws by which it runs (the so-called *natural laws*), and set it in motion; they believe, besides, that God has continued to take an active interest in the evolution of his creation, often manifesting himself in its history by performing miracles and answering petitionary prayers.

Theists often accuse deists of being inconsistent in their belief, maintaining that a God who loves his creation would take an active interest in seeing that it turns out as he intends and wants. Deists return the charge by arguing that a God who is omniscient and omnipotent would be able to arrange for the world to evolve into what he intended it to be without having to intervene afterward to correct mistakes.

However, even if deism is consistent with the belief in the Judeo-Christian God's existence, both Judaism and Christianity traditionally have been theistic in their outlook. Even those arguments that attempt to prove the existence of God often are referred to as "the theistic proofs," and we will be following custom when we refer to a person who believes in the Judeo-Christian God as a theist. Given this backdrop, therefore, these proofs fail to provide a sound basis for Christianity and Judaism in proportion to their failure to prove, not simply that a God having the attributes of the Judeo-Christian God exists, but, in addition, that such a God is active in the affairs of the world.

The portrait of God that takes shape—when his metaphysical and his moral attributes are conjoined and set against the background of theism—is that of an eternal, immutable spiritual being who, out of his infinite love and wisdom, and by use of his infinite power, brought the physical universe into existence *ex nihilo*, and who continues to manifest his concern for the well-being of man and all other sentient creatures by playing an active role in the history of the world. It is when 'God' is understood to refer to a being having these attributes that we will understand the question, "Does God exist?"

"TRUTHS OF REASON" AND "TRUTHS OF FAITH"

It is possible to believe in the existence of the Judeo-Christian God on faith and to concede or insist upon the impossibility of proving the truth of one's belief. Many thoughtful, intelligent persons have done so. It is worth noting, however, that these persons have first familiarized themselves with and gained a thorough understanding of the attempts to prove God's existence; they have not dismissed the proofs as inadequate before examining them. To dismiss the proofs before examining them, they realized, would be to exhibit the same kind of closed-mindedness that they think often prevents nonbelievers from becoming believers. These same persons have also set forth arguments to defend their belief that belief in God does not have to be proven true in order to be worthy of their acceptance. Such persons, therefore, are as convinced that their belief about the impossibility of proving God's existence *can* be supported as they are convinced that sound support *cannot* be given for the belief that this God exists. Finally, let us note that those persons who agree that God's existence need not be proven in order to be credible do not all agree on *why* this is true. Often they have conflicting arguments, and conflicting conceptions of what faith is. To suppose that we can avoid the heat of controversy or to slip past the need to think clearly and critically about belief in God merely by saying that "It's all a matter of faith; either you believe or you don't" is, therefore, to give testimony, not only to our beliefs, but also to the fact that we do not fully understand them.

A useful way to begin to think about belief in God is to think in terms of Saint Thomas Aquinas's (1225–1274) distinction between truths of reason and truths of faith. According to Thomas's conception, a *truth of faith* is any belief about God that man cannot prove to be true but that God has made known to man by means of revelation, as this revelation has been recorded in the Holy Scriptures. Beliefs such as that God is "three persons in one" ("the Blessed Trinity") and that Christ was born of the Virgin Mary are examples of truths of faith that Thomas himself gave. The basis of the Christian's acceptance of these truths rests, finally, on his willingness to trust the authority of the Holy Scriptures, not on his ability to prove them true. Indeed, such truths may not always be completey intelligible to the finite mind of man.

A *truth of reason,* according to Thomas's conception, is any truth about God that the human intellect can both comprehend and demonstrate, independently of any evidence supplied by God's revelation. For example, that God is not a body, that he is not in space, that he is just, and that he is omniscient are examples of truths about God that Thomas thought man could demonstrate by the use of his reason, aided, he thought, by information that we gain a posteriori. Such truths of reason, Thomas thought, of necessity always are in accord with what God has revealed about himself. Thomas thought it impossible, in other words, for man to prove anything about God that is inconsistent with what God has revealed about himself. So, in reaching those conclusions that he did about the nature of God, Thomas always was careful to cite those passages of Scripture that he thought displayed the harmony of his findings with God's revelation. But such truths, he realized, were nonetheless importantly different from truths of faith, in that they had (while truths of faith did not) an additional method of support, and one that did not assume the existence of that being whose nature the Holy Scriptures allegedly depict.

Now, by their very nature, truths of faith will be accepted as true only by those persons who accept the Holy Scriptures as authoritative in matters that pertain to God. As such, there can be no way to persuade a nonbeliever of the truth of a truth of faith, short of persuading him to believe both that God exists and that what the Holy Scriptures say about him is true. Persons can be shown and persuaded of the truth of a truth of reason, however, without their first having to be convinced of the authority of the Bible. Thus, if "God exists" expresses a truth of reason, it should be possible to discover some argument that proves its truth; and this argument, of necessity, would be one that does not make use of or presuppose as true any truth about God that has as its only source of authority the record of God's revelation to man. If "God exists" expresses a truth of reason, in short, then it, like all other truths of reason, need not be supported by one or another truth of faith. It was St. Thomas Aquinas's conviction that the theist's use of the sentence "God exists" does express a truth of reason and is, therefore, a demonstrable truth. Indeed, he thought there were at least five different ways in which its truth could be proven, and the arguments he set forth to accomplish this have come to be known as the Five Ways.

We will not examine all of Thomas's Five Ways, although we will have something to say about one of them (the Second way) in passing, and a good deal to say about another (the Fourth Way). Nevertheless, Thomas's distinction between truths of reason and truths of faith is an intelligible and useful one. Perhaps we will discover that he was mistaken in thinking that the theist's use of the sentence "God exists" expresses a truth of reason; perhaps, indeed, we will find that he was mistaken in supposing that what it expresses is either true or false. But these questions cannot be answered in advance of careful inquiry. The question that remains before us, and to which we now must turn our attention, is whether, as Thomas believed, God's existence can be proven. If it can, it should be possible to construct an argument that is both formally and informally valid, that has 'God exists' as its conclusion, and that contains premises known to be true. We will not be able to consider all of the attempts to provide such a proof, but we will consider a sufficient number of representative kinds so that we may draw some tentative conclusions.

A POSTERIORI ARGUMENTS FOR GOD'S EXISTENCE

Theistic proofs of God's existence are either a posteriori or a priori. There are many a posteriori proofs, but only one wholly a priori proof—the ontological argument, which we will discuss in the next section.

In an a posteriori argument for God's existence, at least one of the premises is said to be known to be true from information gathered by observation. From this a posteriori knowledge, together with whatever else the argument's premises contend to be analytically true, God's existence is inferred. Supporters usually do not believe that these a posteriori arguments are sufficient by themselves to prove the existence of the Judeo-Christian God. But they usually believe that one or another of these arguments is sufficient to prove the existence of a *being* who merits the name "God." Thus, they believe that the identity of this God with the Judeo-Christian God can be established only *after* the existence of a being who merits the name God has been established, for only after this can all the attributes of this being be discovered. In each of St. Thomas Aquinas's Five Ways, for example, the conclusion reached is that a being we can properly call God exists. None of the Five Ways, according to Thomas, is itself adequate to prove that this being is, say, all-powerful or all-knowing. These attributes must be proven by separate, additional arguments. Whether this is true, and, if so, why, are questions we will examine in what follows.

THE ARGUMENT FROM DESIGN

Immanuel Kant, whose criticisms of the theistic proofs rank among the most profound and influential, said of the argument from design that it "always deserves to be mentioned with respect." Kant paid this tribute to the design argument because he thought it was the most natural and least abstract or philosophical of the theistic proofs. It is that argument which, prior to any considered philosophical commitments about the nature of reality, most readily occurs to a person who pauses to ask whether the world we observe provides any evidence for the reality and nature of a God we do not observe. Put very generally, the argument says that the world and the objects in it have been designed; therefore, the world must have had a designer. Since it requires immense power and intelligence to design the world, the designer of the world merits the name 'God'. The naturalness of this line of reasoning might appear to be all the more evident if we suppose that the person who pauses to ask whether the world we observe tells us anything about its originator happens already to believe in the existence of the Judeo-Christian God. For that God is thought to be the creator of the natural universe out of nothing. One would think, therefore, that what this God is like in other respects should be inferrable from what we know about his creation. The thought is so natural it is virtually irresistible. As reflection will show, however, the most natural is not always the best. In all those ways in which an argument can go wrong, the design argument does.

Now, our discussion of this argument assumes that we can agree on what the design argument alleges, an agreement not always easy to secure. Many times an argument will lend itself to different interpretations, or two arguments that appear to be the same will be subtly, but importantly, different. When we speak of *the* argument from design, therefore, we should bear in mind that we may not understand and treat it (or any other arguments in this book) the same way as other people. Certainly our formulation of the design argument differs from the formulation given it by others. Our formulation is along the lines of an *extended* argument, like those discussed in Chapter 2. Formulating arguments this way makes it easier to discuss questions about their formal and informal validity, yet it does not seem to distort either the meaning or the structure of the argument, when its classic expositions are considered. The classic exposition of the design argument is found in William Paley's (1743-1805) *Natural Theology: Or Evidences of the Existence and Attributes of the Deity Collected from the Appearances of Nature,* written in 1802. Besides Kant's criticisms, those of David Hume, in his 1779 *Dialogues Concerning Natural Religion,* rank as the classic critiques of the design argument.

FORMAL STATEMENT OF THE DESIGN ARGUMENT

Steps	*Symbolization*	*Status*
1. If natural objects resemble man-made objects, then the cause of natural objects resembles the cause of man-made objects.	$n \rightarrow c$	Assumption
2. If man-made objects exhibit the adaptation of means to ends, man-made objects are designed objects.	$x \rightarrow d$	Assumption
3. Man-made objects do exhibit the adaptation of means to ends.	x	Assumption
4. Therefore, man-made objects are designed objects.	$\therefore d$	Consequence, from (2) and (3), by *modus ponens*
5. If natural objects exhibit the adaptation of means to ends, then natural objects are designed objects.	$a \rightarrow o$	Assumption
6. Natural objects do exhibit the adaptation of means to ends.	a	Assumption
7. Therefore, natural objects are designed objects.	$\therefore o$	Consequence, from (5) and (6), by *modus ponens*

Steps	Symbolization	Status
8. Therefore, natural objects are designed objects and man-made objects are designed objects.	$\therefore o \,\&\, d$	Consequence, from (4) and (7), by conjunction
9. If natural objects are designed objects and if man-made objects are designed objects, then natural objects resemble man-made objects.	$(o \,\&\, d) \to n$	Assumption
10. Therefore, natural objects resemble man-made objects.	$\therefore n$	Consequence, from (8) and (9), by *modus ponens*
11. Therefore, the cause of natural objects resembles the cause of man-made objects.	$\therefore c$	*Consequence, from* (1) and (10), by *modus ponens*
12. If the cause of man-made objects is man, then the cause of natural objects resembles man.	$m \to r$	Assumption
13. The cause of man-made objects is man.	m	Assumption
14. Therefore, the cause of natural objects resembles man.	$\therefore r$	Consequence, from (12) and (13), by *modus ponens*
15. If it is man's intelligence and power that enable him to design objects, the designer of natural objects must be like man in being intelligent and powerful.	$i \to l$	Assumption
16. It is man's intelligence and power that enable him to design objects.	i	Assumption
17. Therefore, the designer of natural objects must be like man in being intelligent and powerful.	$\therefore l$	Consequence, from (15) and (16), by *modus ponens*
18. If the totality and systems of natural objects (that is, the natural universe) is far more complex than any of man's creations and infinite in its dimensions, then the designer of the natural universe possesses in-	$t \to s$	Assumption

Steps	Symbolization	Status
telligence and power that far surpass the intelligence and power of man.		
19. The natural universe is far more complex than any of man's creations and infinite in its dimensions.	t	Assumption
20. Therefore, the designer of the natural universe possesses intelligence and power that far surpass the intelligence and power of man.	$\therefore s$	Consequence, from (18) and (19), by *modus ponens*
20. If the designer of the physical universe possesses intelligence and power that far surpass the intelligence and power of man, then the designer of the physical universe is a God.	$s \rightarrow g$	Assumption
22. Therefore, the designer of the physical universe is a God.	$\therefore g$	Consequence, from (20) and (21), by *modus ponens*
23. If the designer of the physical universe is a God, then a God exists.	$g \rightarrow e$	Assupmtion
24. Therefore, a God exists.	$\therefore e$	Consequence, from (23) and (24), by *modus ponens*

COMMENTARY ON THE ARGUMENT

The design argument assumes that we can determine, by observation, whether or not an object has been designed. But before we can possibly determine this by observation, we need to know what we are looking for—what would count as confirming or disconfirming the proposition, 'This object has been designed'. The factually necessary and sufficient condition for an object's being designed, the argument assumes, is that it show the adaptation of means to ends: any object that shows this is thought to be a designed object; no designed object can fail to exhibit the adaptation of means to ends. This assumption underlies the reasoning in premises (2) through (8). It is, then, this concept of "the adaptation of means to ends" that is the pivotal concept in the design argument and the one that demands our attention.

The word 'end' is ambiguous. It can mean either the completion of something, as the end of a book or end of a race, or it also can mean the goal or purpose of something, as in the end of an education or the end of marriage. This second sense of 'end' corresponds to the meaning of the Greek word *telos*: the *telos* of anything is what that thing aims at achieving or what it is intended to accomplish. Thus, to give a *teleological* explanation is to explain the existence or activity of something in terms of whatever purpose it is meant or is trying to fulfill. It is in this sense of 'end' that the contention that designed objects exhibit the adaptation of means to ends should be understood. Because the word 'end' here means *telos,* the design argument is a teleogical argument. Moreover, since the *telos* of something was designated its *final cause* by Aristotle, the argument sometimes is referred to as the *argument from final causality.*

Premise (3) of the design argument states that man-made objects exhibit the adaptation of means to ends. Or, said another way, man-made objects exhibit the adaptation of means to the realization of purpose: how a man-made object is made and what it is made of depend upon (are "adapted to") what the *telos* of the object is. Aristotle referred to the material out of which something is made as its *material cause,* and the plan or idea according to which it is made as the object's *formal cause.*

Another way of saying that, in designed objects, means are adapted to ends, then, is to say the material and formal causes are adapted to the final cause. For instance, what a cup is made of and what shape it is made in depend on what its end or *telos* is, or, the fact that pens have their points at one end rather than protruding out of a side is a consequence of what a pen is intended to be used for. Thus, what premise (3) of the design argument commits us to is the view that, if we take the time to observe carefully those objects that man has designed, we will discover that how they are put together and what they are made of depends on what their purpose is. And we will find this to be true of the simplest of objects, such as plates or cups, as well as of the most complex, such as computers and rocket engines.

Premise (6) of the design argument asserts that the same is true of natural objects. By a "natural object," advocates of the design argument mean any object existing in space and time that has not been designed by a human being—stars, amoebas, lettuce, fish, and grains of sand are examples. As such, each exhibits the adaptation of means to the realization of some purpose.

Now, since the number of different kinds of natural objects is enormous, it should not be surprising that advocates of the design argument have failed to work out a complete list of the kinds of natural objects and to explain how each exhibits the adaptation of means to ends. This deficiency can be developed to the point of a serious criticism of the argument. For the present, however, we can ignore this deficiency and, instead, make use of a few examples to illustrate the kind of thinking such a list would have to include.

Consider our teeth. Their purpose is to prepare our food for digestion. Some food is soft and easy to swallow after only minimal chewing. Other food needs to be ripped apart and chewed for some time before it is fit to swallow. Now, our teeth could not fulfill their purpose if they were made out of a fragile material; they would break too easily. Therefore, the fact that they are made out of an extremely hard material can, according to those who adopt this way of thinking, be attributed to the fact that, if they were not so made they could not fulfill their purpose. A similiar explanation can be given, they think, for their location. If our molars were in the front of our mouth and our incisors at the back, then we would have to put food all the way into our mouth before we could rip it apart, and we could not easily bite off a piece of food while still chewing food already in our mouth. The fact that the teeth we use for tearing food are in the front of our mouths, whereas the teeth we use for grinding our food are in the back, should be explained teleologically, these thinkers believe. Moreover, the fact that our mouth is located where it is, they think, should also be explained in this way. It is where it is because it makes it easy for us to *see* what we are eating before we put it into our mouths. Since we eat to survive and since there are many harmful substances around, the purpose of eating is aided by our being able to see what we eat before we put it into our mouths.

Indeed, the fact that our eyes are where they are helps to explain why we have a neck that enables us to turn our heads without turning our whole body. The purpose of our eyes is to show us visual features of our environment both welcome and threatening. If we had to turn our whole body to see, we would not be able to observe potentially harmful objects on the side we were not looking at. We would not need a neck if, like a fish, we had eyes on the sides of our heads. But, given that they are where they are, we can explain why we have a neck that permits us to turn our head without turning our whole body by making reference to the *telos* of our eyes. And explanations of the same kind can be given, according to this way of thinking, of why our eyes are located in sockets and have eyelashes and lids. And so on and on.

Supporters of the design argument thus think that, when examined carefully, natural objects and their constituent parts can be seen to be designed because they show the adaptation of means to the realization of certain ends. Often supporters of the argument go further, believing that the vast physical universe itself exhibits the adaptation of means to ends. The end here, then, is the purpose of nature. According to this view, the means themselves are highly structured systems of natural objects, and the end is that one thing which all the kinds of object in nature work to fulfill. While often it is difficult to determine precisely what this single purpose of nature is supposed to be, those who believe this usually also believe the universe is designed to achieve God's purpose for man. This idea goes well beyond the less ambitious examples of adaptation of means to ends given above, yet the adequacy of the design argument can be assessed fairly without debating which is *the* purpose of nature or how we can hope to know what it is.

DISPUTING THE LOGIC OF THE ARGUMENT

Objections to the logic of the design argument are of two types: (1) those that dispute the claim that the argument is a formally valid proof of, or goes any way toward supporting belief in, the existence of the Judeo-Christian God, and (2) those that dispute the claim that the argument is a formally valid proof of, or goes any way toward lending support to belief in, the existence of *any* God whatever. Objections of this second kind, if sound, make objections of the first type superfluous, but we will consider both.

Before going further, however, we should note that many supporters of the design argument hold that belief in the existence of a designer of the universe is not logically certain but is more *probably* true than any other explanation of the existence and observable character of nature. If the argument is understood this way, then the objections we are about to consider may seem to lose much of their force, for they contend that the design argument is not a valid *deductive* argument. But even when the argument is understood in this less ambitious way, it is open to serious criticism, as we will show in the next section.

Formulations of the design argument usually have the appearance of being formally valid, and we have attempted to preserve this feature in our own formulation of it above. Each step, from first premise (1) to conclusion (24), appears to be logically intact, since each is alleged to be either an assumption or validly derived from other premises in the argument. Thus, if the propositions that are derived in the proof are validly derived, all that would remain for defenders of the argument to show is that the assumptions of the argument are true. On closer examination, however, the design argument can be seen to be riddled with nonsequiturs, some of which render the argument formally invalid, while others reveal a number of questions it begs. Examples of both kinds of fallacy will be considered below.

Why does the design argument fail as a valid proof of the Judeo-Christian God's existence? Recall, first, that one of the attributes included in this conception of God is omnibenevolence. Now, none of the information included in premises (1) through (23), even if we concede their truth, could go any way toward supporting belief in an omnibenevolent God. This is because these premises make no mention of the designer's *goodness*. In a valid deductive argument, however, nothing can occur in the conclusion that is not already contained in the premises. This is why the argument

1. $p \to q$
2. p
3. $\therefore q$

can be and, in fact, is a valid form of argument, while the argument

1. $p \to q$
2. p
3. $\therefore (q \& r)$

is not and cannot be a valid form of argument. The conjunction $(q \& r)$ cannot follow because (r) does not occur in the premises. Since God's ominbenevolence is not mentioned in premises (1) through (23), the conclusion "A God exists and he is omnibenevolent" cannot follow from them either. And since the Judeo-Christian God *is* omnibenevolent, his existence cannot be proven by the design argument.

This same line of reasoning is sufficient to show why the design argument also fails to prove the existence of an omniscient and omnipotent designer. Even granting premise (20)—"The designer of the natural universe possesses intelligence and power that far surpass the intelligence and power of man"—the designer's omniscience and omnipotence do not follow. And we would be guilty of no contradiction to concede that the designer was *very* intelligent or powerful and yet to deny that he was *infinitely* so. And since, once again, the Judeo-Christian God is infinitely so, the design argument cannot be a valid proof of the existence of this God.

In point of fact, the design argument, if it were sound, actually would provide us with grounds for disbelieving in the Judeo-Christian God. For it would establish that the natural universe was put together as a watchmaker makes a watch—the designer of the physical universe arranged already existing matter into novel, highly complex, and interacting systems. The universe would not be any less wonderful for that, but the designer would be considerably less than the creator of the world affirmed by Judaism and Christianity. That God is supposed to be a creator *ex nihilo,* not a (mere) arranger of a preexisting matter. To point out the deficiencies in the design argument, paradoxically, becomes the work of the reflective defender of Judaism and Christianity.

A similar deficiency is that the argument fails to prove the existence of any one specifiable designer. The more the analogy with man's activities as a designer is pressed, the more we must infer that, assuming that the world was designed, it most likely was designed by *many* 'deities'. Many men, and not just one man, work in cooperative ways to build such things as automobiles, appliances, and houses. Should we not conclude that many gods must have worked cooperatively to frame so vast and complex a thing as the physical universe? To limit the designer of this universe to a solitary deity is arbitrary to the extreme, and our presentation of the design argument manages to conceal this arbitrariness only because it commits a fallacy of equivocation in its use of the word 'man'. This word may be used to refer to a particular human being, but it also may refer to *many* (or *all*) individuals, as in "Man is by nature sinful and unclean." When it is said in premise (13), for instance, that "The cause of man-made objects is man," the word 'man' cannot be understood as referring to just one particular man; it must refer to many men—namely, all those who create or design objects. Thus, even if the physical universe was designed by "something resembling man," it would not follow that it was designed by just one human-like being. The more we insist that divine creativity resembles human creativity, the more likely it becomes that many gods are responsible for nature as we find it. The design argument supports polytheism, if it supports anything.

But even if we concede that the argument proves that the universe was designed by a single designer, the conclusion of the argument still would not follow. For the conclusion of the argument states that "a God *exists*," and it does not follow from the fact that the universe *was* designed that its designer *still* exists. It is perfectly possible that, having completed his design, the designer ceased to exist—a not uncommon fact about human designers and their relationship to their creations. This difficulty could be overcome, of course, if the design argument could somehow prove that the designer of the world is eternal. But nothing in the argument can be thought to support this conjecture, so that, at best, the transition from premise (22), "The designer of the physical universe is a God," to the conclusion that "a God exists" is question begging. It assumes what needs to be shown—namely, that this designer is eternal. In fact, however, the analogy upon which the whole argument rests militates against this view. For the more we insist upon the resemblance between human beings and the designer of the physical universe, the more we are obliged to insist that this designer, even assuming that there is just one, and even assuming that he is omniscient, omnipotent, and omnibenevolent, is, like human beings, mortal and therefore liable to cease to exist at any time. Not surprisingly, the more like man God is thought to be, the more liable one's attempts to prove God's existence will succeed in proving at most that nature was designed by a being subject to all the limitations and exigencies of human existence.

DISPUTING THE PREMISES OF THE ARGUMENT

Serious questions can be raised about the truth of several of the premises in the design argument, and two are particularly noteworthy, premise (1) and premise (5).

Premise (1) reads "If natural objects resemble man-made objects, then the cause of natural objects resembles the cause of man-made objects." This premise is not known to be true and is, in fact, so vague as to make questions concerning its truth necessarily imprecise. What are the criteria for the application of the concept of resemblance? What, that is, are the logically necessary and sufficient conditions for its correct application? Advocates of the design argument regrettably are silent on this point. Yet it would seem clear that they must satisfy the demand for conceptual precision before the merits of their underlying assumption can be weighed. Even granting that natural objects resemble man-made objects in *some* respects, is the resemblance sufficient to warrant the inference that their causes resemble each other?

Hume suggested in his criticism, that because the structure and organization of vegetables somewhat resembles that of the remainder of natural objects, why can we not infer that the cause of these other natural objects resembles a seed, which is the cause of a vegetable? This vegetable hypothesis is just as much (or as little) supported by the concept of resemblance, as it is used in the design argument, as is the designer hypothesis. Indeed, even if it were shown that natural objects have a greater resemblance to man-made objects than to anything else, it still would not follow that the cause of natural objects resembles the cause of man-made objects. Before we could reasonably infer this we would have to know that the cause of *some* natural objects resembles the cause of man-made objects. We may not assume that what is true with man-made objects—that they and their causes resemble one another—also is true when natural objects and man-made objects are compared. For whether comparisons of this kind can be made is precisely the question at issue.

The argument cannot be rescued at this point by resorting to the idea that all it attempts to prove is that the designer hypothesis is "more probably true" than other hypotheses. Even if it is true that the probability that a humanlike being designed $x + n$ natural objects is increased if it is known that such a being designed x number of natural objects (and if the objects included in $x + n$ bear a very strong resemblance to those included in x), this in no way increases the probability that a humanlike designer is responsible for all natural objects. In general, in order to increase the probability of the truth of a proposition of the form 'All Y's are Z's', one must first know that some Y's are Z's. Therefore, in order to increase the probability of the truth of 'All natural objects are designed by a humanlike being', we must first know that *some* natural objects *are* designed thus. It is precisely this latter knowledge which the design argument *assumes* we have and it is for this reason that the argument must beg the question. Premise (1), thus, is either vague to the point of obscurity, or, if pressed, it is question begging. In neither case can it be assumed to be known to be true.

Premise (5) reads "If natural objects exhibit the adaptation of means to ends, then natural objects are designed objects." This premise faces even more serious objections than did premise (1). That natural objects exhibit the adaptation of means to ends is not a factually sufficient condition of these objects having been designed by someone. One need not quarrel with the suggestion that this condition is a factually *necessary* condition of design by an intelligent being, but that is not the issue. Let us ignore the possibility that natural objects have the ends they have because of the means they have developed, rather than *vice versa*. We still must ask whether there is any equally plausible or better explanation of "the facts" presented by the design argument that does not make reference to design or to an intelligent designer—"the facts" here being, in particular, premise (6), "Natural objects do exhibit the adaptation of means to ends."

Certainly there appears to be. Natural laws by themselves appear to be sufficient to explain the existence and structure of natural objects, even when (and if) the organization of these objects admits of a teleological explanation. In particular, the theory of evolution would seem to explain whatever "facts" about adaptation advocates of the design argument might make. According to this theory, it is not at all remarkable that living things exhibit the adaptation of means to the end of living. Quite the contrary, it would be remarkable if they did not, since only those species of natural objects that do adapt to the demands placed upon them by their environment are fit to survive. Thus, existing species all exhibit the adaptation of means to ends, not necessarily because an intelligent being designed them that way, but, rather, because if they were not this way they would not now exist. Thus, even to speak of "the argument *from* design" already is to smuggle into the argument the greater part of what it is required to prove—namely, that natural objects can be observed to be *designed* objects. That they can be observed to exhibit the adaptation of means to ends may be conceded. But that is not to concede that they have been designed. Even if all other objections to the design argument could be met, therefore, the argument would remain unsound. Natural objects could exhibit the adaptation of means to ends and yet not be designed.

These, then, are some of the principal objections that can be raised against the design argument. And it is for these reasons that philosophers appear to be all but unanimous in their judgment that the argument is unsound.

THE FIRST CAUSE ARGUMENT

A deficiency of the design argument, as we have seen, is that it fails to prove that there is just one designer or god. As such, that argument cannot be relied upon by anyone committed to monotheism. In this respect, if in no other, the so-called *first cause argument* improves upon the design argument. For, as will become clearer, there can be only one first cause, given the conception of first cause this argument employs.

Expressed generally the first cause argument contends that there must be a first cause since, without a first cause, there could not be any intermediate causes, and, without any intermediate causes, nothing would or could now exist. Since, however, we know that many things do now exist, and that they were caused to exist by other things, it follows that there must be a first cause.

Few philosophers have accepted this argument in so general a form, but it is not an uncommon one for all that. Next to the design argument, it probably ranks as the most frequent argument thoughtful people propose when they first seek to justify their religious beliefs. As we shall explain shortly, however, two very different arguments can be and deservedly are called the first cause argument.

The first cause argument is an example of a type of argument referred to as the *cosmological argument*. Common to all the cosmological arguments is the belief that the existence of a God can be proven from the fact that something other than God exists together with the fact that this thing has not always existed. Sometimes the thing or things alluded to are particular things such as people. At other times they consist of the entire physical universe—a cosmological argument that is called the *argument from contingency* or the *argument from sufficient reason* which, like all cosmological arguments, differs from the design argument in a subtle but important way. The design argument rests its claim to prove God's existence on a particular and, as it turns out, dubious contention about existing natural objects—namely, that, since they exhibit the adaptation of means to ends, they are designed. The cosmological arguments, on the other hand, all rest their claim to prove God's existence on claims about natural objects that do not appear to be in the least bit dubious—namely, that natural objects do exist, and they were caused to exist by other natural objects.

The expression "cosmological argument" is used to refer to a plurality of arguments, and this possibility of confusion is compounded because two

logically distinct arguments frequently are both referred to as "the argument for a first cause" or "the first cause argument." Why is this so?

The problem arises because the concept of cause can be understood in
two different ways—as causes *in fieri* and causes *in esse*. To say that *X*
is a cause *in fieri of Y* means that the past activity of *X* was in whole or
in part responsible for the fact that *Y* came into existence. Parents thus
are causes *in fieri* of their children, as are artists of their creations. To say
that *X* is a cause *in esse* of *Y*, however, means that *X*'s existence and
activity supports or sustains *Y*'s existence. Thus, oxygen and nutritious
food can be said to be causes *in esse* of our existence. But to say that
oxygen is a cause *in esse* of our existence does not imply that it likewise
is a cause *in fieri* of our existence. Oxygen is a cause of our existence, not
in the sense that it conspired to bring us into existence, but in the sense
that, if we were deprived of it for a given length of time, we would cease
to be alive. Similarly, to say that our parents are causes *in fieri* of our
existence does not imply that they also are causes *in esse*. They are causes
of our existence, not in the sense that they now support or sustain us, but in
the sense that, had it not been for their past activity, we would not now exist.

Beings that have causes *in fieri* or causes *in esse* are called *contingent
beings.* Contingent beings are those that depend on other beings for their
existence. Thus, as the examples of oxygen and parents illustrate, there
are two very different ways in which a contingent being can be causally
dependent on other beings. Expressed another way, causes *in fieri* are factually necessary and sufficient conditions for the *coming into existence* of any
contingent beings whereas causes *in esse* are factually necessary and sufficient conditions for the *continued existence* of any contingent being. This
is one reason why talk about a first cause is ambiguous, for the first cause
might be either *in fieri* or *in esse*, and it is conceivable that there could be
a first cause in one sense of 'cause' but not in the other.

A second reason why the expression "first cause" is ambiguous is that
the word 'first' is ambiguous. Let us designate these senses the *temporal*
sense of 'first' and the *nontemporal* sense of 'first'. In its temporal sense,
the word 'first' is used to indicate that something happened or came into
existence *before, earlier than,* or *temporally prior to* something else, as
when we say that "Neil Armstrong was the first man on the moon" or
"the first animals on the earth lived in the sea." In its nontemporal sense,
'first' is used to indicate that something is *most fundamental* or *most basic*,
not that it necessarily existed earlier. The so-called "first principles of
science," for example, are said to be first because they are the most basic
principles of science, and not because they either came into existence or
were discovered before any other bit of scientific knowledge.

Thus, when someone contends that there is a first cause, he could mean
two very different things. First, he could mean that, among those causes

that are causes *in fieri* of a contingent being, there is one cause that existed before all contingent beings and upon whose past activity all contingent beings ultimately depend for their coming into existence. In this sense of first cause, there could be no contingent being that existed earlier than the first cause, and to contend that there was a cause *in fieri* of the first cause would be to utter a contradiction. Moreover, since a contingent being is, by definition, a being that depends on some other being as its cause, it follows that the first cause could not itself be conceived to be a contingent being. But the second way a person could mean "the first cause" is that it is first among the causes *in esse*, and such a cause need not also be that one cause that existed before all others in time. It is, rather, that one cause that sustains all other contingent beings in existence, and which depends on no other being for its continued existence. Once again, therefore, the first cause of causes *in esse* could not itself be a contingent being, since a contingent being, by definition, depends on some other being for its existence.

Given, then, that the conception of "the first cause" can be understood in these two different, logically independent senses, it should not be surprising that two quite different, logically independent arguments might rightfully be called "the first cause argument." Here we will deal with that species of the first cause argument that attempts to prove that there is a first cause *in fieri*. For convenience we will call this the *temporal first cause argument*.

Sometimes it is thought that this argument corresponds to Saint Thomas Aquinas's "second way." However, since Thomas held that belief in the finite duration of the physical universe is a truth of faith, it is extremely unlikely that this is a sound interpretation of his second way. We would be closer to understanding his argument in this connection, therefore, if we read it as the attempt to prove that there is a first cause *in esse*. Even so, some but not all of the objections that follow can be raised against St. Thomas's second way.

FORMAL STATEMENT OF THE ARGUMENT

Steps	Symbolization	Status
1. Either there is a first cause or there is not a first cause.	$f \vee \sim f$	1. Assumption
2. If there is no first cause, then the series of causes stretching from the present back into the past is infinite and does not contain the first cause as one of its members.	$\sim f \to \sim n$	2. Assumption

Steps	Symbolization	Status
3. If the series of causes stretching back into the past is infinite and does not contain the first cause as one of its members, then there is no series of causes connecting what now exists with the first cause.	$\sim n \rightarrow \sim s$	3. Assumption
4. If there is no series of causes connecting what now exists with the first cause, then there are no intermediate causes that existed between what now exists and the first cause.	$\sim s \rightarrow \sim i$	4. Assumption
5. If there are no intermediate causes that existed between what now exists and the first cause, then there were no causes that existed prior to what now exists.	$\sim i \rightarrow \sim p$	5. Assumption
6. If there were no causes that existed prior to what now exists, then nothing existed in the past to cause what now exists.	$\sim p \rightarrow \sim e$	6. Assumption
7. If nothing existed in the past to cause what now exists, then nothing that exists now could have been caused to exist.	$\sim e \rightarrow \sim c$	7. Assumption
8. But we know of many things that exist now that have been caused to exist.	c	8. Assumption
9. Therefore, there must have been something that existed in the past to cause what now exists.	$\therefore e$	9. Consequence, from (7) and (8), by *modus tollens*
10. Therefore, there were causes that existed prior to what now exists.	$\therefore p$	10. Consequence, from (6) and (9), by *modus tollens*
11. Therefore, there were intermediate causes that existed between what now exists and the first cause.	$\therefore i$	11. Consequence, from (5) and (10), by *modus tollens*

Steps	Symbolization	Status
12. Therefore, there is a series of causes connecting what now exists with the first cause.	$\therefore s$	12. Consequence, from (11) and (4), by *modus tollens*
13. Therefore, the series of causes stretching back into the past is not infinite and does contain the first cause as one of its members.	$\therefore n$	13. Consequence, from (12) and (3), by *modus tollens*
14. Therefore, there is a first cause.	$\therefore f$	14. Consequence, from (13) and (2), by *modus tollens*
15. If there is a first cause, then there exists a being that depends on nothing for its existence and upon which all other beings depend for their existence.	$f \rightarrow b$	15. Assumption
16. Therefore, there is a being that depends on no other being for its existence and upon which all other beings depend for their existence.	$\therefore b$	16. Consequence, from (14) and (15), by *modus ponens*
17. If there is a being who depends on no other being for its existence and upon which all other beings depend for their existence, there exists a being that merits the name "God."	$b \rightarrow g$	17. Assumption
18. Therefore, there exists a being that merits the name "God."	$\therefore g$	18. Consequence, from (16) and (17), by *modus ponens*

COMMENTARY ON THE ARGUMENT

The essential nerve of the temporal first cause argument is that it denies the possibility that causes *in fieri* can proceed backward indefinitely. It is important, therefore, to understand the thinking that underlies this denial.

The germinal idea is very simple—namely, that if we deny the existence of a contingent being's cause *in fieri,* then we make it impossible, as a matter of fact, for that particular contingent being to come into existence. For example, if we deny that our parents existed, then it would be physically impossible for us to come into existence; if we deny the existence of, say, Picasso, then we deny that any of his paintings exist as well. Or if we deny the existence of Smith's great-great-grandparents, then it would follow that his great-grandparents could not have existed, nor his grand-parents, nor his parents so that if his great-great-grandparents had not existed, it would now be impossible for Smith to exist. This example illustrates how causes *intermediate* between a being that now exists and a being that existed in the past cannot exist if the past being's existence is denied.

Perhaps this idea can be made clearer if we let the letters of the alphabet symbolize the existence of things and let the symbol $\rightarrow$ represent the idea "is the cause *in fieri* of." Then, if we begin with the existence of something, A, that now exists, we can construct a series of causes *in fieri*:

$$H \rightarrow G \rightarrow F \rightarrow E \rightarrow D \rightarrow C \rightarrow B \rightarrow A$$

Suppose the existence of H is denied. Then it would follow that any cause intermediate between it and A (namely, G, F, E, D, C, and B) also could not exist, with the result that A could not exist either. For B, we are assuming, is the cause *in fieri* of A. And a similar denial of other combinations of intermediate causes would be implied if we denied the existence of, say, F or D.

Suppose someone believes that one of the causes in the series of causes *in fieri* is the first cause of that series. Let us symbolize this first cause Z and symbolize the first being whose existence Z brought about as Y, the second being as X, and so on. Given, then, that Z is one of the members of the series of causes *in fieri*, there could be causes intermediate between it and, say, A. But now suppose that someone contends that the series of causes *in fieri* is infinite so that there is no first cause, Z. Then, it is argued, there can be no causes intermediate between Z and A. For there can only be causes intermediate between Z and A if *both* are members of the series of causes *in fieri*. Since Z is denied membership in this series, however, then there can be no causes intermediate between it and A. But this implies, it is argued, that A could not now exist. For the causes intermediate between Z and A include H, G, F, E, D, C, and B, and if any one or all of these causes *in fieri* had not existed, then A could not now exist. Thus, since we know that A exists, we must conclude that there are causes intermediate between it and Z. But this, it is argued, implies that there *is* a first cause, Z.

Such is the core of the temporal first cause argument. The power of this argument to persuade is not to be denied, and the apparent validity of it is, it seems, well captured in our formal statement of it. Nevertheless, like the design argument it is open to serious objection, from the standpoint both of the logic of the reasoning employed and of the truth of the premises used Each kind of objection shall be considered in its turn.

DISPUTING THE LOGIC OF THE ARGUMENT

The temporal first cause argument is plainly inadequate as a valid proof of the Judeo-Christian God's existence. Since there is nothing in the premises of the argument to suggest that the first cause is omniscient, omipotent, or omnibenevolent, the argument, considered by itself, provides no basis for the identification of the first cause with the Judeo-Christian God. Indeed, nothing in this argument provides any basis for supposing that the first cause, even assuming that one does exist, is in the least a *personal* being, so that, in this respect, if in no other, the design argument enjoys a small success over the first cause argument. Like the design argument, however, the temporal first cause argument is unable to prove the *present* existence of the being whose existence it endeavors to demonstrate. For even if there was a first cause that existed in the past, it does not follow that the first cause exists right now. This can follow only if it is assumed that it is the first cause's nature to exist eternally, and to make this assumption begs the question at issue—namely, "Is it part of the first cause's nature to exist eternally?" Thus, even if we were to concede to the argument steps (1) through (14), premise (15) can be seen to beg the question. And since the subsequent reasoning in the argument depends on this, the remainder of the argument is question begging as well.

DISPUTING THE PREMISES OF THE ARGUMENT

To concede steps (1) through (14) to the argument would be to concede to it far more than it warrants. In particular, we should examine premise (2), "If there is no first cause, then the series of causes stretching from the present back into the past is infinite and does not contain the first cause as one of its members." Now, part of this premise is true: if there is no first cause or first member of the series of causes *in fieri*, then that series is infinite. But the rest of the premise is not true. For while it is true that the first cause cannot be the first member of an *infinite* series of causes, it does not follow that any *particular* cause (including any cause thought to be first) is excluded from membership in this series.

We can make this clearer by examining the ambiguous character of the proposition 'There in no first cause'. Suppose someone denies that Columbus was the first Caucasian to set foot on the North American continent. Now, clearly, to say that Columbus was not first does not imply that he did not set foot on North America at all. It means that, among those persons who have set foot upon it, some other Caucasian did so before Columbus. Or suppose again the question arises as to who was the first person on the scene of an accident. If someone denies that John was first, it hardly follows that John was not there at all. Rather, it follows that, among those persons who were there, someone other than John was first to come upon the accident. Now, suppose that someone does deny that there is a first cause. How should this be understood? Exponents of the first cause argument understand this as the denial that some *particular* cause existed. For it is only if it is understood in this way that they can go on to argue that this denial implies that there are no intermediate causes between the present and that *particular* cause called the first cause. But this is not how this denial should be understood. To deny that there is a first cause no more implies the nonexistence of something than does the denial of John's or Columbus's being first implies that John was not at the scene of the accident or that Columbus did not set foot on North America.

This can made clearer in the following way. If a person believes that there is a first cause, then he must believe that it has an identity and occupies a particular place in the series of causes—namely, first place. Suppose that we symbolize this first cause by the letter Z. Then we can represent its relationship to other things as

$$Z \rightarrow Y \rightarrow X \rightarrow W \rightarrow V \rightarrow U \rightarrow T \rightarrow S \rightarrow R \rightarrow Q \rightarrow \text{ and so on.}$$

Now, suppose someone denies there is a first cause. Clearly, this denial is not logically equivalent to the denial of Z's existence. In denying that Z is the *first* cause, one does not deny Z's existence but rather Z's *position* with respect to other things—namely, that Z is first. In denying that Z is the first cause, one is contending that something else existed before Z and was the cause *in fieri* of Z. Thus, in denying that there is a first cause, one is contending that, take whatever member of the series of causes *in fieri* you like, there always are causes that come before it and that were causes *in fieri* of it. Thus, rather than denying the existence of any member of the series of causes *in fieri,* the denial that there is a first member commits one to *insisting* upon the existence of all the members of the series. And to insist on the existence of *all* the members, of course, is to insist on the existence of an *infinitely* large number.

Once it is clear that to deny there is a first cause is not to deny the existence of any particular cause, premise (2) can be seen to be false. The antecedent of the premise can be true and the consequent false. In other words, even if there is no first cause, so that the series of causes stretching from the present into the past is infinite, this series can contain whatever particular cause one might care to nominate as the first cause as one of its members. For yet another reason, therefore, this attempt to prove the existence of a god a posteriori fails.

THE A PRIORI ARGUMENT FOR GOD'S EXISTENCE

At first, the idea of proving the existence of anything wholly a priori might strike us as odd indeed, so much are we accustomed to supposing that what is real can be seen, heard, touched, smelled, or tasted. And so it has seemed to many, perhaps most, philosophers—even after the most careful examination. But this fact has not deterred others from accepting such a proof as possible, and it did not deter the philosopher-theologian Saint Anselm (1033–1109) from developing the so-called ontological argument as a proof of God's existence. This argument was not the only one developed by Anselm. What he sought to accomplish by it, however, and what he thought his other proofs failed to demonstrate, was a proof of *both* the existence *and* the attributes of God. And since he believed in the Judeo-Christian God, what he sought to demonstrate in one fell swoop was not only the existence of a being that deserved the name "God" but a being who had all those attributes definitive of the Judeo-Christian God.

We already have seen how two traditional a posteriori arguments fail because they do not show that the being whose existence they endeavor to prove has the attributes of the Judeo-Christian God. Moreover, once we see why these arguments fail, we see why no a posteriori argument can possibly demonstrate the existence of an omniscient, omnipotent, omnibenevolent creator *ex nihilo*. For all a posteriori arguments, by their very nature, must be based on our observation of reality, and since our observation of it is limited, it will always be a nonsequitur to infer from our limited observation the existence of a limitless being. Indeed, the more we insist that the world as we observe it provides us with a basis for saying what its creator is like, the more we have to say that its creator is not the Judeo-Christian God. For the world we observe contains evils not of man's own making, such as insanity, congenital birth defects, and the vast suffering of the animal kingdom. Clearly, logic can never sanction the inference from "evil exists in this world" to "an all-good, all-knowing, all-powerful God created this world." This is not to say that these two beliefs might not both be true. Perhaps they are. But neither can serve as *evidence* for the truth of the other. We will have more to say about evil toward the end of this chapter.

Once we understand that and why a posteriori arguments fail, we can empathize with Saint Anselm's dissatisfaction, and we can experience some of the same puzzlement in searching for an argument to remedy these deficiencies. It could not be yet another a posteriori argument, it is certain, and thus must be wholly a priori. But to know the type of argument required is far from knowing the form the argument should take. As an exercise in our own thinking we might pause here to see what possible lines of argument occur to us. Nothing can make the genius of an idea more apparent than to experience the difficulty of discovering it.

The idea that struck Anselm, and the one that forms the heart of the ontological argument, is this: rather than try to prove the supreme perfection of God by attending to the fact that something other than God exists (as in the first cause arguments) or to presumed facts about how it exists (as in the design argument), we might prove his existence by dwelling on the idea of supreme perfection itself. At first Anselm regarded a proof based exclusively on the idea of supreme perfection as impossible, but finally he set forth the argument we know as the ontological argument (a name given by Kant, not Anselm). Although Descartes also developed a version of it, Anselm is still its undisputed originator. Kant considered the ontological argument to be the most fundamental of the proofs of God's existence, meaning that the soundness of the ontological proof was assumed by all the other proofs, so that if the ontological proof was unsound, all other proofs of God's existence necessarily were unsound. Kant's judgment here is disputable. But the fact that so careful and original a thinker should fix the importance of the argument in this fashion does much to suggest the singular position it has occupied in the history of reflective thought.

Now, in order to discuss an argument, as we said above, the debaters must agree on and understand what the argument contends. Sometimes this agreement is impeded because the name of the argument is ambiguous (as in "the first cause argument"), but sometimes it is because of genuine difficulty in determining just what the argument alleges. This is true of the ontological argument, for whether Anselm had just one argument is much disputed. He himself seems to have thought there was just one, but we can probably better understand it if we examine it as *two* logically distinct arguments: "the first ontological argument" or "the first form of the argument" and "the second ontological argument" or "the second form of the argument."

THE FIRST FORM OF THE ONTOLOGICAL ARGUMENT

In this form of the argument, Anselm can be understood as trying to show that God must exist because to deny his real existence would be a contradiction. We can understand his reasoning if we give it a formal presentation.

FORMAL STATEMENT OF THE FIRST ONTOLOGICAL ARGUMENT

Steps	*Symbolization*	*Status*
1. The Judeo-Christian God is a supremely perfect being ("a being the greater than which cannot be conceived").	s	1. Assumption
2. If the Judeo-Christian God is a supremely perfect being, then he lacks no attribute that is a perfection.	$s \rightarrow {\sim}l$	2. Assumption
3. Therefore, the Judeo-Christian God lacks no attribute that is a perfection.	${\sim}l$	3. Consequence, from (1) and (2), by *modus ponens*
4. If the attribute of real existence is a perfection, then the Judeo-Christian God does not lack real existence.	$r \rightarrow {\sim}e$	4. Assumption
5. The attribute of real existence is a perfection.	r	5. Assumption
6. Therefore, the Judeo-Christian God does not lack real existence.	${\sim}e$	6. Consequence, from (4) and (5), by *modus ponens*
7. If the Judeo-Christian God were to exist as an idea in the understanding alone, he would lack real existence.	$u \rightarrow e$	7. Assumption
8. Therefore, the Judeo-Christian God does not exist as an idea in the understanding alone.	${\sim}u$	8. Consequence, from (6) and (7), by *modus tollens*
9. If the Judeo-Christian God does not lack real existence, then he exists in reality.	${\sim}e \rightarrow g$	9. Assumption
10. Therefore, the Judeo-Christian God exists in reality.	g	10. Consequence, from (6) and (9), by *modus ponens*

COMMENTARY ON THE ARGUMENT

To understand this form of the ontological argument, we must first understand premise (7), "If the Judeo-Christian God were to exist in the understanding alone, he would lack real existence." We must also understand the basis of this claim—in particular, premise (5), "The attribute of real existence is a perfection." Let us discuss premise (7) first.

In speaking of "existence in the understanding," known as existence *in intellectu,* Anselm was engaging in a practice common to his scholastic contemporaries. A being that exists *in intellectu* is one whose description is understood; it exists in the sense that we understand the concepts that apply to it. For example, if we understand the description of the Eiffel Tower, then we can say that the Eiffel Tower exists *in intellectu.* If we understand the description of the Straits of Magellan or the present King of France then these, too, may be said to exist *in intellectu.* Notice that, as the example of the present King of France is meant to illustrate, it seems to be possible to have the concept of an object, and thus for that object to exist *in intellectu,* despite the fact that no such object exists in fact (exists *in re*). Indeed, it seems those objects whose actual existence we deny must at least exist *in intellectu,* since otherwise we could not understand just what it is that we are denying, if we deny that such an object exists *in re.* If true, this is far from a trivial point, especially within the context of Anselm's argument. It implies that anyone who denies the existence of the Judeo-Christian God *in re* at least must understand what that God is. Accordingly, the Judeo-Christian God must at least exist *in intellectu,* even for those persons who deny his real existence (his existence *in re*).

Given the foregoing, we can enumerate the following possibilities concerning the existence of any object. (1) The object exists *in intellectu* but not *in re.* (Such would seem to be the true of the present King of France, gremlins, and abominable snowmen.) (2) The object exists *in re* but not *in intellectu.* (Such is the case of any object whose real existence is forever unknown by us or unknown prior to its discovery. For example, radio waves and the microscopic world.) (3) The object exists both *in intellectu* and *in re.* (Such is true of the Eiffel Tower.)

Now, since any reasonable person who denies God's existence at least must understand his description, God exists at least *in intellectu.* What Anselm proposes to show is that, given that the concept of God is the concept of a supremely perfect being, God *cannot* exist only *in intellectu* but must also exist *in re.* Part of the basis on which Anselm rests this claim is premise (5), "The attribute of real existence is a perfection." Let us see what sense we can make of this contention.

Notice, first, that if real existence is an attribute, then those things that do exist *in re* have something that is lacking in things that do not exist or that exist *in intellectu*—and this "something" is named, described, or other-wise indicated by the word 'exists'. Thus, to say the Eiffel Tower exists *in re* is to say it possesses the attribute *real existence*, an attribute that the concept of the Eiffel Tower lacks. But the doctrine that the attribute of real existence is a perfection also involves the idea that this something called "real existence" is valuable, so that things that have it are *better* than things that do not. In other words, to the extent that anything exists *in re*, it is good, and to the extent that anything that exists is evil, it can be understood as lacking what is proper to it—as blindness in the eye, for example, is not anything positive, but is the negation of what makes the eye what it is. Thus, evil can be understood alternatively as the absence of good or the absence of being.

How valuable real existence is supposed to be often is unclear, but it would seem to rank as the most fundamental value, since, if anything lacks it, then it cannot be valuable in any other way. Whether this view is justi-fied or not is a question we shall return to directly. However, it might well seem to embody another view familiar to us and to which we might all give our assent—namely, that poor eyesight, say, or a deformed hand is better than none at all.

With these two points clarified, Anselm's argument should now be more intelligible. Since the Judeo-Christian God is, by definition, a supremely perfect being, he cannot lack any perfection. And since a being that exists *in re* is, according to Anselm, better or more perfect than one that exists only *in intellectu*, it follows that God, who exists in the understanding even of those who deny his real existence, must exist *in re*. To suppose that he does not is to withhold a perfection from the supremely perfect being, which is contradictory.

DISPUTING THE LOGIC OF THE ARGUMENT

If otherwise sound, the ontological argument does appear to overcome many of the objections that can be raised against the design and first cause arguments. Whereas these arguments fail to establish that the God whose existence they purport to demonstrate has any of the moral attributes of the Judeo-Christian God, the ontological argument provides a basis for attri-buting these attributes to the God whose existence it purports to prove. For once it is conceded that omnipotence, omiscience, and omnibenevolence are perfections—that they make the object that possesses them better than if it did not possess them—then these attributes must belong to the su-premely perfect being—"the being the greater than which cannot be thought."

The belief that there is just one God also seems to be guaranteed by Anselm's argument, if we agree that a being is greater or more perfect in proportion to its independence. That is, the less a being depends for its existence on other beings and the more others depend on it, the more perfect it is. Given this criterion of perfection, it is clear that the *most* perfect being would be one who depended on no other being for its existence and upon whom all other beings depended for their existence. And it is equally clear that there could be but one such being.

In these respects, then, Anselm's argument marks an important improvement over the a posteriori arguments discussed earlier. Nevertheless, most philosophers believe this first form of the argument fails as a proof of God's existence, partly because of the premises and partly because of the logic.

Perhaps we can best understand how the argument's logic can be contested if we consider the last premise, (10), "If God does not lack real existence, then God exists in reality." This premise perpetuates an important ambiguity that influences the whole argument. What, precisely, are the antecedent and consequent of premise (10) about? That is, to what does each refer? Ostensibly, both are about or refer to God. But a closer examination shows that whereas the consequent seems to be about the *being* God, affirming that there is such a being, the antecedent seems to be about our *concept* of the being God. The antecedent alleges that our concept of God includes the fact that he exists or, less ambiguously, that if anything is to be God it must exist *in re.* In other words, nothing nonexistent can be God.

And it is not to be denied that, if true, this is an interesting fact about our concept of God. Indeed, what is to be insisted upon is that it is just that—an interesting fact about our *concept* of God. For what does not follow logically from this is that there is a being *meeting* this conception. That is, the idea that no being could be supremely perfect if it lacked real existence does not mean that such a being exists. For it could be the case *both* that nothing nonexistent can be God *and* that God does not exist. Thus, the consequent of premise (10) does not follow, even if its antecedent is true, and our inclination to suppose otherwise results from the ambiguous reference in the use of the word 'God'.

The difficulties inherent in this aspect of the first ontological argument go deeper. If an advocate insists that premises (1) through (10) do establish the real existence of God, then a new, damaging objection can be developed, as was raised by the monk, Gaunilon, a contemporary of St. Anselm. For precisely the same line of reasoning can be used to prove the real existence of things all reasonable men agree do not exist.

Gaunilon used the example of the most perfect conceivable island, arguing that, given Anselm's assumption that real existence is a perfection, and given that we can conceive of there being such an island that does exist *in re,* it follows that there really is such an island. And it is easy to see how analogous arguments could be developed to 'prove' the real existence of the most perfect conceivable Santa Claus, unicorn, or leprechaun. The consequence, then, of insisting upon the first argument's logical power to prove God's existence, is that it shares a similar power to prove the real existence of the most perfect specimen of whatever one might care to imagine. Which is to say, the first form of the argument cannot be relied upon as proving the real existence of anything. And if the advocate replies that it can be relied upon to prove the real existence of *one* being—God— we can charge the defender with begging the question. For the question at issue here is whether and, if so, how the argument ever succeeds. To be told in so many words that, yes, it does succeed, just in the one case of God, is not even to begin to explain why or how it works in this one case and not in any other. Not surprisingly, perhaps, the second form of the argument can be understood as an attempt to overcome this, as well as the foregoing criticism of the first form's logic.

DISPUTING THE PREMISES OF THE ARGUMENT

As mentioned earlier, the main criticisms of the first form of the ontological argument are aimed at the argument's premises, especially premise (5), "The attribute of real existence is a perfection." Let us refer to this premise as "the doctrine that the attribute of real existence is a perfection" or, more simply, as "the doctrine." Philosophers seem to be all but unanimous in rejecting the doctrine, either because they believe it is false to classify real existence as an attribute (or property or predicate), or because they think it makes no sense or is false to contend that real existence is a perfection. The former is the more frequent of the criticisms, but the latter deserves brief mention. First, though, let us clarify the doctrine.

It is easy to misunderstand the doctrine. When someone says that things that exist *in re* are better than things that do not, it is easy to suppose that they are saying that things that exist *in re* are pleasant or useful, whereas things that do not exist are neither. Thus, poor (existing) eyesight is better than blindness, and a poor (existing) horse is better than no horse at all. But this would seem to be because even poor eyesight or a poor horse is more useful or otherwise beneficial to us when we need them than if we lacked them altogether. And while this would seem to be true and noncontroversial, it is not what the doctrine maintains. The doctrine maintains the quite different view that things that exist *in re* are better *in themselves* than things that do not exist *in re,* which means that *they are better independently of any relationship they might have to other existing things, including people.* The value that real existence confers upon those things that have it is intrinsic to them. Thus, if we were to imagine a horse that existed on some uninhabited planet, and if there never was or would be any person to gain pleasure from or make use of it, that would not in any way diminish its value as an existing object. In itself, that horse would not be any less perfect or valuable than any existing horse, and both it and every other existing horse would be alike in having the attribute of real existence that nonexistent horses lack.

It is when the claim that real existence is a perfection is understood in this way that it lacks a clear sense. For while it makes sense to compare the value of two existing objects, it is unclear how the value of a nonexistent object can be compared with values that do exist, at least in the sense that the doctrine would require that such comparisons be made. Of course, we can imagine situations in which someone might say "This horse is better than no horse at all," but such situations are those in which it would be *better for some person* to have a horse around than not, because of some need or interest of the person. But as we have seen, this is not the sense the doctrine would give to "This horse is better than no horse at all." It would have us understand such claims as meaning that, in itself, an existing horse is better than a nonexisting one. And it is just not at all clear how such a comparison between the intrinsic values of an existing and a nonexisting horse could be carried out.

However, even if a clear sense could be given to the idea that real existence is a perfection, there appear to be good grounds for denying both that it is a perfection and that it is an attribute. The fact that real existence must be treated as an attribute by anyone who would uphold this form of the ontological argument often is an unspoken assumption of the argument, and we have taken the liberty of making this explicit in our formulation of it. But that they must so regard real existence can be seen if we recall that an upholder of the first form of the argument must think it can prove God's real existence merely because it analyzes the concept of a supremely perfect being.

But what is it to analyze a concept in general, or the concept of a supremely perfect being in particular? It is to discover the logically necessary and sufficient conditions for correctly applying the concept. Thus, in the particular case of the supremely perfect being, it is to discover those attributes or properties the possession of which is logically necessary and sufficient if a being is to be supremely perfect. Now, since an advocate of the first ontological argument would believe that it proves God's existence, he clearly would be committed to the position that real existence is an attribute. Otherwise he could not consistently believe that this method of reasoning proves that real existence must be included in the concept of God, since *only* attributes can be included in this concept. It is not unfair to the first form of the argument, therefore, to state explicitly that, according to this argument, real existence is an attribute.

Now, there are good reasons for denying that real existence is an attribute. A concept of an attribute is one we make use of when we *describe* objects. To describe an object, that is, is to say what its attributes are. For example, to say the thief who broke into your house was about six feet tall, in his early thirties, weighed about two hundred pounds, walked with a limp, and had a scar across his left cheek is to begin to enumerate the thief's attributes or to describe him. You cite those attributes you noticed that could be used to distinguish the thief from other persons. If, then, after having given your description, you should add, "Oh, and he exists," it would be odd indeed to suppose that "he exists" adds to the description of the thief, and an investigating officer would rightly wonder what the point of your utterance was.

This is not to deny that propositions of the form 'x exists' have a clear point, but rather to deny that their point is to describe x. For when we say something of the form 'x exists', we do not describe x but *posit that there is something to which the concept of x applies.* Thus, for example, to say "The Loch Ness monster exists" is not to impart any information about the monster—it is not to describe it. But that does not prevent the proposition from being intelligible, even to someone who does not understand what the Loch Ness monster is. For anyone who understands the language understands that what is meant is that there is an object to which the concept of the monster applies.

Now, since propositions of the form 'x exists' do not perform the function of describing x, and since existence can be correctly classified as an attribute if and only if propositions of the form 'x exists' do function to describe x, it follows that existence cannot be correctly classified as an attribute. Moreover, if existence cannot be correctly classified as an attribute, and if the perfections of a being must be among that being's attributes, then it also follows that existence cannot be correctly classified as a perfection. Now, it seems evident that the *intrinsic* perfections of a being must be included among that being's attributes, since otherwise these perfections could not serve to distinguish the being from other things. It follows, therefore, that existence is not a perfection. Thus, since the first form of the ontological argument assumes that existence is both an attribute and a perfection, when, in fact, it appears to be neither, it follows that the first form of the argument rests on a false premise. Even if the first form were logically in order, therefore, it would fail as a proof of God's existence.

THE SECOND FORM OF THE ONTOLOGICAL ARGUMENT

The principal defect in the first form of the ontological argument is the doctrine that the attribute of real existence is a perfection. It is because of this assumption that Gaunilon could raise his objection. For only if existence *in re* is considered a perfection can one argue that the perfect island must exist *in re,* since one that existed only in the imagination would be less than the most perfect conceivable island. The difficulties one encounters in interpreting Saint Anselm's thought are due, in part, to his response to Gaunilon's objection. In writing his response, Anselm writes as though he is adding nothing to his original statement of the ontological argument. At the same time, however, something new does seem to be included, and it is this "something new" that provides us with a basis for distinguishing between the two forms of the ontological argument. What is different about the second form is its contention not only that God exists, but that he cannot *not* exist or that he exists necessarily. We will first give a formal statement of this argument, then clarify how one of its premises, premise (5), differs from its counterpart in the first form.

FORMAL STATEMENT OF THE SECOND ONTOLOGICAL ARGUMENT

Steps	Symbolization	Status
1. The Judeo-Christian God is a supremely perfect being ("a being the greater than which cannot be thought").	s	1. Assumption
2. If the Judeo-Christian God is a supremely perfect being, then he lacks no attribute that is a perfection.	$s \rightarrow \sim l$	2. Assumption
3. Therefore, the Judeo-Christian God lacks no attribute that is a perfection.	$\therefore \sim l$	3. Consequence, from (1) and (2), by *modus ponens*
4. If the attribute of necessary existence is a perfection, then the Judeo-Christian God does not lack necessary existence.	$n \rightarrow \sim e$	4. Assumption
5. The attribute of necessary existence is a perfection.	n	5. Assumption
6. Therefore, the Judeo-Christian God does not lack the attribute of necessary existence.	$\therefore \sim e$	6. Consequence, (4) and (5), by *modus ponens*
7. If the Judeo-Christian God were to exist contingently, he would lack necessary existence.	$c \rightarrow e$	7. Assumption

Steps	Symbolization	Status
8. Therefore, the Judeo-Christian God does not exist contingently.	$\therefore \sim c$	8. Consequence, from (6) and (7), by *modus tollens*
9. If the Judeo-Christian God does not lack necessary existence, then the Judeo-Christian God exists necessarily.	$\sim e \rightarrow g$	9. Assumption
10. Therefore, the Judeo-Christian God exists necessarily.	$\therefore g$	10. Consequence, from (6) and (9), by *modus ponens*

COMMENTARY ON THE ARGUMENT

The obvious differences between this and the first form of the ontological argument lie in the revision in premise (5) and in what is alleged to follow from it. Instead of saying, as in the first form, that "the attribute of *real* existence is a perfection," we now find the claim that "the attribute of *necessary* existence is a perfection." These two propositions are not logically equivalent, as even the argument's most caustic critics would agree. Therefore, the falsity of the second proposition does not follow from the falsity of the first. Assessment of the truth of this reformulated premise, however, must await its clarification.

What we need to understand is the distinction between two concepts: the concept of a *contingent being* and the concept of a *necessary being*. Contingent beings are those that have not always existed and may not always continue to exist in their present form; the existence of a contingent being, that is, has a beginning and may have an end. Thus, it is not part of the nature or essence of a contingent being to exist, and we can have a complete understanding of the concept of a contingent being and not know whether it exists or not. For example, we could completely understand what a being would have to be like to be the Loch Ness monster and still be uncertain whether there was such a being. In other words, the fact that a contingent being exists, if it does, must be explained by appealing to the causal activity of some other being, since it is not its nature to exist. Thus, in saying that it is a contingent being we mean that it *depends* on the causal activity of other beings for its existence—both those that first brought it into existence and those that sustain it.

Now, a necessary being is not a contingent being, and what characterizes it is the contradictory of what characterizes a contingent being. The existence of a contingent being has a beginning and may have an end; the existence of a necessary being does *not* have a beginning and cannot have an end. It is not part of the nature or essence of a contingent being to exist; it *is* part of the nature or essence of a necessary being to exist. The existence of a contingent being must be explained and accounted for by the activity of some other beings; the existence of a necessary being *cannot* be explained and accounted for by the activity of some other beings. A necessary being, in short, is eternal and exists because of its very nature; it is self-existing; it has the property of *aseity*. Thus, *if* a necessary being exists, it could not not exist, owing to its nature, whereas, if there now exists no necessary being, then none could come into existence.

With this distinction in mind, and adding to this a third possibility, we can conceive of three possible accounts of how any particular being, *X*, exists: (1) *X* exists owing to *X*'s nature, in which case *X* would be a necessary being. (2) *X* exists owing to the activity of other beings, in which case *X* would be a contingent being. (3) *X* exists, not owing to its own nature or to the activity of other beings, but as a result of chance, in which case, once again, *X* would be a contingent being, since, if it had not been for chance, *X* would not have existed in the first place.

If now we consider the concept of "a being the greater than which cannot be conceived," we may ask, "What kind of being would such a being be?" Surely not contingent, for if God were contingent, then his existence would depend on some other being or on the whims of chance, and this would be to diminish his power and, with this, his perfection. The being the greater than which cannot be conceived must, then, be a necessary being, and it is in these terms that premise (5) and the remainder of the second form of the ontological argument should be understood. Anselm is contending, that is, that a being is greater ("more perfect") if it is a necessary being than if it is a contingent being. Thus, what he is alleging in the case of the being the greater than which cannot be conceived is not only that such a being exists, a claim that, even if true, would leave unspecified *how* this being exists; what Anselm is alleging is that a supremely perfect being cannot *not* exist, because of its very nature. In a word, Anselm's second argument attempts to prove not simply that God exists, but that he *must*. And it is by virtue of this difference, and the concepts that underlie it, that Anselm has a reply to Gaunilon's objection. For the concept of any particular being that either does or might exist in the physical universe is the concept of a contingent being. Thus, the concepts of Gaunilon's perfect island, a perfect Santa Claus, or a perfect leprechaun are of contingent beings, and to ascribe necessary existence to a contingent being is to utter a contradiction. Regarding the *second* form of the ontological argument, therefore, we cannot use its method of reasoning to prove the real existence of *any* contingent being. Thus, at least one classic objection to the first form of the argument seems to be countered by the second.

DISPUTING THE LOGIC OF THE ARGUMENT

The second form of the argument may still be open to an objection that also applies to the first—namely, that it commits a fallacy of equivocation. Once again there is an ambiguity of reference in the use of the word 'God'. Sometimes the word is used to refer to the *being* called God, and sometimes to our *concept* of the being called God. This difference is crucial. We can concede to Anselm that our concept of a supremely perfect being requires he must be a necessary being and that in showing this Anselm contributed much to our understanding of what such a being would have to be to merit the name 'God' and our worship (as distinct from our fear). But all we would be conceding are analytic truths about the *concept* of God, just as we would concede an analytic truth about the concept of a triangle in saying that it has three interior angles. But analytic truths tell us only about the meanings of words or the logical form of propositions; they do not tell us whether anything exists. Thus, even if the concept of God is the concept of a necessary being, it does not follow that such a being exists. As Kant contended, the idea only shows that *if* God exists, then a necessary being exists. But *whether* God exists cannot be settled merely by understanding the concept of a supremely perfect being. Thus, the inference contained in premise (9)—"If the Judeo-Christian God does not lack necessary existence, then the Judeo-Christian God exists necessarily"—is made invalid by a fallacy of equivocation. For the antecedent is a claim about the *concept* of a supremely perfect being, and the consequent a claim that there *is* such a being. Accordingly, we can concede the truth of the antecedent and deny the truth of the consequent, without committing a logical mistake. Even in the case of the second form, therefore, the ontological argument contains a nonsequitur.

DISPUTING THE PREMISES OF THE ARGUMENT

This last criticism of the logic of the second form is important because the objections raised against the argument's premises seem less than decisive. There are two principal objections—namely, (1) that existence is not an attribute and (2) that the concepts of a necessary being and of necessary existence are unintelligible. Let us consider each in turn.

To say *existence* is not an attribute does not raise an objection against the second form of the ontological argument, for the claim that it is an attribute occurs nowhere in this form of the argument. Thus, to concede (as we should) that existence is not a property does not jeopardize this form of the argument. For it claims that *necessary* existence is an attribute, and it appears that necessary existence could be—indeed is—an attribute, though existence is not. For if a being the greater than which cannot be conceived cannot be a contingent being, then the claim that such a being exists necessarily, if such a being exists at all, seems to specify an attribute of that being that would distinguish it from all others. Thus, adding the idea of necessary existence to the concept of the being seems to add to the being's description, so the concept of necessary existence seems to specify a distinguishing attribute of a supremely perfect being. Therefore, the first objection to the premises of the argument seems unfounded.

Similarly unfounded is the second principal objection. The point of this objection is to take up where the first objection leaves off. For necessary existence can be an attribute of God only if the concept of necessary existence is intelligible. If it is not, then the answer just given to the first objection is robbed of its basis. What, then, are the grounds for this second objection? They are that the concepts of necessity (and contingency) can be correctly applied *only* to propositions and not, as the second form assumes, to beings. Now, it is a fact that the concepts of necessity and contingency are correctly applied to propositions. What is dubious is how this fact is supposed to show that propositions are the *only* things they can be correctly applied to. The reasons given to support this view seem generally to lack force.

However, even without examining these reasons, we can make a case for the propriety of applying the concepts of contingency and necessity to beings. For the concept of contingency is correctly applicable to anything that *depends* on something else. If X depends upon Y, it is correct to say that X is contingent upon Y. Thus, if beings depend on other things for their existence, they are contingent beings. Moreover, if a being can be conceived of that does not depend on any other thing for its existence, then it would be apt to say that the concept of this being is the concept of a *non*contingent being. And to conceive of such a noncontingent being is to conceive of a necessary being, for what is necessary does not depend on other things. Thus, although it is true that in speaking of God as a necessary being we are not declaring the proposition 'God exists' is necessarily true, it does not follow that the application of the concept of necessity to him is unintelligible.

The two principal objections raised against premises in the second form of the ontological argument seem, then, to be weak. But a defense of the argument against these criticisms does not mean it is sound, since the logic is open to serious question. However, our defense of the premises (if sound and if no other objections can be raised against it) suggests that how sound the argument is depends *entirely* on its logic. And even if Saint Anselm's argument were not unique in any other way, it would be unique in this.

IS 'GOD EXISTS' A PSEUDOPROPOSITION?

Both proponents and critics of the theistic proofs discussed so far assume the theist's use of the sentence "God exists" expresses a genuine proposition. They do not differ on the question, "Is it either true or false that God exists?" (both imply affirmative answers), but rather on the question, "Can God's existence be proven and, if so, how?" But many philosophers, particularly positivists, would dispute this assumption. They would not accept the idea that the theist's use of the sentence "God exists" expresses a genuine proposition merely because it is a complete sentence in the indicative mood. And they would not be satisfied that it does express a genuine proposition for reasons that are analogous to those we gave in an earlier chapter in conjunction with Smith's use of the sentence, "People visit my room when I'm not there." In that case we argued that what this use of the sentence expresses is not verifiable, in practice or in principle, and it was on this basis that we said that the positivist would say that Smith's use of this sentence fails to express a genuine proposition. Precisely these same grounds can be and have been invoked to deny that the theist's use of the sentence "God exists" expresses a genuine proposition.

The importance of this argument, if sound, is difficult to overestimate. If sound, it not only would show that those who affirm their belief in God's existence are misguided; it would also show that those who deny God's existence, in the sense that they believe that it is false that he exists, are equally misguided. For if it is *neither* true *nor* false that God exists, then those who deny his existence are just as confused as those who affirm it.

The positivist's argument here assumes that the theist's use of the sentence "God exists" does not express an analytic proposition. This assumption is one the theist himself would concede, for when he affirms God's existence, he takes himself to be affirming the reality of God, not making an observation about the meaning of the word 'God'. Thus, this assumption of the positivist seems to be a reasonable one.

Notice what follows from this assumption. What follows is that *if* the theist's use of the sentence "God exists" does express a proposition, it must express a *synthetic* proposition. At least this follows if we assume, as we have from the beginning, that there are but two kinds of propositions, analytic and synthetic, and the positivist does assume this. So what the positivist asks is whether the theist's use of the sentence "God exists" expresses a synthetic proposition; to determine if it does, he thinks, we must ask if what it expresses—namely, that a particular being exists—is verifiable by observation, in practice or in principle.

The fact that the positivist thinks this is how we should proceed here is very important, for it means he thinks there is no synthetic a priori knowledge. If the theist's use of "God exists" expresses a synthetic proposition, the positivist maintains, it must express one that is verifiable *by observation,* either in practice or in principle. To suppose that it or any other use of any other sentence expresses a synthetic proposition that is not verifiable by observation (which, notice, would be the case if we could know that some synthetic propositions are true *a priori*) is, the positivist thinks, to indulge in the very kind of nonsense his use of the verification principle is intended to detect. We should bear in mind, therefore, that, when the positivist asks whether the theist's use of "God exists" expresses a synthetic proposition, he means, "Does it express an *empirical* proposition, one whose truth could be verified by observation?"

IS GOD'S EXISTENCE VERIFIABLE?

The difficulties of verifying by observation God's existence are straightforward. Let us first ask whether we have any grounds for supposing that God's existence is verifiable *in practice.* That is, are there any observations that we can *now* make, aided or not by instruments, that could verify the existence of the Judeo-Christian God? Once we recall the attributes ascribed to this God, we see that we have no grounds for supposing this.

Consider the attribute of asiety or self-existence. Even if our senses are adequate to determine whether or not a thing exists, it does not follow that they are adequate to verify that something exists owing to its own nature. What would we have to look for to establish that an existing being had aseity? There are no observations we could make, it seems, that could verify the presence of this attribute in some being. Or consider the attribute of immateriality or spirituality. With our present powers of sensory observation and the present state of our technology, there is no way that we can observe, with our senses, the existence of a being who is lacking altogether in materiality. Of course, elaborate instruments have been used to try to detect ghosts, and various pictures have been taken that show shadowy, semitransparent outlines of humanlike figures. But a being *totally* lacking in material properties will not appear in one of these pictures, no matter how fine the exposure. Thus, with our present capabilities we are not able to verify that a being exists who possesses the attributes of aseity or of immateriality. And since the Judeo-Christian God is supposed to have *both,* it follows that his existence is not verifiable *in practice.*

What, then, of the possibility of verifying God's existence *in principle?* That is, can we *conceive* of any observations that could verify the existence of the Judeo-Christian God? Again, probably not, for in trying to verify God's existence our limitations are not just due to our *present* sensory capacities.

Consider again the question of verifying, by sensory means, that an immaterial being exists. Such verification seems impossible, for no matter how fine our eyes might conceivably become or how discriminating the cameras of the future might conceivably be, they could still detect only things with spatial properties—something "thus and thus wide" and "so and so high." But a being who is *im*material lacks all spatial properties, and thus could not conceivably be detected by the human eye, aided or not by instruments. And the same is true of our other senses as well. They too are incapable of detecting an *im*material being, and we cannot conceive of a way they might be used to do so. On just the basis of the attribute of immateriality, therefore, we can maintain that the existence of the Judeo-Christian God is not verifiable, either in practice *or* in principle.

Problems arise for the theist no matter what attribute is discussed. Consider the moral attributes of omnibenevolence, omniscience, and omnipotence. Can we verify, in practice, that there is a being having these attributes? It appears not. Even though we have ways to observe whether a being knows some things, has some power, and is to some degree good, we lack at present any way to determine whether a being has these qualities to an *infinite* degree. Nor can we even conceive of how we might verify this, given the theistic view that humans are limited creatures. To verify that a being is, for example, omniscient, we would have to suppose that we could be omniscient ourselves. Only if *we* could be omniscient could we have the power to verify the omniscience of another being, for to determine whether another being knows everything, we would have to check this being's claims to knowledge to ascertain whether the being did really know. But the theist contends we are by nature limited in what we can know, so it follows that we cannot even conceive of verifying that a being is omniscient or, for similar reasons, omnipotent or omnibenevolent.

Given, then, positivism's verification principle, and assuming that the foregoing is sound, the theist's use of the sentence "the Judeo-Christian God exists" fails to express an empirical proposition. And given these same assumptions, what this sentence expresses is *neither* true *nor* false—a consequence that would support the positivist's position that both those who affirm and those who deny God's existence are equally confused. Given all the above, in short, it is not true that God exists, but it is not false either, so to debate God's existence is as idle as to debate with Smith whether or not persons, of the kind conceived by Smith, visit his room when he is out.

Christians and Jews have realized that the posivitist's critique of belief in the Judeo-Christian God is very serious and that it cannot be dismissed out of hand. They have endeavored in various ways to meet the challenge of positivism, and though we cannot here explore them all, we should note that it is unlikely that theism and positivism can be shown to be consistent. For the reasons given above, it does seem to be the case that God's existence is not verifiable by means of our senses, either in practice or in principle, and those who would seek to show that it is seem destined to fail. The positivist's critique, in short, cannot be met on the positivist's terms.

Where the positivist's critique can be most seriously challenged, however, is over his view that *all* synthetic propositions must be empirical—that is, verifiable in practice or in principle. This view can be challenged in two ways, as will be described in the next two sections. First, we might dispute the adequacy or completeness of the positivist's analysis of an empirical proposition. Secondly, we might dispute the positivist's view that all synthetic propositions must be, in his sense, empirical.

IS GOD'S EXISTENCE FALSIFIABLE?

What does this question mean? Asked another way, it means, "Are there any observations that we can or conceivably could carry out that would show that God does *not* exist?" Let us see how this question found its place within the greater debate about God's existence.

Earlier we said the positivist maintains that a proposition is empirical if and only if it can be observationally verified, in practice or in principle. Now, this may not be an adequate analysis of the concept of an empirical proposition. For whether a proposition is an empirical one might also be determined in another way—namely, by asking whether there are any observations we might make from which we could conclude that the proposition is *false*. In others words, it seems to be the case that, if a proposition is empirical, we must at least be able to conceive of what we would have to observe to show that it is false. So there may be two ways to determine if a proposition is empirical: we can ask, as a positivist does, if it is verifiable, and we can ask if it is falsifiable by observation, either in practice or in principle.

The reasoning underlying this second way seems sound. For a belief or proposition to be empirical, it cannot be consistent with anything and everything that we might observe. There must be some things that might exist such that, if observed, would prove the proposition false. For example, the proposition 'All swans are white' is a clear example of an empirical proposition. But its truth is not consistent with everything we might observe to exist or happen. If we observe a swan that is not white, then we would have to call the proposition false. And the same is true of all those propositions that are empirical: they must be falsifiable, by observation. That is, even if they are *really* true, as a matter of fact, we can at least *conceive of* certain things occurring that, if we were to observe them, would show the proposition empirically false. In the particular case of those who aver God's existence, then, we can inquire into the empirical status of their belief by asking, as the positivist does, "Is God's existence observationally verifiable?" *or* by asking, for the reasons just given, "Is God's existence observationally falsifiable?" Let us explore this latter question.

Again, let us ask: Is there anything that might conceivably exist or happen, such that if a person already committed to belief in God were to observe that it did, he would thereby be obliged to concede that his belief in God was false? First, then, consider this fantastic case. Suppose that during the night, while no one was watching, the stars were rearranged, and that they spelled out the words "The Judeo-Christian God does not exist!" The case is fantastic, but it is conceivable. And what we want to ask is: would it count as evidence against God's existence? It is difficult to see how it could, at least to a person fully committed to belief in God's existence. "It's the work of the devil," such a believer might say. Or, "It's just another of those temptations to disbelief we must overcome. It's God's way of testing the strength of our belief." And so on. The point is, faced with a fantastic situation of this kind, a devoted believer would seek and find some explanation that made the fantastic occurrence perfectly consistent with his belief in God. And if he would seek and find some explanation that made these facts perfectly consistent with his belief in God, it is clear that the existence of these facts could not in any way count as evidence *against* his belief.

Consider another example that is not fantastic but all too common. Suppose a natural disaster, such as a hurricane, a tidal wave, or an earthquake occurs, killing and injuring hundreds of thousands of people and inflicting incalculable property damage. Would such an event count as evidence against the truth of the theist's belief? Once again, a firm believer might seek an explanation of these facts that he thought made them perfectly consistent with his belief: "The Lord works in mysterious ways, His wonders to perform," or "It's God's way of controlling the population."

Finally, suppose that after death we continue to go on living. And suppose that the life we experience is different from what the believer expected it to be. For example, suppose that there is no experience of union with God and no experience of pain that would suggest that we were in Hell. Instead we experience simply a long period of peaceful rest, as though in a dream, but without the appearance of God. And suppose we experience this for thousands of years, still without God's presence. Would this afterlife experience count as evidence against belief in God's existence? It seems unlikely. The person fully committed to belief in God's existence would, once again, seek some explanation of these facts that would reveal that they were consistent with the truth of his belief—for example, "This is just another of God's ways of testing our faith" (a contention not necessarily limited to what transpires in our earthly life). Thus, no matter what actually happens, and no matter what we may conceive might happen, either in this life or in the next, the believer will, it seems, interpret it so that it is perfectly consistent with the truth of his belief.

But if nothing can count as evidence against belief in God's existence and if, further, a proposition must be falsifiable if it is to be empirical, then we have additional support for the view that the theist's use of the sentence "God exists" does not express an empirical proposition. This result is important. If true, it helps us see that belief in God is not empirical in nature; that even the most devout believers can be confused about the nature of their own belief, thinking it is empirical when it is not. Whether the preceding argument is sound, therefore, is a question of great importance. Thus, let us give a brief formal statement of this argument and see how it might be challenged:

Steps	*Symbolization*	*Status*
1. If what is expressed by the theist's use of the sentence "God exists" is not falsifiable, then what is expressed by the theist's use of this sentence is not an empirical proposition.	$\sim f \to \sim e$	Assumption
2. What is expressed by the theist's use of the sentence "God exists" is not falsifiable.	$\sim f$	Assumption
3. Therefore, what is expressed by the theist's use of the sentence "God exists" is not an empirical proposition.	$\therefore \sim e$	Consequence, from (1) and (2), by *modus ponens*

The argument is formally valid, and no case can be made, it seems, for the claim that it commits an informal fallacy. Thus, the question of its soundness becomes the question of the truth of its premises. As we have said, no proposition can be empirical if it cannot be falsified by observation, either in practice or in principle. And if this is true of every empirical proposition, then, of course, it would be true in the special case of 'God exists', assuming that this is a proposition. Thus, premise (1) seems to be true and known to be so.

But premise (2) is something else again. For it is unclear how we could *prove* that what the theist says is not falsifiable. But the burden of proof here is on those theists who think that belief in God is an empirical belief. It is up to them to present us with a case that would falsify 'God exists', if empirical propositions must be falsifiable and if 'God exists' is an empirical proposition. They must try to explain what they would have to observe to convince them that their (empirical) belief in God was mistaken.

We cannot discuss all such attempts by theists, but we will discuss one that seems the most promising—namely, the case of unnecessary or gratuitous evil in the world. Let us first describe the kind of situation these theists have in mind here and then go on to assess the adequacy of their argument.

Two kinds of evil have been distinguished. The first is _moral evil, which is man's inhumanity to man_—murder, theft, rape, beatings, blackmail, and so on. It results from human decision making and action and is, therefore, evil for which man himself is said to be responsible. The second type is _natural evil—hurricanes, earthquakes, cancer, birth defects, the suffering of the animal kingdom, and so on._ Evils of this type result from the operation of natural laws, and thus man cannot be said to be morally responsible for them.

Now, a great deal of evil of both kinds exists in the world, and has led some thinkers, including Hume, to deny that an omniscient, omnipotent, omnibenevolent God exists. For, they have argued, if God is omniscient, he must know that this evil exists; and if he is omnibenevolent, he must want to get rid of it; and if, finally, he is omnipotent, he must have the power to eliminate it. Thus, these thinkers conclude, the existence of evil shows that God is not all-knowing, all-good, and all-powerful, or, in short, that God, if there is one, is not the Judeo-Christian God. Other thinkers, however, have argued that it is possible for both evil and the Judeo-Christian God to exist. Who is correct with respect to this debate (known as "the problem of evil") it is not our present interest to try to determine. What we want to do is to see how the idea of unnecessary evil can be clarified by what we have just said.

The background against which this idea can be understood is that of God's plan for the world. We are to suppose that God, with all his knowledge, power, and goodness, has created the universe such that, though there is some evil in it, it is somehow all necessary in the divine scheme of things. For, being omniscient, God knew how much evil would exist, and, being all good and all powerful, he could have eliminated any evil that was unnecessary. There is no evil that does not, therefore, somehow or other contribute to the realization of God's plan. None is wasted, all is essential— at least this is the view taken by many theists. And, crude though our account of this view is, it is sufficient to provide us with the means of explicating the idea of unnecessary evil. For unnecessary evil would be any evil that did _not_ fit into the realization of God's plan; it would be evil that is inessential or superfluous.

How might the theist make use of this idea of unnecessary evil? He might say, "You have challenged me to show that my belief in God is an empirical belief, and, to do this, you have required that I show that my belief is falsifiable. The idea of unnecessary evil enables me to do this. I can conceive of something such that, if I observed it, I would most definitely conclude that an all-good, all-knowing, all-powerful God does not exist. This 'something' is unnecessary evil. Of course, since I happen to believe that God does exist, I do not think that I ever shall observe superfluous evil. But, still, such a case is conceivable, and that is all that is required if, on your own view, belief in God's existence is to count as an empirical belief."

This argument may be challenged in two different but related ways. First, it is unclear that any committed theist *would* ever be moved to say that he had found out that the universe contains unnecessary evil. For he would have to find out that an instance of evil was unnecessary in the sense that God could just as well have realized his plan without it. Suppose we think we have found just such a case and call the attention of the theist to it. It is doubtful that he would agree, if he was a devout believer. Instead, he probably would say, "But can we *really* be sure it is unnecessary? Might it not only *appear* to be? Who are we, frail mortals that we are, to judge what is and what is not necessary for God to achieve his plan?" In short, no matter what possibly unnecessary evil we might cite, the believer would probably respond by saying that we cannot be sure that it is *really* unnecessary. And he is, of course, free to do this. Only then the theist cannot use the argument about unnecessary evil to show that belief in God is an empirical belief because it is falsifiable. For so long as the theist responds as we have imagined he would, he makes it impossible for his belief to be falsified by reference to the idea of unnecessary evil.

Moreover, it is unclear whether any theist *could* respond in the way we've supposed. For, to know that some evil was unnecessary he would have to know that it was inessential in the realization of God's plan. But to know this, of course, he would first have to know what God's plan is and what is essential to its realization. But no theist could consistently credit man with the ability to possess such knowledge, since he believes that man is by nature *limited* in what he can know in this regard. Thus, this line of reasoning is not open to the theist.

We have seen, then, that there are very serious questions that arise concerning the nature of belief in God. This belief may not be what many presume it is—an empirical belief—for if it were, it would have to be verifiable or falsifiable. We have not been able to consider every possible way a theist might try to show that his belief is verifiable or falsifiable, but the ways we have discussed have all failed. Thus, we have some reason for thinking that belief in God is not empirical. Whether any conclusive reasons can be presented either for or against the view that it is not empirical is a question each of us must try to understand and think about more fully as future experience allows. For it is a question of vital importance, especially for those who do believe in God. This is because, prior to answering it, no believer can be credited with understanding what he or she believes.

DOES GOD EXIST?

The positions we have argued for in this chapter are the following:
(1) God's existence cannot be proven a posteriori.
(2) God's existence has not been proven a priori.
(3) God's existence is not observationally verifiable, either in practice or in principle, in either this life or the next one (assuming there is a next one).
(4) God's existence does not appear to be observationally falsifiable, given a committed theist's belief that He exists, a contention that, if true, does seem to show, together with (3), that belief in God cannot be an empirical belief.

If the arguments in support of positions (1) and (2) are sound, then we have good reason to deny that anybody knows, either from observation or independently of it, that God exists. Moreover, if the argument in support of position (3) is sound, then we have good reason to deny the oft–heard belief that after we die we will find out whether God exists or not. For if God is a being whose existence *cannot* be verified by us, then we will never be able to verify his existence, even in the next life, assuming there is one. Finally, if the argument in support of position (4) is sound, then we have grounds for wondering just what belief in God does amount to, since, if both (3) and (4) are true, this belief does not appear to be empirical. Even those who would simply profess their *belief* in God, and disclaim any knowledge concerning his existence, in other words, have their philosophical work cut out for them. For they cannot be credited with understanding what it is that they profess to believe unless or until they have clarified the nature of the belief in question.

At this point, many persons throw up their hands and say they "just believe, that's all there is too it!" But they can be understood to be erecting a defense against the unremitting challenge to think carefully and clearly, even about matters that concern us deeply—indeed, especially about these! To accept the challenge does not make life any easier. But it holds the promise that the beliefs that stand up under the heat of philosophical scrutiny are more apt to be true than those that do not.

In response to the question, "Does God exist?," then, we seem to be justified in responding, "We don't know." But this does not imply that we do not know anything at all about the question of God's existence. On the contrary, if our arguments in this chapter are sound, we know a good deal more than we did at the beginning. One point in particular needs to be stressed: we now know how *not* to conduct our thinking on the question of God's existence. Once we recognize that it is logically impossible to prove God's existence a posteriori or verify it observationally, then we should realize that nothing we might do or observe could prove God's existence. And this should come as a liberating experience. It should free us from a prejudice we may well have had about how to answer the question, "Does God exist?" But more importantly for our purposes, it should direct our attention back to the one argument that is untouched by all the criticisms we raised against the a posteriori proofs and all the difficulties connected with the questions of observationally verifying or falsifying God's existence. This argument is the ontological argument of Saint Anselm. Because it is wholly a priori, it is immune to the above criticisms and difficulties. For this reason, too, Anselm's use of the sentence "God exists" would not express, nor would it be intended to express, an empirical proposition. One can begin to sense, therefore, the significance that philosophers like Kant have attributed to this argument.

Is it *possible* to prove—as Anselm and other rationalists affirm, and as positivists deny—the existence of a being wholly a priori? Such a question goes to the heart of the difference that separates rationalist from positivist, as does the question, "Are all synthetic propositions, as the positivist claims and the rationalist denies, verifiable, in practice or in principle?" Later on, toward the end of the next chapter, we will indicate *some* synthetic propositions that are not empirical in the sense that the positivist understands this concept. And this, if true, is a point of great importance. For if there are synthetic propositions that are not empirical, then one cannot assume, as the positivist does, that since the theist's use of the sentence "God exists" does not express an empirical proposition (a view we tried to defend in the above), it does not or cannot express a synthetic proposition either. The theist *might* express a synthetic proposition by his use of the sentence "God exists" even if he is *not* expressing an empirical proposition. This possibility should be explored with rigor and patience, and there is no better place to begin than with Anselm's argument. For when Anselm uses the sentence "God exists," he does *not* think he is asserting an empirical proposition, but he *does* think he is asserting a synthetic one.

Anselm's argument, then, demands further consideration that cannot be given here. And that is a shortcoming that we must acknowledge. Nevertheless, we should not count our effort as wasted. If our arguments are sound, we have been able to pinpoint areas where further reflection is most likely to yield the knowledge and understanding we seek. And this we could neither have known nor understood in advance of the inquiry we have conducted here.

FOR FURTHER READING

Hick, John, *The Philosophy of Religion.* Englewood Cliffs, N. J.: Prentice-Hall, 1963. Perhaps the finest introductory book on the subject. Contains short, intelligible summaries of the classical arguments discussed above, as well as a helpful commentary on the problem of theology and falsification. Chap. 1 parallels and supplements above discussion of God's nature.

_____ ,ed., *The Existence of God.* New York: Macmillan, 1964. A fine collection of essays on God's existence.

Paperback collections of essays devoted more or less exclusively to the individual proofs and problems discussed above include the following, which also have valuable bibliographies:

Burill, Donald R., ed., *The Cosmological Arguments.* Garden City, N.Y.: Doubleday, 1967.

Platinga, Alvin, ed., *The Ontological Argument.* Garden City, N.Y.: Doubleday, 1965. With an introduction by Richard Taylor.

Flew, Antony, and Alasdair MacIntyre, eds., *New Essays in Philosophical Theology.* New York: Macmillan, 1955.

Two particularly noteworthy books that discuss in depth the problem of religious knowledge are:

Blackstone, William, *The Problem of Religious Knowledge.* Englewood Cliffs, N.J.: Prentice-Hall, 1963.

Ferre, Frederick, *Basic Modern Philosophy of Religion.* New York: Scribner's, 1967.

EXERCISES

1. How do God's metaphysical attributes differ from his moral attributes?
2. What is the difference between theism and deism? Between both these views and pantheism?
3. According to Saint Thomas Aquinas, how do "truths of reason" differ from "truths of faith"?
4. How does an a posteriori proof of God's existence differ from an a priori proof?
5. Give a summary statement of the argument from design and indicate how the validity of its reasoning can be challenged and the truth of one of its premises can be disputed.
6. Distinguish between a cause *in fieri* and a cause *in esse.*
7. Give a summary statement of the temporal first cause argument and indicate how the validity of its reasoning can be challenged and why the truth of at least one of its premises can be disputed.
8. Clarify the ideas of existence *in intellectu* and existence *in re.*
9. Clarify the doctrine that existence is a perfection.

10. How does the second formulation of the ontological argument differ from the first formulation? What, if any, are the criticisms that can be raised against the first that cannot be raised against the second?

11. Does the theist's use of the sentence "God exists" express a proposition? If it does, how can God's existence be verified or falsified? If it does not, what *does* the theist's use of this sentence express?

12. What role, if any, do you think that the proofs of God's existence play in the final determination of whether to believe in his existence or to disbelieve?

5 Is Man Free?

The belief in man's free will has been a central idea in the *Weltanschauung* of Western civilization. How should the concept be understood? What are the grounds (and how good are they) for saying that man has or does not have free will?

THE IDEA OF FREE WILL

The word 'free' is used in different ways. We speak of the freedom *to do* certain things (speak, vote, marry) and of the freedom *from* certain things (hunger, fear, repression). We speak of the "free world," "free love," "free enterprise," "fighting for freedom," "escape from freedom," "the truth shall make you free."

'Free' is used in many ways, and we should keep this in mind. For the sense of 'free' we shall be dealing with—what we shall call its *metaphysical sense*—is not the only way the word might be used, though it is a profoundly important one.

Let us first distinguish between involuntary and voluntary actions. *Involuntary actions* are actions we do not *choose* to perform: our knee jerks when it is struck by a hammer, our eyes blink when a rock is thrown toward them. These are actions all physiologically normal human beings perform, automatically, given the same stimuli. We do them *in spite of*, not because of, what we may decide. *Voluntary actions*, on the other hand, are ones we choose to perform. Not all physiologically normal people respond automatically to the same stimuli; different men perform different voluntary actions, given the same stimuli. For example, two men in the same cafeteria line, presented with the same dishes, may make quite different selections.

Voluntary actions may be deliberate or habitual. In a *deliberate* voluntary action a person is faced with an alternative between doing two things —say, studying for an exam or seeing a movie. He considers what he stands to gain or lose by doing each, then makes his choice. In a *habitual* voluntary action he does not deliberate; he just decides to do something—automatically out of habit. Smokers often light a cigarette without thought to the wisdom of smoking it. We put on shoes and socks or start a car the same way. Unless we are just learning how to do such things, we do not think about what we are doing before we do them—we simply do them, without deliberation. But these actions are not involuntary. We had to learn how to do them, whereas we perform involuntary actions without instruction.

Now, the question philosophers ask is, "Do we ever *freely* choose to do any of those voluntary actions that we perform?" Obviously, we do not *choose* to do what we do involuntarily, so of course there can be no question of our *freely* choosing to do so. But for voluntary actions, both deliberate and habitual, we do choose to perform them—and so we must ask whether the choices are free ones.

What do we have in mind when we ask whether any of these choices are *free* ones? To make the meaning of "free choice" clear, imagine that in a certain situation a person can do only one thing; there are no alternatives, no options, open to him—only the one thing he can do. Now, we would never say that a book or pencil freely chose to fall, when we removed support from them, for there really is nothing else the book or pencil can do— they *have* to fall. Similarly, if a man has no options in a certain situation, he *has* to do what he does—his doing it is unavoidable. So we would deny he freely chose to do what he did, even if he deliberated at length before he did it. To say he freely chose to do it suggests he did it *instead of* something else—which implies he might have chosen to do something else, which, of course, he could not have done, if the *only* thing he could do is what he did do.

What, then, is free choice? To say someone freely chose to do something is not merely to say he chose to do it voluntarily; it is also to say that he did it *instead of choosing* to do something else and that he *could have chosen not to do it.* So, our question about free will can be reformulated to read: "Is it ever the case that we could have chosen to do something different from what we have chosen to do?" Let us consider why this question is important, both for theoretical problems in science, for instance, and also for practical, everyday issues.

FREE WILL AND MORAL RESPONSIBILITY

When we hold people morally responsible for what they do, we are judging that they deserve to be praised or blamed, on moral grounds, for their behavior. A person is morally responsible for what he has done if what he has done is either morally right or morally wrong (one cannot be held morally responsible for an act that is morally indifferent). But this condition is logically necessary only; it is not sufficient. For if we supposed no one ever really has any alternative but to do what he does, that, in other words, no one is free in the metaphysical sense, then we could not rationally hold people morally responsible for what they do.

To make this clearer, let us suppose a person saved a number of elderly people from a fire—and really had no choice but to do what he did. Of course, we would be grateful that the man acted as he did and the elderly persons might thank their lucky stars, but we would have no reason to praise him for his behavior. For if he had no choice but to do what he did, then he contributed nothing to his decision to do it. So why praise him? Similarly, if he set the fire and if he had no choice but to do it, we would doubtless bemoan the suffering and loss of property caused, but we would not blame him. For, if there were nothing he could have done to prevent his action, then this should call forth our pity, not our moral outrage.

What this line of reasoning, if sound, shows is that at least two logically necessary conditions are involved in our thinking that someone is morally responsible for what he has done, neither of which also is sufficient. These conditions are (1) we must think that the person's act was either morally right or morally wrong, and (2) we must think that he could have chosen not to do what he did, so that he can be said to have freely chosen to do it.

Thus, as condition (2) makes plain, our belief in human free will is logically related to our belief that people are morally responsible. Moreover, once we see that these two conditions are involved in our concept of thinking that people are morally responsible, we can see part of what is involved in asking whether people are *actually* morally responsible for what they do, in addition to being *thought* so. For a person to be morally responsible for his behavior, (1) his action must actually be either morally right or wrong and (2) he must actually have freely chosen to do what he did. Thus, if nothing is really morally right or wrong, then, although people may *think* that some men are morally responsible for what they do, no one really would be, just as if no one has free will, then no one would be morally responsible for what he does.

Whether anything really is right or wrong is the principal question of ethics, and we cannot pursue it here. However, we can pursue the question of man's free will. But first let us notice how the philosophical problems surrounding this idea touch each of us personally.

REGRET, REMORSE, AND GUILT

From time to time each of us experiences various emotions about what he has done, including guilt or remorse. Perhaps we have been insensitive toward someone we love or taken advantage of a friend's trust. Whatever it is, we know how uncomfortable and unpleasant those moments are when our conscience bothers us.

But is it ever appropriate to feel guilt or remorse or regret? Not if there never is any way of avoiding acting as we do. In that case, there simply would be nothing else we *could* do. And it cannot be reasonable to regret doing what you simply cannot avoid doing.

Thus, feelings of guilt, remorse, and regret are like the practice of holding persons morally responsible. They are appropriate only if we assume we can choose to act otherwise than we do, that we have free will. And since we not only do experience such feelings but are bothered by them, it is worth asking whether it is reasonable to feel these ways.

FREE WILL: WHAT THE PROBLEM IS

The "problem" of free will comes down to the question of whether man is free in the sense that, for some of the voluntary actions he performs, he could have chosen to act differently than he did. If man is free in this sense, then we are justified in holding him morally responsible for what he sometimes does, and our feelings of regret, remorse, and guilt could have a rational basis. But if man is not free, the practice and these feelings are not reasonable.

Now, the reason there is thought to be a "problem" of free will is because there are other beliefs that people accept that appear inconsistent with the belief in free will. That is, the proposition 'Man has free will' seems logically incompatible with other propositions, so the free will proposition cannot be true if the other propositions are. And many careful thinkers believe these other propositions *are* true. The "problem" of free will, then, is not simply whether man has free will but whether he can *possibly* have it, if certain other propositions are accepted as true.

What are these "other propositions"? It depends. There is a plurality of propositions that different thinkers have thought are (1) true and (2) inconsistent with the proposition that affirms man's free will. We will examine two principal ideas that have been thought to be inconsistent with human freedom–first, the belief in divine omniscience and, second, the belief in the causal principle or the belief that every event has a cause.

FREE WILL AND DIVINE OMNISCIENCE

Fundamental to the Judeo-Christian view is the belief that man is a morally responsible being—that in following God's commandments he does what is right and in violating them does what is wrong. Naturally, in this view man has free will. Indeed, so central is this idea of free will to the Judeo-Christian world view that it appears in the Old Testament story of God's creation: the fall of Adam and the expulsion of Adam and Eve from the Garden of Eden clearly depict Adam as being endowed by God with free will and, as such, as a being who deserved to be punished for choosing to violate God's commands.

The belief in the existence of God and the belief in the existence of human free will, many philosophers maintain, are inconsistent, although others affirm their consistency. One way of formulating the argument against their consistency is the following.

FORMAL STATEMENT OF THE INCONSISTENCY BETWEEN DIVINE OMNISCIENCE AND HUMAN FREE WILL

Steps	Symbolization	Status
1. If God is omniscient, then he knows everything that each of us will do before we do it.	$g \rightarrow k$	Assumption
2. If God knows everything that each of us will do before we do it, then the only thing we ever can do is what God knows we will do.	$k \rightarrow o$	Assumption
3. Therefore, if God is omniscient, then the only thing we ever can do is what God knows we will do.	$g \rightarrow o$	Consequence, from (1) and (2), by chain argument.
4. If the only thing we ever can do is what God knows we will do, then we never can act otherwise than as we do.	$o \rightarrow {\sim}a$	Assumption
5. Therefore, if God is omniscient, then we never can act otherwise than as we do.	$g \rightarrow {\sim}a$	Consequence, from (3) and (4), by chain argument.
6. If we never can act otherwise than as we do, then we do not have free will.	${\sim}a \rightarrow {\sim}f$	Assumption
7. Therefore, if God is omniscient, then we do not have free will.	$g \rightarrow {\sim}f$	Consequence, from (5) and (6), by chain argument.

COMMENTARY ON THE ARGUMENT

Even the severest critics of this argument would, it appears, concede its formal and informal validity. Thus, the issues that divide the critics and proponents of this argument concern the truth of its assumptions. Let us examine these assumptions, then, beginning with the least controversial, premise (1). If God is omniscient, then he must be supposed to know *everything*; and if he knows everything, then he must know what each one of us will do before we do it. Indeed, if God's omniscience excludes his ever learning anything (for if he knows everything, how could he learn something he did not already know?), then we must suppose that God always has known what we will do at any given moment—and he has known this for as long as he has existed as an omniscient being. And since God is said to be eternal, then he has known, from all eternity, exactly what each of us will do at any given moment. Therefore, there is a necessary connection between the antecedent in premise (1) ('God is omniscient') and the consequent ('He knows what each of us will do before we do it'). Thus, premise (1) appears to be a clear example of an analytic truth, and both the proponents and opponents of this line of reasoning appear unanimous in conceding its truth.

The same can be said for premise (6). This premise affirms an analytic truth that we already have commented upon. This leaves premises (2) and (4) as possible targets of criticism, both of which are highly controversial. Let us first look at premise (2).

Premise (2) affirms that there is a necessary connection between the proposition 'God knows everything that each of us will do before we do it' and the proposition 'The only thing we ever can do is what God knows we will do'. The premise rests upon a more general view about the logical connection between the concept of *knowing* that p is true, on the one hand, and p's being true, on the other. For if someone *knows* that a given proposition, p, is true, then it follows that p is true. To say that a person "knows that p," in other words, entails p's truth. For if p happened to be false, then we could not say that he *knew* that p. Of course, we might say that he *believed* that p was true, and this is an important point to notice. A person can believe that something is the case and be mistaken; a person can have a false belief. But no one can have false knowledge; no one can have knowledge of what he is mistaken about. If he is mistaken, then he does not know, which is why the truth of p does follow from the truth of the proposition that someone knows that p is true.

The relevance of this entailment to the free will debate can be explained as follows. As we have seen, to know that p is true entails that p is true. Now, suppose that p describes what someone will do at some future date—for example, that Smith will shoot Jones at a particular time in a particular place. And suppose Brown knows that *p* is true. What follows from this assumption? The truth of *p* does. And what follows from the fact that *p* is true? Quite a bit, it seems—namely, that at that time and place specified in *p*, Smith *must* shoot Jones. For if it is *true* that he will, then this is what he *must* do; if it is *true* that he will, then there is *nothing else he can do*. Thus, it seems that, if Brown *knows* that Smith will shoot Jones, at a particular time and in a particular place, then the *only* thing that Smith can do, at that time and place, is shoot Jones. If Smith were to do anything else, then Brown would not know what he (Smith) would do, which is contrary to our assumption that he does know this.

Now, substitute God for Brown. Exactly the same entailment holds. If God knows that Smith is going to shoot Jones, at a certain time and place, then it is true that this *is* what Smith will do. And since it is true that this is what Smith will do, then the only thing he could do is shoot Jones. Nor can we avoid this result by saying that God did not know what he (Smith) was going to do. For God is supposed to be omniscient. And since God's omniscience entails that he knows what each of us will do, in every situation and at any time, one can contend, as backers of premise (2) do, that "If God knows what each of us will do before we do it, then the only thing we ever can do is what God knows we will do."

Now consider premise (4), 'If the only thing we ever can do is what God knows we will do, then we never can act otherwise than as we do'. This premise, too, rests on the more general truth that if there is only one thing a person can do, then there is nothing else he can do. Thus, if the only thing a person can do is what God knows that person will do, it follows that there just is nothing else that person can do, no other real possibilities between which he might choose. The only thing he can do is what he does do.

Thus, if the logic of this argument is conceded to be valid and if, as we have been urging, the assumptions are true, then the truth of the conclusion must be conceded as well: free will and divine omniscience must really be incompatible. But before we can be satisfied that this is so, at least one criticism of the argument must be considered.

DISPUTING THE ARGUMENT

The criticism we should consider here involves an important objection frequently raised against premise (2). This premise frequently is attacked in the following way. Suppose that Jim and Bill are good friends. They spend a lot of time together and know one another very well—so well that they often are able to say how the other will react to something or what the other will do before he does it. They are sensitive to each other's habits, interests, and moods and can predict one another's behavior. Now, suppose that Bill knows that Jim will go to the show rather than study, if a mutual friend, Don, asks Jim to go to the show. If Bill *does* know this, then, of course, Jim must elect to go to the show, when Don asks him. Since it is true that this is what Jim will do, then this is the only thing Jim could choose to do. But no one would be tempted to say, this criticism goes, that Jim "was not free to decide" to go to the show—that Bill's knowledge of what Jim would do *made* Jim do it. Bill's knowledge, in other words, did not *cause* or *force* Jim to go to the show. It is still Jim who chose to go to the show; it is just that Bill happened to know what choice Jim would make, prior to Jim's making it.

This same line of reasoning, it is alleged, can be applied to God's omniscience. As an omniscient being, God must know what Jim will do, and know that Jim will decide to go to the show, when Don asks him. But, this line of reasoning goes, God's knowing that this is what Jim would do would not cause, force, or make Jim do it. Thus, proponents of this criticism contend, to know what someone will do, before he does it, is perfectly compatible with that person's freely choosing to do it. And since they think these two ideas are compatible, they think God's omniscience is not inconsistent with human free will. God knows what we are going to do before we do it. But we ourselves can freely choose to do it.

DEFENDING THE ARGUMENT

How adequate is this criticism? An important deficiency is that it appears to commit a fallacy of *ignoratio elenchi* (that is, a fallacy of irrelevance). For the question at issue is not whether God's knowledge *forces*, *causes*, or *makes* us do what we do; clearly neither God's nor Bill's knowledge of what Jim will do has causal power. Rather, the question is whether God's reputed omniscience is compatible with the idea that we could act otherwise than as we do. And the answer is that these two beliefs do not seem consistent. For if God knows that Jim will choose to go to the show when Don asks him, then it is true that this is what Jim will do. And since it is true that Jim *will* do this, there is ample reason to say he *must* do it. For if he were to do anything else, then God would not know what he was going to do—which, of course, is impossible, if God is presumed to be omniscient. The concept of God's knowing what a person will do, before he does it, seems to imply nothing less than that it is necessary that the person do it. Thus, if it is *necessary* that he act as he does, then he could *not* act otherwise than as he does—not because God's knowledge causes him to act as he does, but because, say, going to the show is the *only* thing Jim could choose to do, given that God is assumed to know that he will do it.

And it is easy to see how we can generalize on the basis of this one example. If God's knowing what Jim will do, before he does it, is inconsistent with the view that Jim freely chooses to do it, then, clearly, God's knowing what anybody will do, before he does it, is inconsistent with the idea of any person's freely choosing to do what he does. And since Jews and Christians agree that God is omniscient, it follows, if this reasoning is sound, that man is not free (in the metaphysical sense) which, in turn, implies that man is never morally responsible for what he does. The two propositions, then—that 'God exists and is omniscient' and that 'Man has free will'—appear to be genuinely inconsistent, which, if true, must force the thoughtful Jew or Christian to give up either one or the other of two of his most cherished beliefs.

FREE WILL AND DETERMINISM

The general thesis of the above argument is that if a person knows what another person is going to do, before he does it, then the person who does it cannot be said to have had a free choice to do or to refrain from doing it. The person's choice may be voluntary (as opposed to involuntary), and he may have thought long and hard about his choice before making it. But the act is still something he *must* do, if we know that he will do it.

This general thesis has nothing in particular to do with God or his omniscience; it is a very general thesis about how anyone's knowledge of what another will do excludes the latter person's free choice. Thus, if we can show that some people do know what other people are going to do, before they do it, or if human beings are such that, in principle, it is possible to predict what everyone will do, then we would have substantial grounds for denying the existence of free will. For if we could correctly predict the behavior of everyone, then everyone would be bound or necessitated to behave as we predict they will. What everyone does could be seen to be the only thing they could do, and thus it could be seen that no one is really free or, therefore, morally responsible.

Such a view of the world in general and of human behavior in particular underlies *hard determinism*. It is an outlook that, historically, has been intimately connected with the development of the natural and the behavioral sciences, although its roots go back to the ancient Greek idea of *Moira* or fate. Let us first clarify some of the hard determinist's leading ideas before attempting to relate his position formally to the question of human freedom and moral responsibility. We will begin with the general idea called determinism.

Determinism may be summarized as the view that *every event has a cause*. Thus, a *determinist* subscribes to the principle of causality or the causal principle, discussed in Chapter 3. What this principle expresses is the thesis that the cause of an event *determines* the event—that is, determines what event will occur as well as when it will occur. Thus, determinists maintain that, for everything that occurs, something else, called its cause, determines when and how it will occur.

We can express this view in a somewhat more technical manner as follows. The claim that every event has a cause is equivalent to the claim that every event has a *factually sufficient condition*. (For stylistic reasons, we will refer to such a condition as simply "a sufficient condition.") This means that, for every event that occurs, there is some condition or set of conditions that is sufficient for the occurrence of the event. This, in turn, means that, *given* that those conditions are fulfilled, the event *will* occur. There will be nothing that can prevent the event from occurring, so that, in *this* sense, the occurrence of the event is necessary. This does not mean, of course, that the occurrence of the event is necessary in the sense that it is logically impossible for it not to occur. Rather, it is necessary in the sense that nothing can, as a matter of fact, prevent it. Once the sufficient condition has been fulfilled, the occurrence of the event is unavoidable. Indeed, this seems to be what is involved in saying that the occurrence of the event is *determined*.

Now, one difficulty we can have understanding determinism is due to its high degree of abstractness; it is a view about *all* events, and it alleges that something is *always* true of them. This is apt to make determinism appear very strange or hard to comprehend, but it need not be. The way to get over this reaction is to think about a few everyday examples. Consider what happens when we flip a switch to turn on the lights. In a perfectly ordinary sense, *that* the lights come on is an event. It is something that happens, occurs, or takes place. The determinist would contend something must have caused the lights to come on, that they did not just come on "all by themselves." When we flip the light switch, an electrical circuit is opened and the current is permitted to run through the switch to the socket containing the light bulb. If the light bulb has not blown, the light *will* go on. Indeed, the light *must* go on—given that the world observes the causal laws it does, nothing else could happen.

The sufficient condition of an event's occurring can be, and usually is, very complex. Even in the simple case of the lights going on it is difficult to completely specify its sufficient condition. For example, we would have to include not only the fact that the bulb had not blown, but also that the fuse had not blown, the switch had not broken, the wiring carrying the current to the house was operational, the transformer converting the current for house use had not become defective, that the distant generator had not broken down, and so on. To say that the lights coming on had *a* sufficient condition, therefore, does not mean it has a simple cause. The statement of the cause can be long and complicated indeed, though for practical purposes, we normally do not complicate our lives by seeking a full specification of the conditions that caused something to happen.

Once we see how the determinist's causal principle applies to a case such as the lights coming on, we should be able to imagine how it would apply to numerous other day-to-day occurrences. For example, we can view the boiling of water as an event or series of events, and can inquire into its cause. Other instances are when we start a car, ring a door bell, throw an object into water. In all such cases, something happens and, the determinist would contend, causes were present: what took place was determined.

CAUSAL LAWS

Causal laws are an important concept in the free will debate, so we must have some familiarity with them.

We have said that, according to determinism, every event has a cause. This implies that no event, E, can occur in the absence of some cause, C; moreover, if C is the causally sufficient condition of E's occurring, then if C is the case, E will occur. To clarify the concept of a causal law, let us ask what we would be committed to if we *universalized* the claim about the causal connection between C and E. The result would be the proposition 'Whenever C is the case, E will occur' or, alternatively, 'Every time C is the case, E will occur'. Thus, if we universalized the claim, we would be committed to the view that the connection between any cause, C, and the event, E, that it causes holds *in all cases*. So the mere fact that the sufficient condition, C, might be fulfilled at different times is irrelevant to the question whether an event of type E will occur or not. Given that C is the causally sufficient condition of E's occurring, then if C was the case at some time in the past, E must have occurred at that time, just as if C is the case at present or will be the case in the future, E will now occur or will occur in the future. Thus, although all events must occur *in* time, the time at which an event occurs is not itself part of the cause of its occurring.

Now, a causal law is affirmed by any true proposition of the form 'Whenever C is the case, E will occur'. Thus, to maintain that events observe causal laws is to believe there are true propositions of this form. To maintain that every event observes or is governed by a causal law is to believe that, for every event that occurs, some true proposition of this form can be applied to the event to explain its occurrence. Whether to accept determinism necessarily commits one to the view that every event observes a causal *law* is an open question, but most determinists have accepted this view.

PREDICTABILITY

The kind of truth scientists seek is never about *particular* objects— for example, about this falling object or that case of typhoid. It is instead universal or general in scope—truths about *all* falling objects, *all* cases of typhoid. And this explains why one goal of the scientist is to discover causal laws. For propositions affirming causal laws, as we have seen, have that degree of universality that seems to characterize the knowledge the scientist seeks.

Possessing knowledge of causal laws helps us to predict what will happen before it does. And the reason is as follows. Suppose we know a causal law that says whenever X is the case, Y occurs. Then, besides this causal law, all we need to know to predict that Y will occur is that X is the case. For example, a causal law states that, whenever blue litmus paper is put in an acid solution, the paper turns red. If we know this law and know a particular solution is an acid, we can predict what will happen, when we submerge the litmus paper in it. We *know* what will happen, before it occurs.

Now, clearly, the more such knowledge we have, the more we can predict what will happen. And if we knew *all* the causal laws observed by things in this universe, and if we had a *complete* description of things in the universe at any moment of its history, then we could predict everything that ever will happen in the future. Such is the inevitable consequence of the determinist's point of view—a consequence the determinists have not been reluctant to draw. Of course, even the staunchest determinist would concede we are far from possessing such knowledge. But suppose we did have it— suppose we could predict *every* event that will occur. What would follow from this?

If we could know everything that anyone ever will do, every choice he will ever make, then no choice anyone will make could be free. The idea that a person has freely chosen to do something appears to be inconsistent with the idea that we know what choice he will make (as we argued in our discussion of man's free will and God's omniscience).

Once we recognize this implication of determinism, two questions come to mind. First, "Is determinism true? Does every event have a cause?" Second, "Even if determinism is true, does it really follow that no one is free and, therefore, that no one is morally responsible?" These questions are the heart of the nontheological problem of free will, and we will investigate them now. We will soon discover that philosophers, not surprisingly, differ sharply on the first question: many think determinism is true, many others think it is false. Surprisingly, however, there are different opinions on the second question, with some philosophers thinking that determinism and free will are compatible while others think they are not.

HARD DETERMINISM

Hard determinism is the view that man is not free, nor, therefore, morally responsible, *because* determinism is true. Hard determinists believe that free will and determinism are incompatible: if a choice someone made were free, then it could not have been caused (determined); if a choice someone made were caused (determined), it could not have been free.

Let us set forth the hard determinist's position with greater rigor.

FORMAL STATEMENT OF THE HARD DETERMINIST'S DENIAL OF MORAL RESPONSIBILITY

Steps	Symbolization	Status
1. If every event is caused, then no event is avoidable.	$c \to a$	Assumption
2. Every event is caused.	c	Assumption
3. Therefore, no event is avoidable.	a	Consequence, from (1) and (2), by *modus ponens*
4. If human choices are events, then no human choice is avoidable	$h \to n$	Assumption
5. Human choices are events.	h	Assumption
6. Therefore, no human choice is avoidable.	n	Consequence, from (4) and (5), by *modus ponens*
7. If no human choice is avoidable, then no one can act otherwise than as he does.	$n \to {\sim}o$	Assumption
8. Therefore, no one can act otherwise than as he does.	${\sim}o$	Consequence, from (6) and (8), by *modus ponens*
9. If no one can act otherwise than as he does, then no one is morally responsible for what he does.	${\sim}o \to {\sim}m$	Assumption
10. Therefore, no one is morally responsible for what he does.	${\sim}m$	Consequence, from (8) and (9), by *modus ponens*

COMMENTARY ON THE ARGUMENT

The objective of the hard determinist's reasoning is to show that no one can act otherwise than as he does. If he can show this, then clearly no one is morally responsible for what he does. The truth of premise (9), therefore, would be conceded by all the parties to the free will debate, and the validity of the reasoning in premises (8) and (9) would be conceded also. But critics dispute whether the hard determinist has shown that premise (8) is true. It is clear why the hard determinist thinks so: if the causal principle is true, as the hard determinist thinks (premise (2)), then it seems to follow that nothing can be avoided. For to say that every event has a cause is to say that every event has a sufficient condition. And if this condition is fulfilled, the event for which it is sufficient will occur—it is unavoidable. Thus, if our choices can be accurately classified as events, then they, too, are unavoidable. So it seems that we never could choose to do something other than what we actually choose to do. And if we concede the hard determinist this point, then it seems we must concede that no one can act otherwise than as he does. For the only way we could truly be said to have the capacity to *act* otherwise than as we do is if we have the capacity to *choose* otherwise than as we do. Once we concede that we never can choose otherwise than as we do, therefore, we must conclude, it seems, with the hard determinist, that (Step 10) 'no one is morally responsible for what he does'.

Critics of hard determinism are by no means of one voice on where they think hard determinism is vulnerable. Some philosophers think that free will is inconsistent with the truth of the causal principle—thus agreeing with the hard determinist, who also thinks they are inconsistent—but they differ in maintaining that man *is* free and the principle of causality is false. But not all such thinkers agree on how the concept of free will should be understood. *Indeterminists* think the concept refers to the idea of *chance. Libertarians* think the concept must be understood according to certain assumptions about the *self* or what it is to be a *person. Soft determinists* (or *reconciliationists*) believe the debate among hard determinists, indeterminists, and libertarians has rested on a false assumption—the idea that free will and determinism are incompatible—whereas, they allege, it is perfectly possible for a choice to be both caused and free at the same time.

We will now consider how the indeterminists, soft determinists, and libertarians have sought to criticize the hard determinist's position. But, as we will see, each view seems to encounter serious difficulties peculiar to itself, and it is difficult to defend the claim to know that any one of the positions is true.

INDETERMINISM

Indeterminism is the view that at least *some* events are not determined in the sense the determinist says they are. According to the indeterminist, not all events have sufficient conditions; some events are uncaused.

To make this view clearer, we need to understand what the indeterminist commits himself to. Suppose that at a certain time, T_1, and given the fulfillment of certain conditions, C, a certain event, E, takes place. Then the indeterminist is maintaining that, if E was not determined, it might just as well have not have happened at T_1, and that, at some time other than T_1, the very conditions, C, might be fulfilled and some event other than E might occur. To the indeterminist such uncaused or undetermined events are not only conceivable, they actually do occur, and it is a matter of *chance* whether they occur or not. There are no causally sufficient conditions to guarantee that event E will occur, which implies that there are some events that do not observe causal laws. One cannot truly say that "whenever C is the case, E occurs." Sometimes E occurs, sometimes it does not. No general causal truth will tell us when it will and when it will not. We could not predict, in all cases, when it will or when it will not occur, even if we had complete knowledge of all the causal laws that events observe as well as a complete description of the universe at any moment.

If we ask, then, how the indeterminist is critical of our formal statement of hard determinism, the answer is that he denies the hard determinist's most basic contention—premise (2), 'Every event has a cause'. He denies determinism. And he alleges not only that this premise is not known to be true, but that it actually is known to be false. For he believes that some events occur as the result of chance, not of causality, and their occurrence cannot be explained by one or another hard and fast causal law.

THE UNCERTAINTY PRINCIPLE

What events are these? Some examples are those that occur in the atomic and subatomic world of electrons, protons, neutrons, and mesons. Stretching terms a bit, we could call this subatomic world the submicroscopic world, and call the world of grosser objects—planets, billiard balls, water drops, salt crystals—the macroscopic world. Then we can say that many, perhaps most, scientists take a thoroughly deterministic view of the macroscopic world, but adopt an indeterministic view of the submicroscopic world. In dealing with gross objects such as planets, these scientists would maintain that there are universal causal laws that can be appealed to to explain and predict their behavior. For example, if we know the location, mass, and velocity of a planet at any given time, then we can, using the laws of classical mechanics, predict its future position and velocity. Not so with an electron, however; there simply is no way we can predict, with certainty, its future location and velocity.

Why is this so? Very generally, the reason is that the methods we might use to record the behavior of an electron actually themselves influence the electron's behavior in fundamentally important ways. If we choose a means that would permit us to locate the position of the electron, this very means of locating it will influence its velocity; if we choose a means for observing its velocity, this very means will change the electron's position. Thus, we cannot locate an electron and *at the same time* measure its velocity in such a way that neither its location nor its velocity is influenced by our effort to observe both. Thus, since we cannot determine both at the same time, we cannot predict and confirm the future real location and real velocity of the electron at any given moment in time. If the original real location and velocity cannot be fixed, neither can any future real location and velocity be predicted. Such is the heart of what is called *the Uncertainty Principle* in physics.

TWO CONCEPTS OF PROBABILITY

A conclusion we might draw from these facts is that the submicroscopic world cannot be studied scientifically. And we might draw this conclusion because of the close association between determinism and the development of science. If the submicroscopic world really is indeterministic, we ask, how can it be studied scientifically? The answer lies in the concept of *probability*.

From the indeterministic point of view, it is true, sometimes there are no universal causal laws of the form "Whenever *C* is the case, *E* occurs" that apply to the submicroscopic world. What can be discovered and empirically confirmed in such cases, however, is the *probability* of *E*'s occurring, given that *C* is the case, and the type of laws that can be formulated are what frequently are called *statistical laws*. Such laws do not enable us to predict whether, say, a particular electron will strike a given point on a screen, but they enable us to state the *probability* of its doing so.

Here we must be careful not to misunderstand how the physicist uses the concept of probability. In everyday life we use this concept in a way that is perfectly compatible with determinism. For example, we say that "the probability (or chances) of a coin coming up heads is fifty-fifty." But suppose that we knew all the causal laws relevant to the flight and behavior of a coin such as a quarter; and suppose we were able to control exactly the force with which the quarter was flipped, as well as the angle at which it was held just prior to flipping, and so on. Then, it seems, we could predict with certainty whether and when the coin would come up heads. In everyday life, therefore, when we say that something might only "probably" happen, we often mean that *we do not know enough* to be certain that it will occur. But that we do not *know* does not exclude the possibility that we *could* know this; it certainly seems possible we could predict with complete accuracy which way a coin would come up, if we knew the relevant data and laws. This is why our use of 'probably' in everyday life frequently is consistent with a thoroughgoing deterministic outlook.

The indeterminist, however, uses the concept of probability in a different way. He uses it to exclude the possibility of our being able to predict what will happen before it does. In other words, when he speaks of "the probability of the electron impacting at point *B* is so and so," he implies that we *cannot* know if it will or will not impact at *B*. And the reason we cannot know this, he contends, is because each time we try to find out if it has, *we* influence what the electron does. We make it behave differently than it would have behaved, had we not tried to observe it. Thus, in a fundamental sense, there can be no such thing as "the observation of an electron" or "an observation of an electron's effects." There can only be "an observation of an electron's position or velocity as these have been influenced by the observer." Now, since it is impossible to know what the initial position of the electron is (what we "observe" always will be the position of the electron as influenced by our attempt to locate it), it also is impossible to predict its future real position with certainty. For *its* real position never can be known, according to the indeterminist. The most we can do is to speak of *its* position in terms of probabilities.

SOME PROBLEMS FOR THE DETERMINIST

Not surprisingly, the determinist has responses to the objections raised by the indeterminists. However, his basic response exposes his own view to very serious problems indeed. His basic response is this: Even if we cannot know both the location and the velocity of an electron at any given time or predict its future location and velocity, it does not follow, the determinist contends, that electrons themselves do not observe causal laws. They might well observe causal laws whose existence we simply cannot verify—or falsify—not only in practice but also in principle, because of the consequences that flow necessarily from any attempt to verify or falsify their existence.

But this response is itself open to serious objections. First, to speak of causal laws whose existence *cannot* be verified would not make any sense, given the positivist's verification principle. To claim that something exists but that we cannot verify its existence is utter nonsense, given this principle. At the very least, therefore, the determinist, in his effort to avoid the criticisms of the indeterminist, will have to face the challenge of the positivist, if he responds in the way we have just described.

A more serious objection is that determinism, despite its historical alliance with science and despite the widespread belief that all scientific claims are empirical, is not itself an empirical thesis. This can be shown in the following way. The proposition, 'Every event has a cause', cannot be verified by observation, either in practice or in principle. This is because no one could observe every event. For example, no man could observe his own conception or birth. Nor, in fact, is this proposition falsifiable, given the determinist's understanding of it. For suppose we cannot find a cause for the behavior of, say, electrons; they appear to behave in a random way, so that we are not able to say what they will do on the basis of what they have done in the past. This case, indeterminists think, shows that the causal principle is false.

But the determinist would disagree, saying perhaps electrons have causes we have yet to discover. Perhaps they do. But then we ask the determinist just what it *would* take to show him that they do not have causes. We have to ask him, that is, just what it is that he would have to observe in order to concede that he had been mistaken in thinking that every event had a cause. And the determinist's difficulty is that he will not be able to tell us what he would have to observe to know that any given event was uncaused. For no matter what he might observe—say, electrons behaving in a random way—it would not be sufficient to show him that something is uncaused; it would always be possible that it had a cause which is as yet unknown. Indeed, precisely this line of reasoning underlies the determinist's basic response to the indeterminist. So in interpreting him as we do here, we are not being unfair to him.

Now, if the determinist's use of the sentence "Every event has a cause" does not express a proposition that is either verifiable or falsifiable by observation, either in practice or in principle; and if, furthermore, a proposition cannot be empirical if it is not observationally verifiable or falsifiable, in practice or in principle (a position we endeavored to justify in the preceding chapter); then it follows that, when the determinist uses the sentence "Every event has a cause," he fails to express an empirical proposition.

This is an important consequence, for scientific claims are empirical, we are told; they are all observationally verifiable or falsifiable, in practice or in principle. And it is easy to suppose, therefore, that if science presupposes the truth of a particular proposition, then that proposition, too, is empirical. But what we have shown makes it clear that this is not so. Even if it is true that all scientific claims arc empirical, it is not truc that the causal principle is. Thus, even if it is true that science must assume the truth of determinism (a highly controversial assumption, to say the least) it does not follow that determinism itself is a scientific theory.

Indeed, what we can show is that, given certain assumptions we have been making throughout our inquiry, the determinist must be driven to concede that his position turns out to be a priori rather than empirical. This can be shown in the following way. First, the causal principle is not analytically true—on this all parties to the dispute agree. Thus, if the determinist expresses a proposition by his use of the sentence "Every event has a cause," then the proposition must be synthetic. But if it is synthetic and if it is not empirical (cannot be known to be true or false by observation) then the only way we could know it, it seems, is a priori. And if this is the only way this proposition could be known, then the determinist would have to concede that he is committed to a rationlist epistemology, according to which we can know that certain synthetic propositions are true a priori.

What does this argument show? It does not show that determinism is false or that indeterminism is true. What it does show, if it is sound, is that the determinist cannot maintain that the causal principle is an empirical truth. It shows that, *if* determinism is true, it can only be known to be so, not by observation, but a priori. Thus, it leaves open the question of whether determinism is true and specifies instead only how we could know that is is true, if we do.

But there is another thing that our argument also shows, if it is sound. It shows that the determinist cannot consistently regard the causal principle as true *and* maintain that he has good empirical evidence for it. For if he does know that it is true, he can only know it a priori, in which case there is no need to gather empirical evidence for it (nor could any be provided) by what we observe. Thus, it would be inconsistent of the determinist to say that the indeterminist has not provided "good enough empirical evidence" that, say, electrons are not caused to behave as they do. For this suggests both that the indeterminist might be able to provide empirical evidence that is good enough to show this, and that the issue that separates the determinist and the indeterminist could be settled if we could only determine who had the best empirical evidence. In fact, however, the question about the truth of determinism has no relation whatever to any question about empirical evidence, a fact that determinists themselves too frequently ignore. For they, and not just their critics, often are guilty of misunderstanding just what is at issue, when the issue is "Is determinism true?"

In asking if determinism is true, then, the issue is whether there are grounds to suppose the causal principle can be known a priori. Here philosophers disagree. Positivists would deny that we could know this principle a priori, and perhaps they are right, though we cannot resolve this question here. We must be content to understand just what kind of question is the question "Is determinism true?" as well as how the truth of determinism would affect the question of man's free will.

And what we shall see in this latter regard is this: The hard determinist sometimes is confused about the nature of the causal principle, thinking it is an empirical proposition when it is not. But he is not mistaken when he thinks this principle implies that man is not free. For if determinism is indeed true, then man is not free—a proposition whose truth will be apparent after we have assessed the attempt to show that determinism and free will are compatible. First, however, let us assess the adequacy of indeterminism, as it relates to the problem of free will. Here we shall see, with a clarity that is infrequent in philosophy, that a philosophical thesis can be dismissed as totally inadequate.

THE INADEQUACY OF INDETERMINISM

The indeterminist maintains the following propositions about human decision making:

(1) Human choices are events.

(2) If a choice is caused, it cannot be free, and vice versa.

(3) If a choice is uncaused, it is free, and vice versa.

(4) Some choices are uncaused.

(5) Therefore, some choices are free.

(6) A person can freely choose to do something that is morally right or wrong.

(7) Therefore, a person can be held to be morally responsible for freely choosing to do what is either morally right or wrong.

These contentions can be challenged at several places. For example, is is unclear how the indeterminist thinks he could establish the truth of (4), though this is not his most serious problem. Let us concede to him claims (1) through (6), bearing in mind that when he speaks of "freely choosing to do something" he means that an uncaused choice has occurred.

We now see that his fundamental problem is that under his account of "freely choosing to do something," people cannot be held morally responsible for what they do. For if a person's choice to do something is uncaused, in the sense that it is a matter of chance, it follows that the person himself has not caused the choice to be made. So how could it be reasonable to hold *him* responsible for choosing to do what he has done? *He* did not make it happen: rather, his decision to do it "just happened," it was not caused by anything. Thus, an indeterministic account of human freedom cannot provide us with an adequate basis for holding people morally responsible for doing what they do. Accordingly, we seem to have the following dilemma:

If man's choices are caused, then man is not morally responsible.

If man's choices are uncaused, then man is not morally responsible.

Either man's choices are caused or they are uncaused.

Therefore, man is not morally responsible.

SOFT DETERMINISM

A group of thinkers that would dispute this dilemma is the *soft determinists,* who include such thinkers as David Hume (1711–1776), John Stuart Mill (1806–1873), and Moritz Schlick (1882–1936). The view they present is sometimes referred to as *reconciliationism* or *compatibilism,* because these philosophers set out to show that certain ideas can be reconciled, that certain propositions are compatible. In particular, they think they can reconcile the ideas of human free will and determinism: they think a choice can be both caused and free. Thus, the soft determinists dispute the assumption shared by hard determinists and indeterminists that free will and causality are incompatible. They deny the first premise of our formal statement of the hard determinist's position, the premise that alleges, "If every event is caused, no event is avoidable." Soft determinists contend there are many events—namely, human choices—that are caused but that are avoidable in the sense that the person who has made such a choice could have acted otherwise.

Soft determinists do not necessarily agree with one another on the *reasons* they give to support the view that free will and determinism are compatible, but they agree in general on *why* determinists and indeterminists have been misled on this point. They believe that this is due to a series of mistakes involving key concepts, including those of causality and freedom. They believe that free will and determinism appear incompatible only so long as we are confused about the concepts involved in the traditional problem of free will, and that, once these confusions are removed, we see there is no problem after all, that free will and determinism are perfectly compatible.

CAUSALITY AND COMPULSION

The principal confusion the soft determinist seeks to remedy is in the hard determinist's and indeterminist's concepts of causality and freedom. Imagine a case of someone doing something we think is wrong—say, killing another person—but where we would insist that the person who did the shooting was not morally responsible for what he did. For example, suppose an American GI, Private John Smith, is captured while serving in Southeast Asia and imprisoned for five years during which he is subjected to torture, deprivation, and brainwashing. His captors gain control of his mind and plant within it a plot to kill the President of the United States. In time Smith is released and returns home, where he undergoes an intensive period of reacclimatization. He appears ready to begin living a normal life again. Soon an awards ceremony is planned, and when the President steps forward to decorate Smith for gallantry and service to his country,

Smith pulls a pistol from his pocket and shoots the President, who dies instantly.

Now, granted, the case we have imagined is a fantastic case. "It never really could happen," we might say. But whether or not such a series of events would ever really happen is irrelevant. The question is, "What would we think, *if* they did? In particular, would we hold Smith morally responsible?" Clearly the answer is no. To hold Smith responsible would be grossly unfair to him. If his mind really was controlled by his captors, then there really would be nothing else he could do but shoot the President. Though he did something wrong, he could not help it and so cannot be held morally responsible.

But, the soft determinist asks, what leads us to deny Smith's responsibility? That Smith's shooting was *caused*? This seems indequate, the soft determinist thinks: it is not merely *that* Smith's behavior was caused but *how* it was caused that underlies our assurance that he is not responsible. Shooting the President was not something Smith himself wanted to do; he was made to do it. And it is the fact that Smith's behavior was caused by *constraining* or *compelling* causes that the soft determinist thinks underlies our insistence that Smith is not responsible.

Consider a less fantastic case. While Jones is walking on a city street at night, he is stopped by a man who pulls out a pistol and demands that Jones hand over his wallet. Now, Jones might try to get away or in some other way avoid handing over his wallet. But this possibility is so obviously fraught with danger, in Jones's mind, that he hands his assailant his wallet and watches him flee off into the city's darkness.

Did Jones "freely choose to give his wallet to the holdup man?" Hardly. He was forced or compelled to do it. Giving the man his wallet was not something Jones wanted to do; he was made to do it. How might we convey this idea of "being made or forced to do something"? By saying that Jones's decision to surrender his wallet was "caused"? Such a way of putting things, the soft determinist would suggest, is clearly inadequate. Again, it is not the mere fact that Jones's choice was caused that leads us to say that he did not freely make the choice; it is, rather, the fact that the cause was constraining or compelling: the assailent, after all, had a gun.

These two examples illustrate a general thesis that is central to the soft determinist's position—namely, that the opposite of freedom is not causality, but is constraint or complusion. In other words, the soft determinist maintains that free will and constraint are incompatible in the sense that if a choice is free it cannot be constrained, and *vice versa*. This is why, according to the soft determinist, neither Smith nor Jones can be thought to have made a free choice. Each man's choice was compelled.

But what the soft determinist denies is the idea that causality and constraint are the same or logically equivalent ideas. For if these two concepts were equivalent, then it would be redundant to say, for example, "Smith's behavior was caused by a constraining cause." If the two concepts were equivalent, this would be the same as saying "Smith's behavior was caused by a cause." But these two sentences do not appear to say the same thing, which, if true, seems to show that the concepts of causality and constraint are not logically equivalent.

Notice what appears to follow. If causality and constraint are not equivalent, and if the opposite of a free choice is a choice that is constrained, then we cannot conclude that the opposite of a free choice is a choice that is caused. On the contrary, this argument tends to support the view that a choice can be both caused and free at the same time. And this is precisely what the soft determinist hopes we will see. A recurring way in which people are led to suppose that a free choice cannot be caused, the soft determinist thinks, is by getting them to believe that causality and constraint are logically equivalent concepts. Once we see, however, as in the above, that these two concepts are not equivalent, then, the soft determinist thinks, the supposed grounds for believing that causality and freedom are incompatible begin to disappear.

FREEDOM AS THE ABSENCE OF CONSTRAINT

Of course to say that some choices *can* be both caused and free does not tell us much about those choices that *are* both caused and free. What is needed is some positive characterization of such choices. Now, since the soft determinist maintains that a free choice is a choice that is *not* compelled, the problem of giving a positive account of what a free choice is becomes the problem of describing what is involved in the concept of an uncompelled choice. The main elements can be seen in the two examples we have considered. What led us to say that Smith and Jones were "compelled to choose" as they did was the idea that they were forced to do something they did not want to do. So, it seems, a free choice, since it is opposed to a constrained one, must be one in which a person chooses to do what *he* wants to do, rather than something he is forced to do. And this concept of free choice is *not* inconsistent with determinism. For a free choice *is* a caused choice, not "uncaused," as the indeterminist would have us believe. It is a choice that is caused by the person's own wants or desires. And what makes it a free choice is precisely the fact that *it is caused by the person's own wants and desires,* rather than being forced upon him, without regard for what he might want to do.

At this point, two possible criticisms may be raised, and we can get a deeper understanding of the soft determinist's position when we see how he responds to them.

TWO KINDS OF LAW

The first objection can be set forth as follows. "The soft determinist believes events are caused, in the sense that they have sufficient conditions; and he also believes events are governed by causal laws. Now, if events are governed by causal laws, they must occur; the laws make them occur. And if the laws make them occur, how can the soft determinist contend that there can be such a thing as a free choice? If a free choice is uncompelled, and if the choices we make are compelled by one or another causal law, then there cannot be such a thing as a free, uncompelled choice?"

The soft determinist's answer is to distinguish between *civil* laws and *scientific* laws. Civil laws are man-made laws created by a person or persons with legislative power. They are laws enforced by judicial means. These laws *prescribe* behavior, most often what people are *not* to do. People who disobey these laws, if detected, run a risk of being punished. Moreover, civil laws often run counter to some desires of the persons subject to them— a law against stealing might conflict with a person's desire for an expensive stereo when he has no money to buy it.

Scientific laws are different in that they are not man made, not the result of legislative power, but are instead discovered by man. If no man had ever existed, no civil law would ever have existed either—but scientific laws might very well have. Also, scientific laws do not prescribe behavior— the laws of celestial mechanics, for example, do not tell the planets they had "better behave or they'll be punished." These laws *describe* how the planets behave. Finally, the scientific laws that apply to human beings— for example, laws discovered by psychology or sociology—do not "conflict" with what a person wants. These laws merely describe what a person will want or will do given certain conditions. And since these laws merely describe that a person *will* want or *will* do such things, they cannot themselves conflict with what a person wants or does.

In view of these distinctions between civil and scientific laws, it is misleading to say, as in the argument above, that events are "governed by causal laws," that these laws "make us" do what we do, that "the choices we make are compelled by one or another causal law," and so on. For this strongly suggests that scientific laws, which merely describe how things behave, should be treated like civil laws, which do not describe but prescribe behavior. A civil law might well compel us to act contrary to the way we would like to, which is why we can say it "governs" us or "requires" us to behave in a certain way. But scientific laws do not govern or require, they *describe*. And since all they do is describe, they themselves cannot compel. And since they themselves cannot compel, it follows, the soft determinist thinks, that there is no inconsistency in asserting that every choice, including those that are free, observes some causal law. This appears inconsistent only if we are confused and regard scientific laws as the same as civil laws.

"HE COULD HAVE ACTED OTHERWISE"

But a second, more fundamental objection might be raised against soft determinism. Any view of free will must show how it is possible that we can sometimes truly say that a person "could have acted otherwise." And the question is, can the soft determinist meet this demand? He would seem to have an especially difficult task precisely because he is a determinist. For he *does* believe that every event has a cause and *does* apply this principle to human decision making.

And let us be sure that we are perfectly clear about what acceptance of determinism does seem to commit one to. It does seem to commit one to the view that if C is the sufficient condition of E, then if C is the case, E will occur—that is, E is unavoidable. Thus, if E happens to be a human choice, then determinism seems to commit one to the view that, given C, this choice is unavoidable.

Now, if the choices we make are events that are unavoidable, then how can we say of anyone that "he could have acted otherwise"? Presumably, he could act otherwise only if he could choose to act otherwise than as he does. But if our choices are unavoidable, then how can someone have chosen otherwise than as he has?

The soft determinist's response to this challenge is to deny the claim that a choice is unavoidable if it is caused. The soft determinist believes a choice can be avoidable, in the sense that we can say a person could have acted otherwise *and,* at the same time, this avoidable choice was caused. Whether the soft determinist is correct on this point is a complex issue, and its final resolution is of fundamental importance for the resolution of the problem of free will. Let us see what headway we can make here.

The issue is what is meant by the words, "he could have acted otherwise." Let's introduce the problems involved here by way of an example. Suppose Brown is deliberating about whether to steal a record from a record shop. He believes he has a duty not to steal it but wants it nonetheless. He thinks about various things he considers relevant to his decision: how much he wants the record; whether he might pay for it instead of stealing it; whether he wants it enough to run the risk of getting caught; whether stealing it would be wrong and violate the store owner's rights. He thinks stealing it would be a cinch, for he has stolen other records from this same shop before and has never had any difficulty. The risk of getting caught, he thinks, is very slight. It is a simple matter of slipping the record inside his raincoat and not losing his cool. His desires take hold and, finally, he decides to take the record. With a deft movement, he takes it from the rack and puts it inside his coat. Then, with an air of casualness, he walks past the cashier at the front of the store and passes through the door. He never is caught, and he enjoys the record very much.

Given this situation we can probably agree that what Brown did was wrong. So the question is whether he is morally responsible for the wrong he did. And this involves our asking how the soft determinist interprets the contention that Brown could have acted otherwise. He might reply thus: Suppose Brown had thought more about what he was doing. Suppose that, having made the judgment that stealing is wrong, he came to have a very strong emotional opposition to stealing. Suppose he did not want to steal such things as records or that he at least wanted to be honest more than he wanted to steal. Then Brown would not have chosen as he did. He would have chosen otherwise; and thus he would have acted otherwise also. So, the soft determinist might conclude, when we say that "Brown could have acted otherwise" we mean that "If Brown had thought more about what he was doing or if his desires had been different, he would have chosen to act differently."

But suppose, we might ask, that no matter how much more Brown thought about it, he would have gone ahead and done the very same thing. People often say just that. Killers sometimes say, for example, that they would do it again, if they had half the chance, even after they have had a lot of time to think about what they did. So what if Brown's behavior would not have been changed by additional thinking?

The soft determinist's response is simple: If Brown's behavior would not have been changed by additional thought, then he truly is not morally responsible for what he has done. He must be mentally defective or otherwise impaired so that he cannot distinguish right from wrong, or else, like a kleptomaniac, psychologically incapable of acting accordingly. Of course, even if Brown was not morally responsible, the soft determinist would say, he should be removed from society for a time. Society, including record-shop owners, has a right not to have others steal property with impunity. Nevertheless, the soft determinist might go on to remind us not to strike a "holier-than-thou" attitude. People sometimes are just incapable of helping themselves or of being helped by others. And if Brown happens to be one of these, then he deserves our pity and understanding, not our moral condemnation.

This example illustrates four claims characteristic of the soft determinist's thinking:

(1) A person is morally responsible for some wrong action he has done if what he did was avoidable.

(2) Those wrong actions a person does are avoidable if they are such that the person would not have done them, if he had thought more

about what it was that he chose to do, or if his desires had been different.

(3) A person is not morally responsible for some wrong action he has done if what he did was unavoidable.

(4) Those wrong actions a person does are unavoidable if they are such that the person would have done them, even if he had thought more about what it was that he chose to do, or even if his desires had been different.

Now if this analysis of "could have acted otherwise" is sound, then the soft determinist has taken a great step forward in showing that free will is compatible with causality. If his analysis is correct, then to say someone "could have acted otherwise" is not to say his choice was *un*caused, but that if the person's thoughts or desires had been different than what they were, then they would have caused that person to behave differently. In short, if the *cause* had been different, the *choice* would have been different also. That is what is meant when we say someone could have acted otherwise, according to soft determinism.

THE INADEQUACY OF SOFT DETERMINISM

Soft determinism is vulnerable to a number of criticisms, and though we cannot hope to cover them all, we should say something about the more important ones.

First, even if we concede to the soft determinist his analysis of free choice—that a choice "freely made" means, roughly, "it was not compelled"—the question still arises as to *how much* freedom people have. The soft determinist tends to assume it is considerable. But is it? It is difficult to see how this could be maintained with confidence in view of what we are learning about the unconscious and how it influences our day-to-day decisions. The soft determinist must face the possibility that, even on his own view, it *might* be that no one is morally responsible for what he does— which would be so if all our morally relevant decisions were compelled by the unconscious.

A second and more important objection is the following. The soft determinist's analysis of "Brown could have acted otherwise" is "Brown would have acted otherwise, if he had thought more about what he was doing" (or, sometimes, "if he had wanted to"). But the question then becomes, "*Could* Brown have thought more about it (or wanted differently)?" And here the soft determinist seems to be in a very awkward position. For as a determinist he must hold that Brown's character or personality is completely determined by causal influences stemming from genetic, environmental, and other sources. Thus, whether Brown is habitually jovial or remorseful, outgoing or introspective, whether he likes music or art, whether he is inclined to steal or not, what he desires and how intensely he desires it—these things about Brown must be susceptible to causal explanation, if determinism is true. And also to be explained is whether Brown thinks much about what he is going to do before he does it, as well as whether, when he does so think, the fact that his actions may cause harm to or infringe upon the rights of another person makes any difference to what he decides to do. The soft determinist must maintain that these aspects of Brown's character are themselves determined.

Thus, our question once again is, "Could *Brown*, being who he was, have thought more than he did about stealing the record?" And here soft determinism is faced with a paradox: if Brown's choice was free, then he would have acted otherwise, if he had thought more about it; but if determinism is true, so that Brown's character, at the time that he made the choice, was causally determined to be what it was, it follows that Brown could *not* have thought more about stealing the record than the amount in which he did. For any additional thought would be *un*caused, which it could not be if determinism is true.

So if Brown really could not have thought more about it than he did, how reasonable is it to hold him morally responsible? The answer is it is not reasonable at all, given the soft determinist's analysis. If thinking more about it than he did is a necessary condition of Brown's acting otherwise, and if Brown, being who he was (and assuming the truth of determinism) could not have thought more about it than he did, then he could not have acted otherwise either. And if he could not have acted otherwise, then he cannot be held morally responsible for his theft. Clearly, the possible adequacy of soft determinism turns on how convincingly its representatives can respond to this, one of its most serious challenges.

Third, we must ask how fully the soft determinist clarifies the concepts in the free will debate—in particular, whether his analysis of "could have acted otherwise" could possibly be right.

Formally considered, the soft determinist's analysis is a conditional proposition of the form, 'If *p*, then *q*'. Moreover the propositions symbolized by *p* and *q*, considered in terms of their content, are not factually true; indeed, they are contrary to fact. The propositions allege that if something had happened (which, in fact, did not), then something else would have happened (which, in fact, did not)—for example, "If Brown had thought more about what he was doing, then he would not have stolen the record." The soft determinist's analysis, therefore, is what is called a *contrary to fact conditional analysis*. We can ask, then, "Could any contrary to fact conditional analysis of 'could have acted otherwise' succeed in capturing what we mean by this concept?"

This is a fundamental question: at issue is the *possible* adequacy of soft deterministic accounts of free will. This issue is also divisive: all soft determinists agree such an analysis can be adequate, but not all agree on the specific content the analysis should have—some think it should include reference to what a person thinks, others, to what a person wants. But not all competent thinkers are prepared to grant even this much to the soft determinist. Libertarians, in particular, deny the adequacy of soft determinism. They contend that "could have acted otherwise" must be given a *categorical* analysis, if we are to do justice to our most enlightened thinking about free will and moral responsibility. What this means, and whether the libertarians are correct on this point, are questions to which we now need to turn our attention.

LIBERTARIANISM

Libertarians reject the soft determinist's attempt to reconcile free will and causality. Like both the hard determinists and the indeterminists, libertarians maintain that a choice cannot be free and, at the same time, caused in the sense that it has a sufficient condition. In this, the determinist's sense of 'caused', therefore, the libertarian maintains that a free choice must be *un*caused. But the libertarian rejects the indeterminist's account of an uncaused choice. Though agreeing that a free choice must be uncaused and while agreeing, also, that there are free choices, the libertarian rejects the idea that chance must be involved in the concept of free choice. For if an uncaused free choice must be explained in terms of chance, it would be irrational to hold people accountable for their 'free' choices. People can be morally responsible only for those actions *they* choose to perform, not for those that occur willy-nilly as a matter of chance.

However, the main problem for libertarians, including Kant, Thomas Reid (1710-1796), and C. A. Campbell (1897-   ) is to explain how a person can possibly make an uncaused choice. These thinkers agree this difficult problem must be solved, if we are to have a thoroughly worked out account of how we can hold anyone morally responsible.

Let us begin with the analysis of "could have acted otherwise." The soft determinist, we saw, thinks that this should be analyzed in terms of some contrary to fact conditional—for example, "If Brown had thought more about what he was doing (or if his desires had been different), then he would have acted otherwise." Thus, the soft determinist affirms the belief that a man could have acted otherwise *only on the condition* that the causal antecedents of his choice, such as his thoughts or desires, were changed. The libertarian rejects this. He contends that when we say a person "could have acted otherwise," it must be understood *categorically* —that is, we are attributing to a person the power or ability to have acted otherwise *without in any way assuming that the causal antecedents of his decision were altered.* When we say, "Brown could have refrained from stealing the record," according to the libertarian, we do not mean "Brown would not have stolen the record *if* he had thought more about what he was doing (or *if* his desires had been different)." Instead, we mean "At the moment that Brown decided to steal the record, he had before himself the equally possible option of choosing not to steal it." Thus, in the libertarian's view—like the indeterminist's and unlike the soft determinist's—situations arise in which two different events can occur given exactly the same causal conditions. That is, to the libertarian as to the indeterminist, there are events that occur which are uncaused, in the determinist's sense of 'caused'.

Let us now examine some grounds for accepting the libertarian's claim that, when we say that someone could have acted otherwise, we are making a categorical claim about what he could do.

THE CONCEPT OF A CONFLICT SITUATION

To understand libertarian thinking here we first need to understand the concept of a conflict situation. In a conflict situation, a person experiences a conflict between what he desires and what he takes to be his duty. Sometimes, of course, our desires and duties coincide, and we experience no conflict. But sometimes we would very much like to do something we think we ought not to do (lie, steal, hit someone); and at other times we may not want to do something we think we have a duty to do (repay a loan, keep a promise). Situations of either type are called *conflict* situations because the person in them cannot, by choosing to do one thing, *both* satisfy his desires *and* fulfill what he takes to be his duty. He must choose *between* the two, so that if he chooses to act as to satisfy his desires, his duty must go unfulfilled, while if he chooses to fulfill his duty, then his desires must go unfulfilled.

A dictum that all philosophers accept as analytically true is that 'ought' implies 'can'. This means that a person can have an obligation to do something only if he can do it. What "can do" means is rather complex but young children, for example, do not have the same duties as their elders, for they simply cannot meet them because of mental and physical limitations. (Incidently, the dictum does *not* proclaim that 'can' implies 'ought', which would mean we have a duty to do everything we can do or are capable of doing—including, say, a duty of stronger persons to kill every young child.) What the dictum declares, then, is not this but rather that a logically necessary condition of any person's being obligated to do some action is that he be able to do it.

The same thing applies even to our *thinking* that we ought to do something. If a person thinks he has a duty to do something, then we must assume he also thinks he can do it. In the second type of conflict situation sketched above, a person must think he can do what he thinks he has a duty to do, just as, in the first type of conflict situation he must think that he can avoid doing what he thinks he has a duty to avoid. Thus, any person involved in a conflict situation must think (a) that he is faced with a genuine choice between two quite distinct alternatives—namely, between doing his duty, as he conceives it, or doing what he wants to do— and (b) that he *can* choose to do either. Moreover, he must believe that whichever choice he actually does make, he could just as well have chosen to do the other instead. Thus, even if he has chosen to do his duty, he must think that he could just as well have chosen not to do it and that he *could* have done what he wanted to instead. If he did not do his duty but followed his desires, he must believe that he *could* have done his duty. For to think it his duty implies that he must think that he could fulfill it.

It is important to note that this argument cannot show that the person in a conflict situation has a *true* belief, when he believes that he can choose between two equally possible courses of action. It only shows he *must believe* he can. And while it is true the person must believe this, the belief itself may be false—indeed would be false, if hard determinism is true, since that view implies that persons never find themselves in situations such that they could just as well choose to do one thing rather than another.

It is apparent how this line of reasoning can be developed to apply to our judgment about what other people could have done. *If* we believe that another person made a choice within a conflict situation, then we must believe that he was faced with the alternative of choosing between two equally possible courses of action—either to do his duty or to do what he desired. Whatever choice he actually did make, we must believe he could have acted otherwise. Of course, we might be mistaken, for perhaps no one ever could have acted otherwise. And determinism seems to commit us to this. But questions about the truth of a belief must be kept distinct from questions about the content of the belief. And the libertarian's thought does help to crystallize what a person does and must believe in a conflict situation, given that 'ought' implies 'can'.

THE CONCEPT OF THE SELF

We now come face to face with the libertarian's principal difficulty, that of explaining how a person can do what the libertarian says he can do— namely, make uncaused choices. For if a person can choose between two equally possible courses of action, and if the conditions do not determine the choice, then his choice must be called uncaused, in the *determinist's* sense of 'caused'. And the next question is, "What kind of a being is a person, if he is able to do such things?" The libertarian's answer is as follows.

A person or self (to use a term favored by libertarians), if he makes free choices, must be capable of making something happen. In a conflict situation it does not matter what choice is made—whether in accord with desires or duty—once it is made, something gets done, some action is performed. Thus, in this view the self must be conceived to have this capacity to cause actions to take place. But the contrary is not true: the self cannot be conceived to be *caused* to make decisions. That is, the self, in a conflict situation, cannot be caused to follow either desire or duty. If it were, libertarianism would be a form of determinism. A free choice must be uncaused, according to libertarianism. The self, then, must (a) have the power to make choices and cause actions but (b) be itself uncaused to do so. Thus, a person must be conceived to be both subject to causal influence as well as standing outside such influence. For example, the fact that a person desires something can be explained in principle by one of the behavioral sciences such as psychology or sociology, so, in this respect, a person observes causal laws. But he cannot be entirely subject to causal laws, for the free choices he makes in conflict situations, libertarians say, are *un*caused; hence, there is no causal law they observe.

Because the self is thus conceived to be orginator of the choice in a conflict situation, rather than a passive recipient, then, according to the libertarian, we can be held to be responsible for the choice we make. Thus unlike the indeterminist, who cannot explain why a person is responsible for what happens as the result of chance, the libertarian, in holding a person capable of choosing freely between various courses of action and thereby making something happen, maintains that people are responsible for those actions they cause to happen by the making of a free choice. That aspect of a person that is capable of making free choices is, then, a kind of *first* cause: Like the first cause discussed in Chapter 4, the self is not caused to choose what it chooses freely, but nonetheless causes these choices to be made. Of course, the self is not capable of causing, by its choices, every action to take place, so that as far as *how much* it can cause to happen, the self differs from the first cause discussed in Chapter 4.

Libertarians do not agree on how often a person can make a free choice, though they agree that the choice made in a conflict situation is a clear example of a free choice. But some libertarians limit the opportunity for free choice just to conflict situations, whereas others believe the opportunity exists in other situations too—for instance, any situation where we must decide between doing two different things we desire to do and where there is no question of what, morally speaking, we ought to do. But this issue is tangential to our discussion, for we are concerned with the question of how free will relates to the problem of moral responsibility.

In any case, all libertarians agree that a person has an opportunity to make a free choice in a conflict situation and so should be held to be responsible for what he does.

Libertarian speculation about the nature of the self has struck many philosophers as wildly implausible or unintelligible. Those who believe that science represents the final test of truth about the nature of reality have been especially critical, for they believe a phenomenon is understood only when it can be explained by some causal law—and that this law can be discovered only by the empirical methods of scientific inquiry. These thinkers throw up their hands when confronted with libertarian theorizing about the self. For the self is pictured as standing outside the domain of natural causes. The choices it makes, though they cause much else to happen, are themselves uncaused, in the determinist's sense and, hence, observe no causal law, not even a statistical one. For this reason, therefore, libertarianism implies that there cannot be a complete science of human nature. There can be no complete science of the self or its activities. And this should be kept in mind, when libertarian's critics take the floor. For although not all critics of libertarianism come to it with the same perspective, many have "the scientific way of seeing things." And to the extent that this way of seeing things does involve the belief that reality is understood only when causal laws can be applied to it, we can well anticipate the puzzlement of those who share this view when presented with libertarian thinking about free (uncaused) choices and the self.

PROBLEMS WITH THE CONCEPT OF THE SELF

Among the many problems that face the libertarian, two in particular deserve to be mentioned. The first concerns the libertarian's view that the self *causes* certain choices or decisions. This use of the word 'cause' is a significant departure from how it is normally used in the free will debate. As we know, the libertarian does not believe that the decision reached in a conflict situation has a causally sufficient condition. Otherwise, the decision would be determined, which the libertarian denies. In this sense of 'cause', therefore, the decision is *un*caused. At the same time, however, the libertarian does maintain that the decision reached is not a matter of chance; it does not happen to the person "against his will," as we say. On the contrary, it is supposed to be something that the person himself causes to happen by an act of his will. But, now, *this* sense of 'cause' is distinct form the sense in which to say that "X is caused by Y" means that "Y is the sufficient condition of X's occurring." And the libertarian's problem here is to explain how *this* sense of 'cause' should be understood; he needs to explain, that is, just what it means to say that a person "causes his choices," bearing in mind that this sense of 'cause' is distinct from the determinist's use of that concept. There are two ways the libertarian might respond.

In the first way, he concedes that it is difficult to give an account of the idea that a person can cause his choices, but he points out that the same is true of *any* attempt to give an account of how any one thing can cause something else to happen. If cause and effect have a necessary connection—that is, if the effect *necessarily* follows from the cause—then any account of causality must include this idea of necessary connection. And to give an analysis of the idea of necessary connection is very difficult. For example, to point out that cause and effect are *constantly conjoined*—meaning whenever the cause is present, the effect follows—is not sufficient. For two things could be constantly conjoined and yet not be causally related. For example, to discover that every time the temperature reaches eighty degrees in Minneapolis a rocket is launched from Cape Kennedy would not mean the first phenomenon caused the second. Thus, the libertarian does not say it will be impossible for the determinist to give an account of his conception of causality, only that it will be very difficult. In this situation, therefore, the libertarian is not unique. Any philosopher who uses the concept of causality for his theoretical purposes will have the same difficulties.

But a second response of the libertarian is to say that he does *not* have to give an analysis of the concept of causality, as he uses it, because the concept of self-causality is primitive and unanalyzable—an argument made by Aristotle, among others. The main thrust of it is that we understand the concept of causality, not by observing the constant conjunction of external events, such as one billiard ball hitting another one, but by our awareness of ourselves being able to cause certain decisions to be made—for instance, by our decision to put forth a certain effort of will and choose to do our duty in a conflict situation. To say that this concept of self-causation is primitive means that it cannot be reduced to any other series of concepts. It means that self-causation is a reality we can be aware of, even if we cannot define it.

In this second line of argument, then, the libertarian is saying he does *not* have a problem of how to analyze the concept of self-causation (because it is simple and unanalyzable), whereas in the first line of argument he tries to show that he is not alone in having to analyze causality. Whichever of the two alternatives the libertarian takes will lead to protracted debate, and the issues raised would be of major importance. But let us now consider a more fundamental problem for libertarianism—its very intelligibility.

THE INTELLIGIBILITY OF LIBERTARIANISM

The question of the intelligibility of libertarianism, especially libertarian speculation about the nature of the self, has been raised by positivists. As we know, they advance the view that a particular use of a sentence expresses a synthetic proposition only if it expresses something that can be verified by observation, either in practice or in principle. Now, it is evident that the libertarian's use of the sentence "the self makes uncaused choices" cannot be so verified. To make the most practiced, detailed observations of people deliberating about what to do and then doing it would show us just that—people deliberating and acting. Nowhere could we observe someone making an uncaused choice. Such occurrences, assuming that they occur, must, by their very nature, remain beyond the ken of our five senses.

To positivists, therefore, libertarianism is a pseudotheory, neither true nor false. It fails to make sense, and the proper response is not to deny its truth but to refuse to discuss it as a serious philosophical position.

Two possible replies should be considered. The first is that all positions on the free will debate, not just libertarianism, are open to the criticism that they cannot be verified by sensory observation, either in practice or in principle. The deterministic principle that every event has a cause most certainly cannot be verified in practice (no one now living can observe *all* events) or in principle (we cannot conceive of anyone observing his own conception).

Indeterminism seems to fare no better. As we saw earlier, not observing a cause for an event does not show that the event has no cause. And so no matter how many observations we make, they will not show the non-existence of a cause.

Both determinism and indeterminism, therefore, seem to involve elements that are not verifiable, so the positivist critique does not apply just to libertarianism but to all parties to the dispute—which is why some positivists regard the whole problem of free will as a pseudoproblem.

The second response we should consider here has a different role. The one just given says, in effect, that every view has the same problem as libertarianism—namely, of making sense, given positivist premises. The second reply involves contesting the adequacy of these premises. For why must synthetic claims be confirmed by sensory observation? There are many things we know about ourselves that we do not come to know from our senses—for example, how we felt when we got up this morning, who we love and hate, what a toothache feels like, what we daydream about. But how did we come to have this knowledge? Not by means of our senses. We do not smell or taste such things. Yet we certainly do seem to be entitled to claim to have such knowledge. And if we are, the positivist account of nonanalytic knowledge must be inadequate. And if a thoroughgoing positivist account of such knowledge must be indequate, it will be no good arguing that we cannot know we are free because we cannot verify statements about the self by observation. If there are synthetic propositions whose truth we can know without relying on observation, then there is no reason, a priori, why propositions about the self might not fall within this class.

But how might we verify that we are free if not by observation? It seems it must be by some kind of *introspection* of our inner experience, particularly in conflict situations. What we need to ask ourselves is whether our inner experience corresponds with what the libertarian says: Have we ever experienced conflict between our desires and what we see as our duty? And we need to ask whether, in our role as the agent trying to decide which alternative to choose, we can doubt that we can choose either one—doubt that our choice of either one is just as possible as our choice of the other. Now, it is highly doubtful whether any mature, thoughtful person would give negative answers to these questions. And this means that even if this "feeling of freedom" is an illusion our affirmative answers here do provide the libertarian with a means of giving a clear meaning to his talk about "uncaused choices," "the self," and so on. Roughly speaking, he can say the self is the power of free choice that manifests itself in conflict situations. True, this "power" cannot be observed by the senses, but that does not mean it is unreal. It would be unreal only if it were conclusively shown we could gain knowledge of reality just with our senses. It appears to be extremely doubtful that this is the only way, however, as we have just noted in the above—a point that, if soundly made, does show, not that libertarianism is true, but that it cannot be shown to be false (or, to be more precise, neither true nor false) by an uncritical use of positivistic principles.

However, even if the foregoing is sound, we have not marked an end to the need to clarify and defend libertarianism. Other problems of both kinds remain, and the principal one among these will be indicated shortly. Nevertheless, we do seem to be in a position to set forth some of the positive results of our inquiry. These are mostly hypothetical, but that does not mean that they are not positive results at all.

IS MAN FREE?

We have argued that if man is free, determinism is false. Not only hard determinism. Soft determinism is also false, if man is free. So we have argued that free will cannot be reconciled with the principle of causality and all it implies, which means a free choice cannot be causally determined. But at the same time, we have rejected an indeterministic account of human decision making. The concept of chance events, as this would apply to the choices people make, could not give a satisfactory basis for holding people morally responsible for these choices. Even if indeterminism adequately explains some phenomena in the subatomic world, it cannot explain the idea of moral responsibility.

So, if man is free, determinism is false. And if man is morally responsible, indeterminism is false. Now, assuming, as we have throughout our discussion, that libertarianism is the only remaining alternative that can account both for man's free will and his moral responsibility, then the conclusion of our discussion is this: *if* man is free and morally responsible, libertarianism is true. And the reverse is also true: *if* libertarianism is true, then man is free and morally responsible. So our initial question of whether man is free and morally responsible reduces to the question, "Is libertarianism true?"

Our results may seem disappointing, for once we see that the free will question reduces to the truth of the libertarianism question, and once we understand the libertarian position, we also see that several problems still must be settled before we can say man is free. One problem, already mentioned, is how to give an account of the concept of the self as the cause of his own choices. Even more difficult is the method of verification that libertarianism seems to recommend—namely, verifying by *introspection*. Introspective knowledge is an elusive concept. One difficulty is how to distinguish genuine introspective knowledge (if it exists) from spurious claims to such knowledge. Or, stated another way, how can we be sure we are not mistaken in claiming to know something introspectively?

Introspective knowledge is not like knowledge based on sensory observation, where if we make a claim about something observable (say, that a particular flower is an azalea) there is a straightforward, public way of determining what is true (we can each go and look, or even call on an impartial person to determine, by observation, whether our judgment is correct). And this is why our claims to sensory knowledge do seem to be testable in such a way that we can distinguish between those that are true and those that are false.

Nothing analogous to this testing procedure appears to hold true in the case of so-called introspective knowledge. There is nothing public for everyone to look at. If we claim to know something by introspection, it is from something private, from our own inner experience. And now the problem of testing this knowledge should be clear: no one else can introspect upon what another introspects upon, namely, his own inner experience So, it seems, no one else can test his introspection the way he does to see if it is reliable. For what could we test his claim against? What could we look for as evidence against what *he* introspects?

The claim that we *know* certain things by introspection is placed in a rather peculiar light. For what kind of 'knowledge' can this be if claims to have it cannot be tested? How could it be distinguished from, say, hunches or feelings, which, however deeply felt and sincerely expressed, are not knowledge?

Finally, could we ever know that *someone else* was free, even assuming that any one person can and does know that he himself is? This is a fundamentally important question. Individuals hold not only themselves responsible but some other people for things they do. Yet, clearly, these other people are responsible only if they have freely chosen to do what they did. And one problem of libertarianism is to explain how we could ever know that *someone else* made a free choice. This is not something we can know by introspection. Even if an individual can know, by introspection, that he is free, he cannot know, by introspection, that *another* person is. But if this cannot be known by introspection, how can it be known? Or can it not be known at all? In short, how, on libertarian grounds, can one person ever be rationally justified in holding another person morally responsible?

This problem of how we can know what is true of another person's experience (or "mind) is not unique to the question about free will, nor is the general problem of knowledge of other minds unique to libertarianism. In fact, we will explore this problem in the next chapter. But it is particularly pressing for the libertarian.

And perhaps this is a fitting place to end our initial investigation of free will—that is, on a problematic note. In fairness to the complexity of the problem before us, we need to realize that, even if the foregoing argument has been both sound and persuasive, so that each of us has been convinced, for good reasons, that man is free and morally responsible if and only if libertarianism is true, we are not by any means through with our thinking about the problem of free will. To affirm or deny libertarianism as true carries with it the obligation to think through other, related problems, including those we have mentioned. To grasp libertarianism and the free will problem is to see that they are logically connected with elusive epistemological issues. It is frustrating (and there is no point denying this) to set out to answer one question, only to find that at the end of our initial investigation we are left with many other questions for which there are no obvious answers. But frustrating though this is, we might learn to accept it as the inevitable destination of our first steps in disciplined inquiry. Indeed, one measure of our understanding of the discipline called philosophy is our ability to see how and why this may be the inevitable destination of our final steps as well.

FOR FURTHER READING

It has been said that more has been written on free will than on any other problem in the history of philosophy. Whether true or not, there is a great deal, and much of the best thinking is available in paperbacks such as follows:

Berofsky, Bernard, *Free Will and Determinism*. New York: Harper & Row, 1966.

Hook, Sidney, *Determinism and Freedom in the Age of Modern Science*. New York: Collier Books, 1961.

Lehrer, Keith, *Freedom and Determinism*. New York: Random House, 1966.

Morgenbesser, Sidney, and J. Walsh, *Free Will*. Englewood Cliffs, N.J.: Prentice-Hall, 1962.

In addition, individual works by authors mentioned in this chapter are worth looking at, including the following:

Campbell, A.C., *Selfhood and Godhood*. Chap. 9.

Kant, Immanuel, *Critique of Pure Reason*.

Mill, John Stuart, *Examination of Sir William Hamilton's Philosophy*.

Reid, Thomas, *Essays on the Active Powers of Man*.

Schlick, Moritz, *Problems of Ethics*. Chap. 7.

A very helpful book on science in general and on science and indeterminism in particular is:

Gamow, George, *Biography of Physics*.

Finally, in the *Encyclopedia of Philosophy*, under the entry "Determinism," which is written by the American philosopher Richard Taylor, is a very lucid, helpful statement of various approaches to the free will problem. See also Taylor's book, *Metaphysics* (Englewood Cliffs, N.J.: Prentice-Hall, 1963), to find a discussion of this and the other problems discussed in this book.

EXERCISES

1. Clarify what is meant by the metaphysical idea of freedom.
2. How is the question of free will related to the question of moral responsibility?
3. On what grounds can it be argued that human free will is impossible if an omniscient being exists? How good is the argument that purports to show this is so?
4. What is determinism? How is it related to the idea of causal laws? How are both of these ideas related to the possibility of prediction?
5. Give a brief account of the position known as hard determinism. How convincing is the argument that attempts to show that hard determinism is true?
6. Give a brief account of the position known as indeterminism. How convincing is the argument that attempts to show that indeterminism is

true? Could it be reasonable to hold man morally responsible for his actions, if indeterminism is true?

7. Give a brief account of the position known as soft determinism. How convincing are the arguments that attempt to show that soft determinism is true? In particular, how convincing is the soft determinist's analysis of the idea that someone "could have acted otherwise than as he did"?

8. Give a brief account of the position known as libertarianism. How convincing are the arguments that attempt to show that libertarianism is true? In particular, is the libertarian's conception of the self an intelligible concept?

9. Is the problem of free will a pseudoproblem? Clarify and defend your answer.

10. Can a person consistently believe in (a) the Judeo-Christian God and indeterminism? (b) the Judeo-Christian God and soft determinism? (c) the Judeo-Chirstian God and libertarianism?

6   Is Man Immortal?

Of all the problems that have attracted philosophers, none has done so more naturally than the problem of immortality. In fact, every person must sometimes ask, "Will I go on living after death?" For many people, indeed, the present life would be meaningless if earthly death marked the final end of existence—and it would be difficult to exaggerate the prominence of this idea in Western civilization. Each of us has been exposed to the idea of an afterlife of eternal duration, to be lived either among the blessed or among the damned. And each of us has doubtless wondered whether such a belief is true. Although today the number of people who believe in heaven and hell is dwindling, many continue to believe it, and others believe in *some* form of personal survival after death.

But certain metaphysical questions must be answered by anyone who believes in life after his bodily death. And these questions are so general and pervasive that every thoughtful person must face them—even those who deny that the person survives death.

In this chapter we will first examine some of the questions that must be asked before we can judge whether the person survives after death. We will ask what it is to be a person, and we will argue that for one to survive his bodily death he must be nonphysical—a mind, soul, or spirit.

But this conception of what it is to be a person encounters very serious problems. What these are, and why they are serious, need to be understood. Then we can examine some of the arguments for personal survival.

VIEWS OF IMMORTALITY

Notice we have been speaking of *personal* survival after death, the belief the *person* goes on living after death. This is one belief in immortality, but there are others. When writers crave "literary immortality," for example, they desire that their name and life be remembered because their work continues to be read after death, and in this way Shakespeare, Chaucer, Tolstoy, Balzac, and Dickens are immortal. But we would not say that the *person* named Shakespeare therefore continues to exist. Perhaps he does, but it cannot be settled by determining whether or not his works are read. The immortality of a person is distinct from the immortality of his works.

The same is true of two other respects in which persons might be said to be immortal. The first involves the idea that the consequences of an action go on after the action itself is completed, as in Lee Harvey Oswald's assassination of President John Kennedy. The actions, however, need not be so famous. Each day we interact with people—some close, some strangers, some in between—and how we act toward them and our environment generally often produces immediate consequences, which lead to consequences of their own, and so on. So, in this sense, the consequences of our actions might continue long after our death, giving us some level of immortality in the survival of our consequences or effects.

But, of course, in this sense the person himself does not continue to exist after his bodily death. And the same is true of the idea that we attain immortality through being remembered by our children, and by our children's children, and so on.

Another view is "the chemical view of immortality." According to this view, a person's body is a particular combination of chemical compounds which, during his earthly life, are more or less stable and whose interactions are more or less confined to within the person's body. All this changes rather dramatically at and after death, however. Then considerable chemical change occurs and, over a period of time, the deceased's body actually decomposes chemically. However, though the body decomposes, the basic chemical elements that comprised it are not destroyed; rather, these elements enter into new compounds and these, in turn, may enter into still further compounds, and so on, for as long as the physical universe continues to observe the same laws it now observes, Thus, although the bodily death of a person does, on this view, mark an end to the person's chemical life, it does not mark an end to the on-going process of chemical life itself. The life of chemicals, in short, is "immortal." Once again, however, this view, though perhaps true, cannot provide us with any reason for believing that the *person* survives death and goes on living.

THE CONCEPT OF A PERSON

None of the views considered above provides us with the least reason for believing in personal survival after death. What they do call our attention to, however, is the fact that a well-thought-out answer to the question "Does the person survive death?" must come to grips with a logically prior problem. This is the problem of what, after all, it is to be a person. So far we have treated this idea as perfectly obvious. A person is not his works or deeds, we have said, and a person is not the memories others have of him. And, indeed, these points do seem true. But their being true should not blind us to the fact that we have been making an assumption throughout our discussion. We have been assuming that we know what a person is, and this assumption needs to be articulated as well as critically examined. This is because we might discover that, at bottom, there are very different ways in which we might conceive of what it is to be a person. Philosophers, in fact, have discovered just this, and part of the problem and fascination of the controversy over personal survival stems directly from the controversies and problems that revolve around this more basic question over the nature of personhood.

We can illustrate the direct relationship between these two questions by considering three different conceptions of what it is to be a person, each one of which fails to provide us with a conception that could make belief in the survival of the person after death a reasonable thing to believe. The three conceptions are (1) that a person just is his body, (2) that a person is a special kind of body called an astral body, (3) that a person is a composite entity, consisting of both a body and a mind or soul. In each case, reflection will show that the view under examination fails to provide us with a rational basis upon which to base the belief in the survival of the person after death.

PERSONS AS BODIES

One way we might conceive of what it is to be a person is to think that a person just is a particular body—namely, what we customarily refer to as *his* body. In other words, the man named Smith just is this particular torso with these particular arms, legs, hands, feet, liver, kidneys, heart, brain, and so on, whereas the man named Jones just is this *other* particular body composed of these *other* arms, legs, and so on. Now, it is true that the human body is a vastly complicated network of nerves, tissues, organs, systems, and the like. But this complexity, according to the view in question, does not show that a person is any less of a body than, say, a llama. All that it shows is that the human body is vastly more complicated and developed than some others. Let us refer to this conception of man as the *materialistic conception,* and let us understand the more general view called *materialism* to be the view, roughly speaking, that everything that exists is either itself material or a property of, or a relation that exists between, things that are material. Thus, materialism involves the denial of the reality of anything *im*material, so that if we conceive of such a thing as the mind (or the soul or the spirit) of a person as immaterial and as irreducible to anything material, then materialism can be seen to involve the denial of the reality of everything mental or spiritual. And since it involves this denial, it follows that it involves the denial that persons have minds or souls that are immaterial. Given the materialistic conception of person-hood, in short, a person neither has nor needs a mind or soul, distinct and different from his body. For a person, once again, *is* just his body.

Suppose, then, that we were to adopt this materialistic conception of what it is to be a person; and suppose that we then went on to ask about the reasonableness of believing in personal survival after death. Given this conception what should be our answer? Surely it should be: "There is no reason to believe that the person goes on living after his bodily death, and every reason to believe that he does not do so." And the justification of this answer, given these presuppositions, also is clear enough. For, first, a person's body gives no bodily indication that it continues to live, once it is dead; indeed, the very idea that it *might* give bodily indications of living after its death seems to be logically impossible, if by a body's being dead we understand that it no longer does or can give any indications of life. And even if we recognize, what is true, that it is unclear exactly when a person has died, viewed from a purely medical point of view, even the most open-minded person would have to agree that this uncertainty does not cover a long passage of time; that is, one might be uncertain whether a person died at exactly 9:22 or 9:23 A.M. on April 4, but one could not be uncertain, for the same medical reasons, whether he died at either of these times in, say, 1935 or 1975. Secondly, there is the plain, inescapable fact that the bodies of those persons who have died actually decompose with the passage of time and cease, in time, to be recognizable as the bodies of these persons. Thus, it seems altogether unreasonable to maintain both that a person is just his body, on the one hand, and, on the other, to maintain that he survives his body's death. Of course, one might take refuge here in the idea that a person's chemicals are "immortal." But this, we know, does not mean that the person is; so, if our objective is to find a concept of what it is to be a person that provides us with a basis for the belief that persons survive death as persons, then the materialistic conception must be rejected.

PERSONS AS ASTRAL BODIES

In the second view, which is less common than the traditional material-istic conception, a person is conceived to have a special kind of body called an *astral body*. This view, which is central to much present-day spiritualism, has not found a very conspicous place in the history of philosophy, but one can find a suggestion of it in the writings of the theolo-gian-philosopher Tertullian (C. A.D. 160–220). According to this view, a person cannot exist and be conscious without some kind of functioning body. However, since it seems clear that our ordinary, physical bodies do cease to function when we die, which implies, given this view, that such bodies are incapable of supporting life and consciousness, one must hypothesize that there is another, different kind of body that makes personal survival without the physical body possible. This body is the astral body, and it is commonly believed that even during our earthly life each of us has an astral body, although it remains distinct from our ordinary body. The matter out of which the astral body is allegedly composed is said to be "higher." What this means is far from clear, but often the suggestion made is that the astral body is more ethereal or vapor-ous than is an ordinary physical body. In any event, each astral body must be conceived to have some spatial properties, to be locatable at various points in space, and, as such, it must be possible to talk about its position in space relative to other astral bodies.

The difficulties with this view are immediate and straightforward. First, it is not altogether clear what sense can be made of the concept of a "higher matter." Presumably this should be understood as referring to a matter that is more refined, more "airy" than the grosser matter that comprises our ordinary physical bodies—presumably, somewhat like how we conceive of ghosts: shadowy, insubstantial, but nevertheless material (in *some* sense) beings. *What* this sense is, is far from clear.

A second difficulty is the lack of credible evidence for believing that persons *do* have astral bodies, composed of this "higher" matter, associated with their ordinary physical bodies. If such bodies really do exist, and if they are said to be "material" in any intelligible sense of this term, then we should be able to gather evidence a posteriori for their existence. Yet no such evidence appears to be at hand. Those few attempts to present evidence for the astral body hypothesis seem to be quite unsatisfactory. For example, it sometimes is argued that this hypothesis is the only one that can account for the fact that one person can appear to another person in the capacity of an apparition. Such would be the case, for example, if John, who was in New York, was to "appear" at Mary's bedside in San Francisco, and when John (the ordinary, physical John) does not leave New York. Now, it is not to be denied that the astral body hypothesis might be developed to explain such facts, *if* they are facts. That is, if people really do have this capacity to transport themselves (or their astral bodies) through space while leaving their ordinary physical bodies behind, then certainly *something* must be hypothesized to explain this incredible phenomenon. But before we try explaining those phenomena, we should first be sure they really do occur. And here it is not at all clear that the kind of phenomena in question are genuine. An equally possible hypothesis is, after all, that 'apparitions' of other people are not real but are only thought to be so by the persons who think they view them, in which case the viewing of an 'apparition' should be classed as an unusual experience, but not as a veridical one—that is, not as an experience that has as its object something that truly exists apart from the experience itself. But to confine our critical examination of the astral body hypothesis to such unusual cases as those of viewing apparitions would be to leave the hypothesis untested by the greater part of human experience, and this, it seems, would be to concede far more to the theory than it deserves. For if persons really do have astral bodies, then why can they not be viewed in ordinary day-to-day encounters with people? And should not we be able to see these bodies depart from ordinary physical bodies when they expire? And there is a host of other questions that would need to be raised, if we were to examine the astral body hypothesis with an eye to rigor and completeness. But enough now has been said, for our purposes, to indicate that there are quite serious logical and empirical difficulties standing in the way to acceptance of this hypothesis, and we should be able to understand why, in general, the great preponderance of thinkers in the Western world have found this view to be less than convincing.

PERSONS AS BODIES AND MINDS

A third, more common way is to conceive of a person as a composite reality. A person is not just a body, physical or astral, but a combination of two different, irreducible things: (1) his body, which is material, and (2) his mind or soul, which is immaterial. In this view, to say that a person retains his identity through time is to declare that both his body and his mind in some sense remain the same, so that to contend that the person survives death in a personal way is tantamount to contending that the person's body and mind are not destroyed by his earthly death but go on existing afterwards.

The prospects are pretty dim that this view can provide us with a rational foundation for belief in personal survival after death. Since it claims that a person is (at least in part) a particular body, it must face the fact that, so far as we can determine, bodies simply do not go on living after death—which would mean that persons do not go on existing either.

To add to the materialistic conception in the manner in which this view does—that is, to insist that persons are not just bodies, but are, instead, bodies *and* minds—adds no new reason for believing in personal survival after death.

However, while this would seem to be obivious and noncontroversial, we may have taken a too narrow view of the idea of the body's living after the person's earthly death, for we have ignored the idea of the resurrection of the body. And it is in conjunction with this idea, some might say, that the claim that the person goes on living both in a spiritual and in a physical sense may be a reasonable contention. Let us examine this view.

To begin with, the doctrine of the resurrection of the body can be understood in at least two different ways. First, it may be held that the bodies of those who have died are not resurrected just at or after death but rather at some point in the future (for example, on the Day of Judgment). Second, it may be held that the body of each deceased person is in some sense resurrected at or just after the person's earthly demise.

Each view encounters serious problems. The first view is consistent with the plain fact that the bodies of dead persons do not mysteriously disappear just after they die, but it must still explain whether—and, if so, how—the person who has died continues to exist during the time between his death and his alleged resurrection. Now, attempts to explain this appear necessarily to encounter the following objection. First, if the person truly *does* go on existing during this interim period, then having his body resurrected is *not* necessary for his continued personal existence (otherwise, *he* could not exist during the interim period). On the other hand, if the person does *not* go on existing between the time of his earthly death and the date of his alleged resurrection, we could not say this resurrected person was the *same* person that died. Rather this "resurrected person" would be a different person; he would resemble the one who died earlier—would remember the same things and have the same interests and desires—but would still not be identical with that former person. The first alternative means this view of resurrection is an unnecessary addition to the explanation of personal survival after death. The second alternative means this view of resurrection fails to account for the alleged fact of personal survival. Thus, this view cannot make a credible contribution to our thinking about personal survival after death.

The failure of this traditional interpretation of resurrection has given rise to a more modern one. In this view, no interim period exists between earthly death and bodily resurrection; the resurrection is supposed to occur just at or after bodily death. But the resurrection here is not claimed to be a resurrection of the very same body that died, a view that would manifestly be false. For cemetaries, after all, abound with the corpses of the deceased. It is rather that, while the earthly body remains behind, a *duplicate* of it is resurrected or, more accurately, "reconstituted" at some other place. In other words, according to this view, the earthly body does go through its inevitable process of decay. But the reconstituted body does not. The reconstituted body remains whole and intact; it continues to be a functioning unity. And so, of course, does the person, it is alleged. The person, in union with his reconstituted body, goes on living also.

How credible is this account? Not very. It too encounters an insurmountable objection. For if, on the one hand, the person does require his earthly body in order to retain his identity, then it seems that it is not just any body that he needs; rather, it would seem to be necessary that he retain his *own* body, and not just some "duplicate" of it, however this idea of a duplicate is to be understood. If, on the other hand, he does not need his earthly body to retain his identity, then it is unclear why he should need *any* body to do so. Now, either he does need his earthly body—which, if true, is at odds with this view's contention that he receives a duplicate—or he does not need his earthly body, which means he does not need any body whatever. Whichever alternative is chosen, therefore, this view of the resurrection of the body seems to encounter quite fundamental difficulties. And so it seems to fail to give us a credible account of the survival of the person after death.

PERSONS AS MINDS

We can summarize our argument to this point as follows: If persons are conceived to be bodies, either in whole or in part, and either of the ordinary, physical variety or of the less ordinary, astral kind, then there is no reason to believe that persons go on living after their earthly death. Indeed, there is every reason to deny it. And here we contend nothing more than what seems patently obvious. And yet many reasonable thinkers insist that there *is* such a thing as personal survival after death.

Now, it seems that no reasonable man can maintain this while at the same time maintaining that persons are bodies. So, those reasonable men who insist on the truth of personal survival after death should dismiss these bodily conceptions of what it is to be a person and put in their place a dramatically different one, which we might call a "spiritual" or "mental" conception. And we may characterize this conception by saying that, according to it, *persons are just minds* or souls or spirits. In other words, according to this view, nothing that is essential for what it is to be a person has anything to do with the nature of body, physical or astral. Persons are not physical beings; they are exclusively spiritual or mental. They are immaterial. They are minds, neither more nor less.

What is the relationship between this view and the belief in the survival of the person after death? It is this. If a person is just his mind, and if a person's mind is distinct from and is not reducible to his body, then, clearly, a person's body might cease to be alive while the person himself (his mind) might very well go on living. In this view, since the person himself is not in any way a body, it becomes possible to believe that the cessation of one's bodily life does not amount to the cessation of one's life as a person. For a person conceivably might go on living after the death of his body.

This view seems to contain the clearest basis for belief in personal survival after death. But there are formidable obstacles to rational acceptance of this view. To accept this view, we would need to be persuaded of the truth of at least two propositions: (1) a person is a mind, and (2) minds go on living after bodies die.

But even more than this is required. For it is possible to maintain that persons are minds *and* that minds go on existing after bodies die and still deny that persons survive their bodily death. Much Eastern thought seems to include beliefs of this type.

Buddhist thought, for example, is characterized by the belief that, during his earthly life, a person consists of two distinct kinds of mind or spirit. On the one hand, each person has a unique consciousness, called *java,* which is his and his alone. It is highly personal—indeed, one might even say that it *is* the person, for it is his awareness of his desires, hopes, memories, emotions, and so on. It is the person's individual consciousness. On the other hand, each person also is thought to partake of or participate in a common mind or spirit, called *atman.* The *atman* of a person is not his and his alone. *Atman* is impersonal; it belongs to no person in particular.

Now at death it is believed that *java* is extinguished, whereas *atman* goes on existing. And this amounts to contending that the person as a distinct, separate reality ceases to exist, while that which is not the person but is nonetheless spiritual or immaterial—*atman*—goes on existing. The credibility of this view, of course, is not here in question. All that we want to notice about it, for present purposes, is how it illustrates the fact that one can believe that something mental or spiritual continues to exist after our earthly death and still deny that persons do. And one does not have to go outside of Western culture to find examples of such beliefs. A view of this same general type seems to be at the heart of Aristotle's speculation about the immortality of what he calls "the active intellect." Like *atman,* the active intellect is conceived by Aristotle to be immaterial *and* impersonal; and it is the active intellect, not the person complete with his memories, hopes, and the like, which, according to Aristotle, survives death, if anything does.

Those, then, who would endeavor rationally to support belief in the survival of the person after death must do more than argue for the truth of the two propositions mentioned above. To these two a third must be added —namely, (3) the mind that goes on living after the death of the body must be the person, not some impersonal spirit.

THE IDEA OF SUBSTANCE

But there is yet another proposition whose truth must, it seems, be confirmed if a case it to be made for the survival of the person after death. To make this clear, let us consider what proposition (3) assumes. It assumes that a person can retain his identity through death. It affirms, in effect, that precisely the same person continues to exist after the death of his body as existed before its death. And it is understandable why this must be insisted upon. For if the person or mind that existed after bodily death were a *different* person than the one who existed before the body's death, then it would be altogether wrong to speak of the *survival* of the person. We would have to speak, instead, of, say, the "alteration" or "metamorphosis" of the person, the change of the person into something other than what he was prior to his body's death.

Thus, one way of making explicit what proposition (3) assumes is to say that it assumes that the person can retain his identity despite the occurrence of quite significant changes in his relationship to other things that exist. In the particular case of death, of course, what changes quite significantly, in this view, is the relationship between the person and his body. And what is being contended is that a person can remain the same person after his separation from his dead body as he was before, when he was somehow associated with it.

But this idea of the person's retaining his identity amid change need not be confined to this special case of death. For what is being assumed here, more generally, is that a person is able to retain his identity, not only through death, but also throughout his entire life. That is, the person that we are imagining has experienced the death of his body is being conceived to be the very same person who, let us suppose, was born into the world eighty-five years ago, grew up from infancy into and out of adolescence, matured during his adulthood, and, eventually, lapsed into senility. Throughout this entire process of development, we are to suppose that something remained constant and unchanging; something did not grow from one thing into another; something did not develop but remained the same. And it is only because there was this "something" that remained the same, according to this view, that entitles us to say that all these developments were developments of *this* particular person. The idea, then, that the person retains his identity—that, in some sense, a person is exactly the same person at every moment of his existence, before death or after—this idea of identity is what proposition (3) seems to assume.

So, to our list of propositions that believers in the survival of the person after death must confront and endeavor to confirm, we must add yet another —namely, (4) a person retains his identity throughout the whole of his life.

Now, there is a special way in which this idea has been understood, and getting clear on the concepts required to make it clear will be helpful both now and in the future. The central idea we need to introduce is the idea of *substance*. There are two characteristics of a substance that need to be understood. First a substance is *that which persists unaltered through change*. Thus, a substance underlies change; it makes change possible while at the same time not itself changing. It is the subject of change, in the sense that the changes that take place are changes *in* it, but not *to* it—as a white chair might be painted red and thereby undergo a change in color without thereby ceasing to be the same chair.

Thus, one way of expressing (4) would be to say that a person must be a substance. Moreover, since those who believe that the person survives death must believe that persons are minds, we can combine this demand with the one just mentioned and say that these thinkers seem required to maintain that a person is a *mental* substance. They seem required to show that a person is a mental or spiritual substance that retains its identity through time and change. It is the person considered as a mind or spirit that is the same at birth as it is at death and as it will be afterward, if it goes on existing.

A second defining characteristic of substance is that it is *capable of existing by itself*. Metaphysically speaking, that is, a substance is independent. If X is a substance and happens to be associated with other things (Y and Z) that are not substances, then Y and Z might cease to exist without in any way causing X to cease to exist. Indeed, even if we were to suppose that X, one substance, is for a time associated with Y, another substance, and that subsequently the association between the two is severed, that would not show that X ceased to exist—or that Y did, for that matter. As substances, both are conceived to be capable of existing independently.

Now, since this idea of independence partly defines the idea of substance, and since those who believe the person survives death seem necessarily to be committed to the view that persons are mental substances, we can see that these thinkers also seem necessarily to be committed to the view that persons are the kind of being who can exist by themselves. But what does "exist by themselves" really amount to? For persons, it means that, although during our earthly life we live in association with our physical bodies, we do not depend on our bodies for our existence. When persons are conceived to be mental substances, that is, their existence and identity as persons do not depend upon their having a body. The body can be taken away and the person can go on existing. The body can die, and the person can go on living. What pertains to the body, in short, has nothing to do with what pertains to the substance that a person is. Considered metaphysically, a person, according to this view, is just a mental substance.

IDEALISM AND DUALISM

Support for the view that a person is a mental substance comes from philosophers of very different metaphysical outlooks. The principal difference to be noted here is between those philosophers who entertain the theory of substance known as *idealism* and those who entertain the theory of substance called *dualism*.

The fundamental difference between idealism and dualism is quite simple to state. Idealists believe that only spiritual or mental substances exist; dualists believe that only some of those substances that exist are mental or spiritual. In addition, the dualist believes there are other, nonspiritual, nonmental substances that are real, and these are said to be bodies or to partake of matter.

Thus, idealism is a variety of a *monistic* (from the Greek *monos* for single) metaphysical theory of substance. It alleges that there is but a single *kind* of basic reality. So idealism is, in *this* respect, like the view called materialism mentioned earlier, but differs in that it affirms that mind or spirit is the single kind of substance, while materialism reserves this place for matter. Dualism, on the other hand, is an example of a *pluralistic* metaphysical theory of substance. Implied in it is the denial of all monistic theories of substance, including both idealism and materialism.

It is worth mentioning here that a philosopher might be, say, a monist with respect to the number of different *kinds* of substance, but a pluralist in response to the question, "How many different *individual* substances exist?" For suppose that an idealist believed that there are *many* mental substances in the world, not just one. Then he would be a monist in his theory of substance but a pluralist in his answer to the question about the number of different individual substances that exist. Indeed, just such a view is held by the English philosopher Bishop Berkeley (1684–1753). And an analogous theory could be set forth by a materialist, as the philosopher Hobbes (1588–1679) maintains.

To take note of yet another pair of possibilities, a philosopher might be monistic *both* on the question about the number of different kinds of subtance *and* on the question about how many different individual things exist. For example, an idealist who was monistic in both these ways would hold the view that there is only one kind of substance, mind, *and* that there is only one individual thing comprising the whole of reality—namely, one mind. The philosopher Hegel (1770–1831) seems to hold such a position. A materialist who was monistic in both these ways, on the other hand, would hold just the reverse of this; he would hold that there is just one kind of substance, matter, *and* that the whole of reality consists of just one thing—namely, a single material substance.

There are other possible combinations of monism and pluralism besides these. What this shows, then, is that the terms 'monism' and 'pluralism' have at least two different meanings in philosophy. Sometimes they are used to indicate a philosopher's answer to the question, "How many different *kinds* of substance are there—one or many?" But sometimes they are used to indicate a philosopher's answer to the question, "How many different *individual* substances exist—one or many?"

We should be aware of these diverging uses of the terms, but we should not be afraid to use them. We should just take special care that we understand how we are using them as well as how they are being used by another. Once we do, in fact, we can use them to state an assumption that appears to be necessary for those who believe that each person can survive his body's death. For any philosopher who contends that *each* person survives his bodily death must, it seems, entertain a *pluralistic* position with respect to the *number of different individuals* that exist. This is because such a thinker is committtted to the belief that different persons survive death, not just some one (impersonal) mind—say, *atman*. Thus, since there are many persons, in this view, proponents of it must believe that there are many different individual substantial things that exist. The view that there is just one individual substance that exists, in short, appears to be logically inconsistent with the view that different persons survive their bodily death.

It does not follow from this, however, that the belief in personal survival is inconsistent with a monistic theory of substance. That is, it appears to be logically possible for it to be true both that there is but one kind of substance—namely, minds—and for it also to be true that there are many such substances. In fact, as noted, just such a view is held by the philosopher Berkeley. But while such a view seems to be a logically tenable position, it nevertheless is not the one toward which the great preponderance of Western thinkers, especially those operating within the context of the Judeo-Christian tradition, have been inclined. Rather, these thinkers have been inclined to insist upon the substantiality, not only of minds or souls, but also of matter or body.

To a great extent, then, our philosophical heritage with respect to substance has been that of dualism. The universe has been conceived as consisting of two kinds of substance—minds and bodies. And although there is a sense in which only the infinite mind, God, is thought to have an existence that is *totally* independent of everything clse, owing to his alleged *aseity*, both finite minds and bodies have been conceived by many thinkers as having the kind of independence within the created world that permits us to regard them as substances. According to this outlook, so long as we confine our attention to the created world, minds are capable of existing by themselves, without bodies, and vice versa.

The view that both minds and bodies are substantial, rather than the view that just minds are or that just bodies are, appears to be the one toward which most people are inclined—prior, at least, to careful reflection. To a considerable extent, therefore, it appears as though thinkers often are driven to accepting either idealism or materialism only because they think they find certain insurmountable objections to dualism. Doubtless this is not a true explanation of why all materialists become materialists or idealists become idealists, but it seems to explain why many thinkers develop the theories they do. In any event, it will be worthwhile to reflect on the merits of a dualistic position with respect to substance. This will be worth our while, not just because many careful thinkers who have gone before us have been so inclined or because so many of us are so inclined initially, but also for the fundamental reason we gave in the preceding argument—namely, dualism seems to provide us with what appears to be a sound basis for the belief that we can survive our bodily death. It is how adequate this basis is that shall concern us in what follows.

Let us now give a formal statement of the argument we wish to examine. This statement is brief compared to others we gave in earlier chapters because we have already presented much of our "commentary." If we have understood what we have argued up till now, we will know all we need to know to grasp the argument that follows.

FORMAL STATEMENT OF AN ARGUMENT FOR THE POSSIBILITY OF PERSONAL SURVIVAL AFTER DEATH

Steps	Symbolization	Status
1. If persons are individual mental substances, then persons can survive the death of their bodies.	$i \rightarrow s$	Assumption
2. Persons are individual mental substances.	i	Assumption
3. Therefore, persons can survive the death of their bodies.	$\therefore s$	Consequence, from (1) and (2), by *modus ponens*.

This argument is not supposed to prove that persons actually *do* survive the death of their bodies, only that persons *can* survive the death of their bodies. The argument endeavors to prove, that, because persons are what they are alleged to be—namely, individual mental substances—it is at least logically possible that persons survive the death of their bodies. For, as individual mental substances, persons would be capable of existing by themselves, apart from their bodies. Whether we actually do so is a question we will discuss later.

Now, clearly, the argument just given is formally valid, and it does not appear to commit any informal fallacy. Therefore, the question of its soundness becomes a question of the truth of its assumptions. Assumption(1) is true, and analytically so. For if persons are individual mental substances, then, by definition, they can exist by themselves, from which it follows that they can exist without the body. Thus, it follows that, as mental substances, persons could survive the death of their bodies. So assumption (1) is true and known to be so.

But what of assumption (2)? Here we come to the heart of the matter. For this idea is as controversial as it is important. That persons are individual mental substances is not self-evidently true (or false, for that matter). Thus, what is needed are some reasons for accepting it as true, either a priori or a posteriori. And it is no exaggeration to say that the questions that arise in this context form the core of the philosophical reflection that has gone into the question about life after death.

Now, it deserves to be mentioned, once again, that we are intentionally limiting our inquiry here to a consideration of how a dualist theory of substance can or cannot contribute to our thinking about the questions of the nature of a person and the person's survival after death. As might be expected, there have been many dualist thinkers who have been great and influential, but none more than the French philosopher Réné Descartes (1596–1650). So recognized is Descartes as a classic spokesman of dualism that it is his name that is most likely to be mentioned first whenever the topic of dualism is discussed. Therefore, we shall look to Descartes's arguments. In particular, we shall ask how his arguments are intended to give support to the view that persons are individual mental substances. And we shall want to ask how convincing are his arguments. In addition, we shall inquire into the problems of this view of what it is to be a person, especially when it is conjoined with the view that, in addition to the many immaterial substances that are alleged to exist, material substances also are supposed to exist, including our own bodies. After we have worked through these issues, we shall consider our second task—namely, that of assessing the adequacy of the reasons for believing that persons actually do survive the death of their bodies. To have to postpone discussion of this topic is apt to be disappointing. But it is the inevitable consequence of trying to discuss the question of survival in a disciplined fashion.

DEFENDING THE ARGUMENT

To understand Descartes, we must understand the novel method he uses. In fact, as we shall see, the novelty of his method is part of the genius of his ideas.

DESCARTES "COGITO"

The method Descartes uses to gain support for the view that persons are mental substances is called his method of *methodological* or *systematic doubt*. In it Descartes resolves to deny the truth of any proposition that he finds it possible to doubt—that is, every proposition except those that are *logically impossible* for him to doubt. If there are such indubitable truths, Descartes thinks, we can perhaps reconstruct the underlying principles of human knowledge. Only by proceeding by the method of doubt, he thinks, can we guard against the hobbling effects of prejudice and assure ourselves that there are some truths that no reasonable man can deny.

Now, the alternative to there being such indubitable truths is, for Descartes, *scepticism*. That is, if we should discover that nothing can be known with absolute certainty, Descartes thinks, we would be obliged to take up the position of the sceptic, who maintains that man can have no knowledge but only opinion. As such, the sceptic must dismiss as improper not only all claims to, say, knowledge of God or knowledge of right and wrong; he must also dismiss as improper all claims to scientific knowledge. Indeed, one might go so far (and Descartes indicates that he, for one, would) as to deny that there could be genuine mathematical or logical knowledge. If, on the other hand, we should happen to discover that there are certain indubitable truths, then, like Descartes, we would think ourselves entitled to dismiss the sceptic's moanings about the nonexistence of knowledge. There would be some things, at least, that we would know for certain, and once we had discovered what these things were, then it might very well be possible to say how they make other kinds of knowledge possible, such as scientific and mathematical knowledge.

In fact, this is precisely what Descartes thinks can be done, so that, fundamentally, what he thinks is at stake, when he asks whether he knows anything for certain, is the possibility of scientific and mathematical knowledge. It is for this reason that he sees himself as attempting to find a new foundation for the sciences (where by "sciences" he means not only those disciplines we nowadays regard as scientific, but also the discipline of philosophy itself). Thus does Descartes see himself, in the course of the six meditations that comprise his *Meditations,* a work that, perhaps more than any other single work in the history of philosophy, deserves the title "classic."

Descartes begins his search by examining what, at first glance, seem to be the clearest and least disputable cases of knowledge. These are those cases where we claim to know that something external to us exists because we observe it by means of our senses—say, the words on this page in this book. For convenience, let us refer to any description of what we are presently aware of by our senses as a *perceptual judgment*. Then we might say that there are different perceptual judgments we can make. For example, we can make the perceptual judgments 'There are words on this page' and 'The words on this page are printed in black'. What could be more obviously true than these judgments? Have we not found already examples of those 'indubitable truths' that Descartes seeks?

Descartes' answer here is no, and the reasons he gives to support it go to the heart of the differences between empiricism and rationalism. The point he makes (and remakes) is that our confidence in the truth of these perceptual judgments rests upon our accepting an unspoken assumption— namely that our senses are a reliable source of and guide to knowledge. When we express our confidence in the truth of these perceptual judgments, we commit ourselves to the soundness of the following argument:

> Since our senses are a reliable, trustworthy source of knowledge, and since they now inform us that something is the case—for example, that there are words on this page—it follows that we know that there are words on this page.

But the soundness of this argument clearly presupposes the truth of its initial premise—'Our senses are a reliable, trustworthy source of knowledge'. Indeed, the credibility of empiricism as the correct view to take in epistemology seems clearly to depend on the truth of this same proposition. It is not disingenuous of Descartes, therefore, to want to know if this assumption can be confirmed. His answer, as we know from our discussion of rationalism in Chapter 3, is that it cannot—at least not without the aid of a foundation supplied by arguments of a distinctively rationalistic bent. Let us review the main outlines of his argument here.

Descartes' argument is an example of a kind of argument we mentioned much earlier, in Chapter 3. He begins by pointing out what everybody would agree. This is that our senses *sometimes* deceive us; that is, some-times our senses present us with data that actually misrepresent the way the world is. A stick placed in water looks bent, but it is not. On a sunny day there appear to be puddles on the road ahead, but there are none. Now, given that our senses *sometimes* lead us to make erroneous judgments about the world external to us, Descartes asks how we can tell when this is the case. In particular, we need to ask how we know that we are not *now* being misled or deceived by our senses? How can we be *certain* that this book actually exists instead of merely appearing to do so?

Or, to recall another argument from Chapter 3, consider the question of dreaming. Sometimes our dreams are so *un*lifelike that, even while having them, we seem to be able to tell that we are dreaming. But at other times they are very lifelike indeed, and we experience the occurrences in such dreams with as much intensity and vividness as we do our ordinary waking experiences. Let us call dreams of such intensity and vividness *realistic dreams*. Then we can say that, somtimes at least, we do have realistic dreams.

Now, Descartes would have us ask how we know for certain that we are not *now* having such a dream? Clearly it cannot be because of the vividness and intensity of what we are at present aware of. Precisely the same is true, by definition, of our dream experiences in a realistic dream. Nor could we hope to settle this issue one way or the other by, say, pinching ourselves. For whatever we might do in waking life we might also dream we are doing while fast asleep. Indeed—and this is quite crucial for Descartes —there is no perceptual judgment that we can know to be true, he thinks, simply because of what we take ourselves to be perceiving. Whatever it is that we might choose to nominate—say, this table or that chair, the ocean or a soft-drink bottle—we might just as well be dreaming that we are perceiving it, in which case, of course, none of these things would have the substantiality we ordinarily assume they do. So impotent are the senses, considered by themselves, as a reliable source of knowledge, that, according to Descartes, they cannot even answer so simple a question as, "How do I know that I am awake right now and not dreaming?"

But Descartes' imagination goes beyond even this. He is aware that many of his contemporaries might scoff at such fanciful ideas and declare that, since a good God exists, and since he has created us such that we rely, by nature, on our senses, then it follows that our senses truly are reliable. But how do we know, Descrates asks, that there is such a being? Indeed, might there not exist a being, just as powerful as the Judeo-Christian God is supposed to be, but one who is not good—one who is, on the contrary, evil or malicious? Descartes refers to this being as "the deceitful demon" or "the malign genius." How do I know, he asks in effect, that such a being does not exist? Might it not be the case that so powerful a demon exists with but one perpose in mind—namely, to deceive me— to make me believe that such things as tables and chairs exist when they do not? Might it not be that nothing else exists—neither things nor people— but only just me and a powerful demon who finds his sole enjoyment in tricking me?

Now, a natural response to Descartes is to declare that he must be either kidding or out of his mind. And Descartes is aware of this view. Only he also thinks that this is not a very reasonable way to dismiss the possibilities he mentions. That it is false, say, that an evil demon exists, is, let us agree, something that all reasonable men are agreed upon. But that fact does not show why it is false (if it is) or what makes it false (if it is). And what Descartes wants is to get beyond our impulsive, out-of-hand dismissal of such speculation as silly, to the difficult question of how we know that it is false. And what he also wants us to see is that we must get to this stage of inquiry if we are to make good our assumption that our senses can be trusted. For that they can be trusted assumes, among other things, that they are not directed by the whims of a deceitful demon.

What Descartes manages to make us aware of, then, is that our claim to know such things as this book exists is not the indubitable truth we quite naturally and uncritically assume it is. There are different grounds on which we might deny, without absurdity, the truth of such a judgment— for example, that we are hallucinating, or that we are dreaming, or that we are being deluded by a deceitful demon. There is no reason why we *must* agree that this or any other perceptual judgment is true. And Descartes hopes that each of us will see that, so long as we trust only the information presented by means of our senses, we cannot determine whether we are awake or dreaming, having a veridical or an hallucinatory experience, or seeing reality or being deceived by an evil genius. We are so far from knowing something by means of our senses alone, he thinks, that we can, without absurdity, doubt that we know anything in this way. And since we can doubt it, then, given Descartes's principle of methodological doubt, he resolves to deny that it is true. And thus he resolves to deny that there are tables and chairs, rivers and trees, beetles and boxes.

But even more must be denied. For why do we think we have a physical body? Presumably it is because we have various experiences, such as hunger and cold, that we think are caused by our bodies, as well as various movements that we think we cause our body to perform, such as when we will to raise our hand and our hand moves as we will it. But if it is not indubitable that such things as tables and chairs exist, why should we suppose our bodies do? It is just as logically possible that the malign genius exists and fools us about the existence of material things such as tables and chairs as that he exists and fools us about the existence of our own bodies. (Indeed, he might take a special delight in making us think we have bodies when we have none. Imagine brushing your teeth that *do not exist* with a toothbrush that *does not exist,* using your arms and hands that have no more substantiality to them than the air.) Clearly, if we allow that we might be deceived about the existence of tables and chairs, we must also deny the reality of our bodies, since we might be deceived about its reality also. Given the principle of methodological doubt, therefore, each of us must deny the reality of the physical world, including his own body, as well as the reality of all other persons. For that other minds in addition to my own exists is not indubitably true.

One might think, then, that there is no synthetic proposition, and perhaps not even any analytic proposition, about whose truth we can be absolutely certain. But this is not so, according to Descartes. We have argued that there is no *perceptual judgment*, no proposition whose truth must be determined by observation, that we can be absolutely certain of. But perceptual judgments do not exhaust the class of synthetic propositions. There yet may be some synthetic propositions we cannot doubt.

In particular, what of the proposition 'I doubt'? Here, Descartes thinks, we arrive at a proposition that cannot be doubted. For in the very attempt to doubt the truth of the proposition 'I doubt', we actually are doing the thing we are, so to speak, trying to doubt can be done—namely, *doubting*. Not even the malign genius could be deceiving in this regard, Descartes thinks. With this simple proposition, 'I doubt', we find, Descartes thinks, a truth that is absolutely indubitable.

And we know this proposition is true, not by making use of our senses, but by making use of our rational capacities, independently of any information derived from observation. Strictly speaking, then, to come to see the necessary truth of 'I cannot doubt that I doubt' is to come to see that something is true a priori. The most fundamental, indubitable truth we can arrive at, therefore, is one that we know to be true independently of observation.

Once again, however, Descartes is not content to stop here. For who is this 'I' that cannot doubt that he doubts? And what is doubting? To take up the latter question first, Descartes says that doubting is a form of thinking; it is to take up a mental attitude of suspending judgment about the truth of one or another proposition. Accordingly, to be the kind of being that is capable of doubting is to be the kind of being that is capable of thinking. What Descartes thinks he has shown, therefore, is that he cannot doubt that he thinks.

But what shall we say of this thing whose ability to think Descartes cannot doubt? Surely, he thinks, we must say that this thing must exist. Surely, he thinks, we must say that it is real. For if it did not exist, then it could not think, and since it can think, then it follows that it must exist. Thus, from the fact that something thinks, Descartes contends, it follows that something exists.

But, further, what identity should we ascribe to this "thing that thinks"? Since it is Descartes who cannot doubt that he thinks, and since it follows from this that something must exist to do the thinking, then it appears to follow that we must identify this thinking thing with Descartes himself. And so Descartes concludes this line of reasoning with his famous declaration, *Cogito ergo sum*—"I think, therefore I am" (or 'I exist'). And it is because of this declaration that the whole of the argument we have characterized to this point often gets referred to as "Descartes' *cogito*" or, more simply, "the *cogito*."

Now, the relevance that the *cogito* has to our interest in the concept of a person is this: What Descartes has endeavored to show is that he cannot doubt that he exists. Indeed, for Descartes, it is the truth of the proposition 'I think, therefore I am' that constitutes, logically, the most fundamental of truths about what exists, since its truth cannot be doubted. At the same time, however, Descartes has argued that he can doubt that he has a body or that his body exists. The proposition affirming the existence of his body, therefore, is not indubitably true, whereas the proposition that affirms his existence is. And from this it evidently follows, he thinks, that this being whose existence Descartes cannot doubt is *not* Descartes's body. In fact, since how Descartes knows that he exists has nothing to do with his having a body or with his gathering information by means of his physical senses, then it also evidently follows, he thinks, that what Descartes is has nothing whatever to do with his body or with his having a body.

Now, what Descartes is, is a thinking thing. Thus, in order to exist as Descartes—which is to say, as a thinking thing—it follows, Descartes thinks, that he has no need of his or any other body. And if this is so, this thinking thing that Descartes is must be something that is not material or physical, which seems necessarily to imply that it must be a mind or soul or spirit. So the conclusion of the argument, according to Descartes, is this: I (Descartes) exist as a thinking thing—that is, as an individual mind.

DESCARTES AND SCEPTICISM

One reason Descartes is sometimes called "the father of modern philosophy" is that he was so aware of the possibility of a radical form of scepticism. His procedure of employing the method of doubt brought to light the possibility of a radical form of scepticism in a way that no previous philosopher had recognized. And it is owing in large part to Descartes's thinking in this regard that philosophers have been so interested in the claims of scepticism. All this, of course, is quite in keeping with Descartes' own preconceptions. As noted, he saw himself as trying to give decisive reasons for claiming that some truths are indubitable and, hence, known with certainty, instead of having to deny this and end by acknowledging that nothing is known for certain—not even, say, that this body exists or that we have arms and legs.

What we have seen to this point, then, are Descartes's reasons for saying that there is at least one thing that he knows for certain—namely, that he exists as a thinking thing. But a few more steps should make us aware of some ideas and problems that are at once interesting and troubling. For even if we were to concede that Descartes has shown that there is one thing about which he can be absolutely certain—namely, that he exists as a thinking thing—the question still remains whether he thinks he can know anything else, or whether, with respect to all else, he must maintain the stance of the confirmed sceptic. Predictably, Descartes thinks he can avoid the sting of scepticism even here.

The way he attempts to do this involves two additional ideas. First, he sets forth what he thinks is a general criterion of indubitable truth. He says, in effect, that any proposition that we understand as clearly and distinctly as the proposition 'I think, therefore I am' is just as indubitably true as that proposition. Thus, in order to discover if there are any further indubitable truths, we are, according to Descartes, to look to see if there are any further propositions that are as clearly and distinctly understood as 'I think, therefore I am'.

Now, instead of trying to proceed directly from this criterion of indubitable truth to the task of showing that we do know that such things as this book and our bodies exist, Descartes takes on a quite different and surprising problem—namely, the problem of proving God's existence! And he endeavors to do this wholly a priori, as indeed he must. For since, at this point, he has given reasons for denying the reality of that physical world we assume we come to know by means of the senses, it obviously would be inconsistent of him to go on to try to prove the existence of God by making use of certain propositions that purport to describe this same world. So he must proceed wholly a priori.

And it is only *after* he has proven the existence of an all good, all-knowing, and all powerful deity—only *after* he has proven the existence of the Judeo-Christian God, to his satisfaction—that he thinks he can provide a rational basis for our belief that the physical world exists outside of our minds or consciousness. Indeed, it is only *after* he has given his proofs of God's existence that he thinks we can justify our conviction that other minds exist in addition to our own. Thus, Descartes' thought tends to turn our ordinary preconceptions upside down. For we ordinarily are disposed to think that the existence of God is something that is far less certain than the existence of, say, this book or our arms and legs. Just the reverse of this is true, however, according to Descartes. God's existence is more certain than the existence of the physical world. Indeed, it is only by appealing to God's existence that we can justify our claim to know that a physical world exists. For our senses lead us naturally to believe this, and an all-good God would not create us so as to be deceived by what we naturally believe.

How satisfactory is Descartes' attempt to avoid scepticism? This is a difficult question. But even if we grant that his *cogito* argument is sound, so that there is at least one thing we know for certain, it does seem clear that the remainder of his argument stands on very precarious grounds. If, as we have argued in Chapter 3, no proof of God's existence is sound, and if, as Descartes argues, we cannot know that the physical world exists unless we first know that God exists, then it does seem to follow that we cannot know that the physical world exists. With respect to our supposed knowledge of the existence and character of the physical world, therefore, it appears that scepticism is the inevitable result of beginning our inquiry into knowledge where Descartes begins. In fact, it is because this does *seem* to be the inevitable result, on the one hand, and because, on the other, it is a result that we are very much inclined to want to avoid, that Descartes's thought has had the influence it has. To a large extent, in short, Descartes is "the father of modern philosophy" not because of the problems he solves but because of the problems he sets.

DISPUTING THE ARGUMENT

There are a number of ways we might dispute Descartes's argument. The English philosopher Bertrand Russell (1872–1969) argued that the most Descartes's *cogito* argument proves is that thought exists. According to Russell, Descartes fails to prove that the thought belongs to *him*; thus, he (Descartes) fails to prove his existence.

Another objection goes as follows: Descartes, in his effort to discover what is true, sets forth the idea that a proposition is true if and only if it is clearly and distinctly understood. But, now, if one needs to have this standard of truth in order to recognize what is true, then Descartes needs this standard *prior* to his *cogito* argument. In fact, however, Descartes uses his *cogito* argument as a basis for this standard of truth. Thus, he is arguing in a circle. On the one hand he is saying that we cannot recognize what is true without the standard of clarity and distinctness. On the other, he is maintaining that this is the correct standard of truth *because* something that we know is true—namely, that to think entails the existence of the thinker—is apprehended clearly and distinctly. Descartes, it appears, cannot have it both ways.

There are, then, serious objections to Descartes's attempt to support the view that each person is a spiritual or mental substance. And even if these objections could be met, there are many other problems to consider. In fact, rather than attack Descartes's argument directly, what we want to do is to examine its implications. That is, we want to see what problems confront the dualist, if, as he assumes, a person is a mental substance who just happens to be, for a time, connected with a physical substance—his body.

THE PROBLEM OF IDENTITY

One problem for the dualist is *the problem of personal identity*—how we can know that any person is the *same* person at different times. Certainly the *cogito* is unable to present a solution to this problem. For even assuming that Descartes can prove his existence as a thinking thing from the fact that he cannot doubt that he doubts, it does not follow that when Descartes proves his existence in this way at two different times he also proves that he is the same person both times.

Nor, for similar reasons, does the *cogito* prove the substantiality of the 'I' whose existence it allegedly proves. If a substance is capable of existing by itself and underlies change without itself changing, then the *cogito* by itself cannot prove that such a mental entity exists. To do this it would have to prove that the same person exists at different times because, at different times, what is ostensibly the same person (say, Descartes) can produce the *cogito* argument. However, as we just noted, the *cogito* is not able to do this, so it follows that it also is unable to prove the existence of a mental substance or self named by Descartes's (or any other person's) use of the word 'I'.

The problem of personal identity is also compounded by the concept of a person that Descartes and his heirs bring to it. For if we begin with the assumption that a person *is* a mind or immaterial being, then it becomes logically irrelevant to cite one or another fact about a person's *body* as evidence for that person's identity. In fact, once we see this, then the only way we can prove that persons do maintain their identity is to use certain alleged facts about minds or mental phenomena.

At least two views of this kind should be considered briefly here. The first is that how we know a person is the same person now as he was before is by the fact that he *remembers* what happened to him in the past. This is a view which receives its major impetus from the English philosopher John Locke (1632–1704), and is the same view that receives its classic critique at the hands of Locke's fellow Englishman, Bishop Butler (1692–1752). The second view is that when we introspect upon our inner lives, we perceive something unchanging to which we can appropriate the name "self." It is this view of personal identity that Hume criticizes in his *Treatise Concerning Human Understanding*. Let us consider each view in turn.

The first view cannot provide us with a satisfactory basis for the belief in personal identity. This view amounts to the claim that a person who exists now is the same person who existed before if the person now can remember having certain experiences at an earlier time. For example, suppose that, at an earlier time and place, Jones experienced terror when his grandfather locked him in the basement. Then if, at present, Jones remembers feeling terrified when his grandfather locked him in the basement, this view contends that Jones is, at present, the same person who had the earlier experience of terror. How one knows that he is the same person today as he was yesterday or fifteen years ago is by being able to remember what happened to him then. And how he knows that some other person is the same person today as he was yesterday or fifteen years ago is by finding out that the second person can remember what happened to him then.

There are two points where this view is vulnerable. First, it would have us believe that a person who is not able to remember what he did at some time and place in the past is *not* the same person as he was then. But this, surely, is a mistake. A person suffering from temporary or permanent amnesia, for example, does not, on that account alone, cease to be the same person that he was before the onset of the amnesia. True, he cannot remember who he is or what he did. But we would not conclude, for that reason alone, that he therefore is not the same person he was before the amnesia set in. But, secondly, this view is so far from providing us with a way to determine whether persons retain their identity that it actually *assumes* that they do. For in order for a person actually to remember something that *he* did, *he* had to do it; he (and not someone else) had to be the person who did what he remembers. Otherwise, he could not remember that *he* did it. Thus, the view that memory alone is the key to the question of personal identity cannot withstand critical objections.

The second view to be considered here appears to fare no better. If we seriously pause to introspect upon our inner lives, it seems, as Hume argued, that we never come across something that is unchanging, let alone spiritual. We never come across any *thing* that is named by the words 'I' or 'self'. Rather, we become aware that we always are aware of something *other than* ourselves—say, some sensation of hot or cold or some idea of fear or loneliness. We can never catch ourself, so to speak, all by itself. And because we never can come to be aware of it all by itself, as a separate, unchanging, immaterial entity, then we really have no right, Hume contends, to speak as though we really do exist in this fashion. So far as we can know, in fact, we do not. And so far as one can say any thing positive at all about himself, it is that he is a particular bundle of perceptions. That is, he is that ever-expanding series of things he is and has been aware of. As for his identity, therefore, who he is constantly changes. Indeed, he changes with the acquisition of every new experience, so that, strictly speaking, he is not the same person at different times, if, at these different times, he finds himself having different experiences. So argues Hume, and many thinkers have found his criticism sound. Yet many of these same thinkers, and Hume himself, have expressed dissatisfaction with Hume's positive account of the self. They declare it leaves unexplained how one person's perceptions constitute an individual "bundle" distinct from any other individual's.

Now, this is not the place to try to solve the problem of personal identity. We only want to show that there is such a problem and that it appears to be particularly serious for those holding the view that persons are minds. That this much is true should be apparent by now. And it also should be apparent that this problem poses special difficulties for those who believe that the person survives his body's death. For if memory is not a complete or final basis upon which to found the idea of personal identity; and if, further, Hume's reports of his introspection are sound, then we might well ask how we can avoid Hume's own positive account of the self—a position that, if true, seems to commit us to the view that the person does *not* and *cannot* survive his body's death.

For to speak of survival here is to imply that the person continues to have experiences after the death of his body. But if he does continue to have such experiences in the afterlife, then, given Hume's position, this afterlife person is a *different* person than the person who died. The *same* person, therefore, could not survive. Thus, those who would work out a thorough basis upon which to ground their belief in the survival of the person after death must show how Hume's criticisms can be met and why his positive account of the self is deficient. Once again, however, these are questions we cannot hope to settle here. But that does not mean that we can pretend that they do not exist.

THE PROBLEM OF INTERACTION

A second, no less difficult problem that Descartes leaves unsolved is *the problem of interaction*. This problem is simple enough to state. It consists in first pointing out what appear to be plain facts of experience. On the one hand, we are all familiar with a variety of cases where what happens in or to our bodies seems to cause us to become mentally aware of various things.

For example, if we step on a tack, we experience pain; if we open our eyes, we become aware of many features of our perceptual environment. Being physically tired can have effects on such mental dispositions as patience and cooperativeness. Various drugs can bring people mentally "up" or "down." Stimulating or removing portions of the brain can have interesting and often dramatic effects upon a person's behavior and personality. From a common-sense point of view, therefore, it certainly appears that the body interacts causally with the mind—that is, that what happens to the body, as well as what state the body is in, often causes various experiences or states of mind.

And the reverse seems also true. The state of one's mind, as well as the experiences one has, seem often to cause various things to happen to his body. For example, there are numerous reported cases of psychosomatic illnesses, including such things as paralysis or blindness, that have no apparent physical cause but that rest instead on what appear to be certain mental causes of which the sufferer is unaware.

Less out of the ordinary but no less real, moreover, are those cases where we are mentally aware of making decisions to do certain things and then find these decisions carried out by our physical movement. During a lecture, for example, a student might hesitate to raise his hand; he might deliberate about doing so a good deal; but then suppose he does decide to do it. Then what happens is that his hand is raised, which seems to be a clear case of the mind's causing the body to move. That is, what seems to occur here, as in countless other cases, is that first a certain event occurs in the mind—namely, a decision is reached—and then this event causes another event to occur in or to the body—in this case, the raising of the hand. So, judged exclusively from the standpoint of our beliefs, prior to any philosophical reflection about them, all of us would allow that causal interaction does take place between what we call the mind and the body, and that it works both ways. Sometimes the mind causes the body to do certain things. And sometimes the body causes the mind to be aware of certain other things. Such is the view called *two-way interactionism*.

The problem dualists encounter with two-way interactionism sets the tone of the problem they must encounter for any type of interaction. For if, as the dualist maintains, the mind is immaterial, how can it cause anything to happen to something that is material? And if, as the dualist maintains, the body is material, how can it cause anything to happen to the mind, which, according to the dualist, is immaterial?

The sense of inexplicable mystery that many have detected at this juncture may be heightened if we pause to consider some of the implications of treating the mind as immaterial and the body as material. For notice that, if the mind is thought to be immaterial, then we cannot suppose that it is located at some point within the body. To locate it within the body would entail assigning it a position in space, and this no mind could have, if, as dualists speculate, minds are immaterial. Indeed, no mind can be located anywhere in space, so to ask "Where is Jones's mind located?" is not an intelligible question. Bodies can be located, to be sure, but not minds.

Now we have an extraordinary suggestion being made here—namely, that a mind, which is not physical and not in space, can cause the body, which is physical and is in space, to do certain things. And we also have the suggestion being made that this can work in the opposite direction— that is, the body, which is material and in space, can cause the mind, which is neither, to have certain experiences. And the question we must ask is, how intelligible and credible are these suggestions? Does a dualist theory of substance that allows for two-way interaction really make our ordinary experience intelligible? Or does it render this experience wholly mysterious and inexplicable—and, if so, then ought we not to abandon a dualist theory of substance altogether?

These questions are difficult and philosophers do not agree on how to answer them. It is fair to say, however, that most thinkers believe that dualists come to grief over the problem of interaction if they (1) concede that interaction takes place and (2) believe that some explanation of how such interaction can occur should be given. For it is very dubious that a reasonable explanation of the kind required can be given.

OCCASIONALISM

The most promising attempt to do so fails conspicuously. This is the view called *occasionalism*. According to this view, neither the human mind nor the body, considered by itself, is capable of causing something to happen in or to the other. What happens instead is that certain occurrences in the one present the occasion for *God*'s causing something else to happen in the other. For example, when a person decides to get out of bed, what causes his body to throw off the covers is not his mind, which is incapable of causing any such thing, but the intervention of God, who, being omnipotent, can do much more than can the limited minds of men.

Occasionalism is a theory developed by some of Descartes's followers, particularly the French philosopher Nicolas Malebranche (1638–1715). It never attracted many adherents, and rightly so, for all it seems to do is replace one mysterious idea with another one. For if it is mysterious how an allegedly immaterial substance, the human mind, can cause certain things to happen in and to the human body, and vice versa, is it not just as mysterious to try to explain it by the intervention of another immaterial, omnipotent substance—God? How does God intervene? And how does the intervention make any more intelligible the fact that mind and matter do interact?

Even if these difficulites could be overcome, a more fundamental one remains–the fact that we do not seem to be entitled to claim to know God exists. We do not seem able to prove his existence, either a posteriori or a priori—which presents a most serious obstacle for occasionalism. For if the upholders of this theory are unable to prove the existence of that upon which they rest their entire explanation of interaction, namely,

God, then it seems reasonable to conclude that their speculation must remain just that—speculation, which, however sincerely intended and devoutly expressed, falls short of the goal of knowledge that philosophers, occasionalists included, set before themselves.

PARALLELISM

There is another way the dualist can try to meet the objections arising from the idea of interaction. This alternative affirms that minds and bodies are metaphysically distinct but denies that the mental and the physical ever interact causally. The German philosopher Gottfried Wilhelm von Leibnitz (1646–1716) originated this idea, and we should take a few moments to indicate how and why he developed it.

Leibnitz developed this position because he thought that no dualist can explain the causal interaction between mind and matter, if such interaction exists. Thus, if the mental really were to interact with the physical, as it *seems* to, then some account of the mind and body *other than* the one set forth by the dualists would, according to Leibnitz, be required to make this interaction intelligible. However, if there is no interaction between the mental and the physical, then dualism cannot be faulted for its failure to be able to explain it. If there really is no interaction, then there really is no "problem" of interaction either, and dualism can escape what appears to be one of its most serious objections.

However, no one can deny that the mental and the physical certainly *seem* to interact. A person's decisions certainly seem to cause his body to move in certain ways; a pin jabbed into his finger certainly seems to cause the sensation of pain in his mind. And Leibnitz, himself, certainly does not want to deny that such appearances exist. But he insists that that is all that does exist—namely, the *appearance* of causal interaction. And he denies that these appearances constitute the reality.

To make this clear, suppose we ask what we are aware of, when, for example, we make a decision to raise our arm and then observe that our body behaves in the appropriate way. According to Leibnitz's thinking, what we are aware of is, first, the occurrence of one event (namely, the mental event of deciding to do something) and, second, the occurrence of another event (namely, the physical event of our arm's moving).

Now, suppose that we discover, further, that these two events are constantly conjoined, that every time we make the decision to raise our arm, the appropriate movement of our body follows. Are we committed, on these grounds alone, to saying that our decisions *cause* our arm to move? Leibnitz answers negatively. Just because two things are constantly conjoined does not prove that one *causes* the other. For example, suppose we set two clocks so that, on the hour, whenever *A*'s alarm would stop buzzing, *B*'s alarm would begin. At one o'clock, then, *A*'s alarm would ring, then stop, and then *B*'s alarm would begin. And the same would happen at two o'clock, and at three, and so on. In other words, the two events are constantly conjoined. But would we conclude that *A* *caused* *B* to ring? Hardly. For us to conclude that *A* caused *B* to ring, we would need to become convinced of a great deal more than the fact that a constant conjunction of events holds true.

So then, Leibnitz argues, the same must be true in the case of the cases of alleged causal interaction between the mind and the body. In order to conclude that the one causes the other to do certain things, we need to know more than that there is a constant conjunction of mental and physical events. However, since Leibnitz thinks this is all that we can know about mental and physical events, it follows, he believes, that we do *not* know that the mind and the body causally interact.

Indeed, the analogy of the two clocks presents us with a dramatically different alternative. For suppose that our minds and bodies stand to one another in the same way as the two clocks. Then whenever a certain "buzz" goes off in our minds (say, we decide to raise our arms), what follows is that the appropriate "buzz" goes off in our bodies (namely, our arm moves upward). And whenever a certain other "buzz" goes off in our bodies (say, a pin is stuck into our fingers), another appropriate "buzz" goes off in our minds (namely, we experience pain.) Thus, it is possible to conceive of the mind and body as two distinct kinds of substance which, although they appear to interact causally, never do so, but run, instead, on parallel courses. They are perfectly synchronized. They come into the world, indeed, in a state of preestablished harmony, events in the one seeming always to be appropriate to what transpires in the other.

This view of Leibnitz's, which is called *parallelism* or *the doctrine of preestablished harmony,* deserves to be mentioned for two reasons. First, it gives a particularly dramatic example of how imaginative philosophical thinking can be; it lets us see how, without abandoning the discipline that philosophy requires, our thinking can soar well above the commonplace. Second, it represents a graphic illustration of just how serious the problem of interactionism appears to be for the dualist. So damaging is this problem, according to Leibnitz, that the only way dualism can be preserved is by denying that causal interaction takes place, a move so drastic that few philosophers have been willing to follow Leibnitz's thinking.

Now, parallelism is not only obviously at odds with common sense, it also stands in need of an explanation of its own. That is, it is appropriate to ask why the mind and the body are in such perfect harmony, as Leibnitz alleges they are. And given the disposition of some philosophers, including Descartes, to call upon God to explain what otherwise must appear to the human mind as mysterious, we should not be surprised that it is God to whom Leibnitz defers for the explanation of the preestablished harmony between mind and matter. Once again, however, this maneuver cannot constitute a credible explanation. If God's existence cannot be proven, then it is sheer speculation to contend that he has arranged the world in the way parallelism requires, and such speculation can never constitute the knowledge that philosophy seeks.

In sum, the problem of interaction represents a serious difficulty for dualists. Attempts to deny that interaction between mind and matter occurs, such as Leibnitz's, appear to be deficient, whereas attempts to explain how interaction does occur, such as the explanation proffered by the occasionalists, appear to lack credibility. And this is why dualists do seem necessarily to face the dilemma of not being able to explain interaction, if it does occur, on the one hand, and, on the other, of not being able to persuade us that there is no problem of interaction because there is no (real) interaction (but only the appearance of the same).

THE PROBLEM OF OTHER MINDS

One final problem that has occupied philosophers since Descartes is *the problem of other minds*. Briefly, this is the problem of how any individual can be entitled to claim to know that minds in addition to his own exist, or, alternatively, that there are other conscious beings in the universe. The contention that there are such beings, as Descartes pointed out, is not an indubitable truth and so appears to need evidence to support it. So the problem of how an individual can know there are other minds besides his own becomes the question, "What is the evidence by which an individual is justified in affirming that other minds exist?"

Like some other philosophical problems we have encountered, this one might strike us as silly. No one, we might think, ever really doubts there are other minds. And possibly this is true (but what about Descartes?) Still, to be told that no one ever really doubts this is not to be told anything whatever about how we are presumed to be entitled to maintain it, and the interesting philosophical questions begin to emerge only after we have gotten past our initial reluctance to do some thinking here to the deep and abiding perplexities that this intitial reluctance often conceals from us.

The problem of other minds is a particularly serious problem for a dualist. For what is it that one observes about other people? Quite generally, he can say he observes their behavior—how they walk and talk, what they laugh and cry about, when they are angry and when kind, when they do silly or stupid things, when they behave wisely or intelligently, and so on. Accordingly, evidence for the claim to know that there are other minds seems to be limited to one's observation of the way certain bodies behave—namely, the bodies of human beings. But, now, the difficulties for the dualist should be obvious. For the mind of a person, given the dualist's position, is immaterial, and it is far from clear how one's observing the physical behavior of a person could provide him with evidence for claiming to know that, in addition to the physical bodies they have, people also have nonphysical minds or souls. The nonphysical, immaterial aspects of being human must, it seems, remain forever beyond the ken of one's powers of observation.

A natural response to this line of reasoning is to argue as follows. Whenever one experiences something—say, pain—he behaves in certain characteristic ways—for example, he winces or moans or cries. One sees that, in his own case, the consciousness of pain, on the one hand, and, on the other, his "pain behavior" are constantly conjoined. Therefore, it seems only reasonable to conclude that whenever another person behaves in an analogous way, one can conclude that the other, too, is aware of the sensation of pain, that he also is a conscious being and has a mind. Thus, although one may not be able directly to observe another person's mind, he can, so this argument contends, infer the existence of that mind from the similarity of behavior with his own.

This argument, referred to as *the argument from analogy,* represents a natural way of thinking. Not a sound way. On the contrary, it falls a victim to a grave objection. Notice, first, that is rests on a wholly unsatisfactory assumption about the concept of evidence. To see this, let us ask ourselves what must be the case if we are to be entitled to view our knowledge that one thing, (a), is the case as evidence for the truth of our claim that another thing, (b), is the case. There are two possible ways in which this may be so. First, if we could establish that *every time* we know that a is the case we also discover or find out that b is the case, then we would be entitled to claim to know that b is the case the next time we found out that a is the case. Second, if we discover that there is not a universal but a *statistical* correlation between a's being the case and b's being the case—for example, if 80 percent of the time, when a is the case, b is the case—then we could argue that, although knowing that a is the case does not *guarantee* that b is the case, it provides us with very good evidence for thinking that it probably is so.

Now, whichever of these two views we take, what is to be noted is that in both cases knowing that a is the case can count as evidence for the truth of the claim that b is the case if and only if we are able to *establish that b is the case* and then see how its being the case is correlated with a's being the case—that is, see whether the two are correlated universally or statistically. For example, that a person speaks with a certain accent provides us with evidence that he is from the South. But that a person *is* from the South can be established independently of discovering any fact about his accent, and it is only because we can do this and then correlate people's way of speaking with their place of origin that we can count their accent as evidence of their birthplace.

Let us apply these ideas to the case at hand. Suppose we ask whether knowing that people behave in certain ways could provide us with any evidence for the truth of the proposition 'They are aware of pain' or 'They are experiencing pain'. The answer here is that such knowledge *could* provide us with evidence *if we already knew* that people actually were aware of pain and *if we already knew* that there was a statistical or universal connection between their being aware of pain and their behaving in certain ways.

However, suppose that we already did know this. Then it would be irrelevant to present the argument from analogy "to show" that we do know this. If we already did know this, what could be the point of "proving" it? Accordingly, the only way the argument from analogy could have any significance is if we do *not* already know that there are other minds capable of experiencing pain (and not just other bodies that behave in certain ways).

However, if we are not supposed to know this, then, given what we have just said about the concept of evidence, it is clear that the way people behave could not provide us with any evidence for the claim that they are aware of something. If we do not know that they are aware of certain things, when they behave in certain ways, then we can never reasonably argue that they are aware of these things on the strength of the "evidence" that they behave in certain ways. Accordingly, the argument from analogy must face the dilemma of being either superfluous (which it would be, if we already know that there are other minds that experience, say, the sensation of pain) or unsound (which it would be, if we do not know this). Whichever alternative is taken, therefore, this argument cannot provide us with a viable solution to the problem of our knowledge of other minds.

How, then, do we know that there are other minds? Or do we really know this? These are difficult questions, and it is because attempts to answer them often seem to fare no better than the argument from analogy that some philosophers have been prepared to deny that we have such knowledge. And many of these same philosophers have gone even further than this. They have joined their scepticism about other minds with their scepticism about the existence and character of the "external world"— that is, the world outside of direct awareness. Out of this union they have constructed the position known as *solipsism*, which is the view that the only thing one can know is just what he is consciously aware of at any given moment.

It is a paradox of the history of reflective thought that Descartes, who understood the potentially lethal effects of solipsism and set out to show its deficiencies, nevertheless set the stage for its emergence. For to deny to Descartes his reliance upon God, and to concede to him the soundness of the *cogito,* has seemed to many thinkers to be tantamount to saddling Descartes himself with the solipsist's yoke.

We cannot examine further the problem of other minds, but we have said enough to show that there is a problem and why. The problem is not unique to the dualist, but it is a special problem for any one who identifies what it is to be a *person* with having a mind. For then the problem of how we know, if we do, that there are other minds in the universe, is equivalent to the problem of how we know, if we do, that there are other *people* in it. It is, then, as Descartes clearly sees, the problem of how I know that I am not completely *alone* in the universe.

The dualist has a lot of unfinished business—such as the problems of interaction, identity, and other minds. The credibility of dualism clearly depends on the success of its spokesman in addressing themselves to these and other problems. To the extent they are unable to do so, dualism's claim to truth is unsupported—and the reasonableness of the belief in the survival of the person after his body's death also is seriously undermined. To take seriously the challenge to think about the problems involved in being human, therefore, since it extends even to thinking carefully about the problem of life after death, imposes on each of us the task of thinking through dualism's credentials. And this, in turn, commits us to reflecting further on the problems we have become acquainted with above.

ARGUMENTS FOR SURVIVAL

Considering the importance of the belief in personal survival after death, it may come as a surprise to discover that relatively few arguments have been advanced to support it. But then, as we have seen, enormous philosophical difficulties must be met and overcome before one can even begin to consider the question of actual survival—problems such as what it is to be a person, how persons retain their identity, whether minds interact with bodies. And it is easy to understand how a philosopher might be obliged to spend the greater part of his time and energy on these more basic problems, so that the question of actual survival might get relatively short shrift. Or it may be that there simply are very few arguments that *can* be advanced for survival.

Even with so few arguments, we will have to be selective. We will not be able to consider all the arguments developed over the ages, but only two of them—the moral argument and the argument from psychic phenomena. Among the arguments that have been advanced for personal survival, these two must rank as among the most persuasive. But how persuasive they are remains to be seen.

THE MORAL ARGUMENT

The moral argument for personal survival is set forth by the philosopher Kant. What Kant endeavors to show is not that we are entitled to claim to *know* that we will survive death as persons, but that it is reasonable to *postulate* we will do so. In Kant's opinion, all our knowledge of what exists must be confirmed by sensory observation, so that he is, to this extent, an empiricist. But he also believes that there are synthetic propositions that can be known to be true a priori, which gives his thought a distinctively rationalistic character. In the case of personal survival, however, Kant maintains that, in this life, we cannot know whether we do or do not survive as persons, either a posteriori or a priori. There are no grounds, either empiricist or rationalist, he thinks, for claiming to have knowledge on this matter. But this fact, he contends, does not mean that to deny persons survive their bodily death is just as reasonable as to affirm that they do. It is more reasonable to postulate continued existence than to deny it, and the grounds for maintaining this are supplied, Kant thinks, by the presuppositions and implications of our beliefs about morality.

What, in particular, is there about our beliefs about morality that Kant thinks supports this contention? Principally, it is the idea that we have a continuing obligation to improve our character. That is, throughout our lifetime, we have, Kant thinks, the obligation to "perfect our will"— to bring ourselves ever closer to a point such that, when we have a choice between doing what is right or doing something else, we always do what is right because it is right.

Now, two points should be noted here. First, no human being ever is able to bring himself to such a high state of moral perfection during his earthly life. All men fall short of the ideal, to some degree. But, second, if it is true, as Kant insists, that we do have the obligation to perfect our will, then it follows that we must believe that we *can* do so. This is a special instance of the general truth, mentioned in the preceding chapter, that 'ought' implies 'can'. We cannot believe that we ought to perfect our will and at the same time deny that we can do so.

We already have noted, however, that no human being can perfect his will during his earthly life. So if our earthly death brought our life to its end, then it would follow that no human being could perfect his will— from which it would follow that no human being could have the obligation to do so either. Thus, in order for it even to be possible for us to fulfill the obligation to perfect our will, we must postulate that we go on living after the death of our bodies, and what we must suppose, minimally, about the afterlife, is that we will there have the opportunity to continue to act and develop toward the fulfillment of the ideal of moral perfection that, Kant thinks, it is the duty of every rational being to achieve. The survival of the person after the death of his body, in short, is, for Kant, a logically necessary condition of the individual's obligation to perfect his will.

DISPUTING THE MORAL ARGUMENT

This argument of Kant's can be attacked on a number of different grounds. One might argue that no one has *any* moral obligations, a view that, if true, would show that no one has the particular obligation to perfect his will. And if it could be shown that this latter claim is true, then one could argue that it is not reasonable to postulate as true whatever is necessary to make the obligation to perfect one's will possible.

Another argument is that the concept of action in general, and of moral action in particular, makes sense only for persons with bodies; that is, if an action must involve some bodily movement, it would be unintelligible to speak of "actions" we might perform in a future, disembodied world.

But the principal difficulty for the moral argument can be raised without denying the contention that we do have obligations and without questioning the intelligibility of speculating that persons sans bodies can perform actions. For the principal difficulty concerns whether we do have the obligation to perfect our will. It is on this point that Kant's argument seems most clearly and fundamentally to run aground. That it does so can be seen by considering the following points.

Suppose we do survive death and go on living and that, in this afterlife, we are able to act and, in particular, are able to do what is morally right or wrong. And let us suppose that at least some individuals grow closer to the ideal Kant sets before us; the will of these persons grows more perfect. Increasingly when they are faced with a moral choice, they do what is right because it is right and avoid doing what is wrong because it is wrong.

Now, let us ask whether, according to Kant, the will of any person will ever reach the state of total perfection. Let us ask, in other words, whether the will of any person will ever reach a state so that it *always* wills what is right, because it is right and *never* wills what is wrong, because it is wrong. Kant's answer is that no human being can have a perfect will, only God, or a being whose will is holy. This is true a priori, according to Kant. Thus, says Kant, the road each person must travel to the goal of total perfection is never-ending, and the state of perfection any human being is able to attain must always fall short, to a greater or lesser degree, of the ideal set before us all.

But—and here we begin our critique of Kant's thinking on this point—if no person *can* achieve the goal of total perfection, how can it be reasonable to say that each person *ought* to achieve it? Quite clearly, it cannot be reasonable *if* the goal, by its very nature, is unrealizable, not only in this life but also in the next one (assuming there is a "next one").

But, now, if it is not reasonable to maintain that we have the obligation to perfect our wills, then it is not reasonable to postulate whatever seems necessary to make this obligation possible. And since continued existence after our bodily death is thought by Kant to be necessary, we must conclude that it is not reasonable to postulate, for the reasons Kant gives, that persons continue to live after the death of their bodies.

Nor will it do to reply here that we have the obligation *to try* to perfect our will. For although this obligation might be one that we can fulfill, and thus, to this extent, be unlike the alleged obligation to succeed in perfecting it, it would fail to provide any basis upon which to postulate continued existence after our bodily death. To try to perfect our wills, if this is an intelligible concept at all, is something we can do in this life; it is not necessary to postulate some future life to make possible the obligation to do so. In either case, therefore, Kant's moral argument must be judged to fail to show that it is more reasonable to postulate the immortality of the person than to deny this.

THE ARGUMENT FROM PSYCHIC PHENOMENA

Kant's moral argument is an example of an a priori argument for personal immortality. In his argument Kant does not make any claim that could be confirmed by observation; instead, he makes a series of claims that, if true at all, must, he thinks, be true a priori. For example, the claim that 'ought' implies 'can' and the claim that we have an obligation to perfect our will are, Kant thinks, a priori truths. The argument we now shall turn to—the argument from psychic phenomena—is set forth on fundamentally different epistemological grounds. It tries to support the contention that persons survive their bodily death on a posteriori grounds. It attempts to show that some facts make the survival hypothesis certain or more probably true than the hypothesis that persons do not survive—and, as the name implies, the "facts" have to do with psychic phenomena.

The expression "psychic phenomena" is used to cover a wide range of experiences, including cases of extrasensory perception (ESP). In cases of extrasensory perception, what happens is that a person apparently acquires factual information by mental operations that do not involve the physical senses. Theoretically considered, then, the problems that confront the researcher in psychical research are (1) to establish that such perception does take place, (2) to distinguish between distinguishable varieties or kinds of such phenomena, and (3) to develop a network of concepts that are sufficient to explain the occurrence of the phenomena in question. Of the three, problems (1) and (2) have met with the most success. There now appears to be quite good scientific evidence for the belief that extra-sensory perception is a genuine phenomenon, and considerable progress has been made toward completing the task of systematically classifying its varieties. As for the third problem, however, much yet remains to be done, and there is at present no commonly accepted hypothesis that explains how what takes place actually does so.

The principle varieties of ESP are telepathy and clairvoyance. *Telepathy* is the name given to thought transference by apparently nonphysical means. Most often, in ordinary life, one person conveys his thoughts to another by using some physical means—for example, his voice, a letter, a code. In telepathy, thought is transferred from a "sender" to a "receiver" without the use of any obvious physical mechanism. *Clairvoyance* is the name given to the ability to know various facts without any apparent use of the physical senses *and* without this information being conveyed by some other mind, as in telepathy.

The difference between telepathy and clairvoyance can be illustrated by contrasting two experiments, both using cards. Suppose, in the first case, that we arrange to have one person look at a series of twenty cards for a certain specified period of time—say, thirty seconds each—and that, while this person looks at each card and thinks about it, we invite another person who is not able to see the cards, to record the identity of the card that comes into his mind. Then, if the second person's success at recording the correct identity of the cards is repeatedly above what chance would lead us to suppose, we could theorize that he had received his correct information telepathically. For our second experiment, suppose that we have just a single person and the same deck of twenty cards, turned face down. And suppose that we ask him to think about each card, record what he thinks it is, and then pass on to the next one, until he completes all twenty. In this case no other person would be aware of the correct identity of the cards, so no other person could "send" this information. Now, suppose that the person performing the experiment repeatedly scores above what chance would lead us to suppose. Then we could speculate that he is clairvoyant; that is, he appears to have the ability to know things without using his physical senses and without coming to know these things tele-pathically.

The two examples we have given can be used to illustrate a very interesting problem in psychical research. For although it is true that, conceptually speaking, telepathy and clairvoyance are distinct, there is no experiment that can test for the existence of telepathy to the exclusion of clairvoyance. For example, in our first experiment, although two persons were involved, it is unclear that we can or should conclude from this that, whenever repeated success is found, it is due to successful telepathic communication. Why may it not be due entirely to the "receiver's" *clairvoyant* capacities? In fact, experiments have been conducted that show that the presence of a "sender" makes no statistical difference to the "receiver's" record of success; that is, those persons who are successful under the guidelines of the first experiment above are just as successful under the guidelines of the second experiment. And this suggests that, so far as success is concerned, clairvoyance explains just as much as telepathy. In any event, reflection on the two experiments we have discussed should make clear why it is very difficult to devise an experiment that tests for telepathy to the exclusion of clairvoyance.

Nonetheless, let us assume for the moment that telepathic communication does exist. How is it relevant to the question of personal survival after death? It is relevant because of alleged communication with the dead —where living persons claim to have come into contact with the spirits of the departed. No doubt many of these cases are fraudulent, but not all of them. Persons said to be gifted at communicating with the dead are called *mediums,* and though many of these persons operate because of the gullibility of other people, some mediums have proven themselves to be quite skilled even under the strictest of controls and before discriminating, intelligent judges. So there is no reasonable way to dismiss mediumship a priori. Still, we must ask just what evidence for survival the medium's apparent success really does provide.

To make the problem clearer, imagine that we go to a medium in an effort to establish communication between ourselves and a deceased friend, Ted, a person who during his earthly life was not known by the medium. Suppose that, after some preliminary meetings, the medium begins, he says, "to communicate with Ted." The medium is able to tell us very much about Ted—his size, color of hair and eyes, his particular interests and aversions, and his father's middle initial. Would not the medium's success show that he really had communicated with Ted? And would not this show that, despite his earthly death, Ted was still living? For how, after all, could the medium communicate with him if he was *not* alive and sending his thoughts?

DISPUTING THE ARGUMENT

These inferences are very natural but not very sound. Indeed, the very thing that makes them appear to be in order—namely, the presumed reality of telepathy—actually serves to show how premature it would be to reason in this way. For *if* telepathy does occur, then it certainly can occur between the medium and those very persons who come to the medium to make use of his services. Thus, the information our medium imparts to us about Ted could just as well have been perceived telepathically not from Ted's mind but from *ours*. In fact, given what we know about the world, even including the world of ESP, this latter inference would be the more reasonable of the two, so that however much success a medium might have in conveying known information to us about a person who has died, it will always be more reasonable to conclude that it is obtained from some persons presently alive on the earth than from some other person whose earthly life has come to an end.

But suppose, someone might argue, that we find out something we did not already know—say, where Ted hid some money. This cannot be explained by saying the medium read *our* minds. This is true. But does it follow from this that the medium therefore must be credited with reading Ted's? Not clearly. Perhaps the medium has succeeded in reading *someone else's* mind. The fact that no one else is present at the séance we attend is irrelevant, since one of the things that has been established is that distance makes no difference in telepathy; that is, two persons can be separated by any amount of distance and still communicate telepathically. Thus, it could be that someone else who knew Ted, but who is unaware of the séance, knew of his hiding the money, and that all the medium has succeeded in doing is receiving this information telepathically from this other person.

But suppose, it might be argued, that it could be shown that no one else could have known what the medium learns. Two problems confront us. First, it is unclear that there ever has been a case where a medium has learned what no else could have known. So this argument assumes a great deal of what it would be obliged to prove. But second, and more important, it would have to be established that the medium could not have acquired the information by *clairvoyance*. For if the medium acquired the information in this way, then nothing whatever follows from this about Ted's continued existence. The fact, assuming that it is a fact, that the medium acquired this information by means of clairvoyance is equally compatible with the propositions 'Ted continues to live' and 'Ted lives no longer'. As such, it cannot be supposed to count as evidence for the former to the exclusion of the latter.

There are, then, severe difficulties in the attempt to base the belief in personal survival after death upon what we know about psychic phenomena, including ESP. To be sure, other phenomena are relevant here—for example, cases of alleged apparitions or of poltergeists or spirits able to move physical objects. And both in fairness to the complexities of the problem before us and in deference to the richness of the world itself, we should go to these phenomena with an open mind, willing to be convinced of all that seems rationally compelling. But this does not mean that we should approach these phenomena without the assistance of our critical faculties. This does not mean that we should accept what is averred simply because it is "interesting" or "more fun than science." The obligation of a rational man to think rationally applies even here, and this is why, despite the allure of the paranormal, we should conclude, for the reasons given above, that no one has yet succeeded in justifying the belief in the survival of the person after his earthly death by appealing to psychic phenomena.

IS THE PROBLEM OF SURVIVAL
A PSEUDOPROBLEM?

That careful thinkers have devoted considerable attention to the problem of personal survival after death does not guarantee that it is a genuine cognitive issue, any more than that the sentence "People will survive as persons after their bodily death" is a complete sentence in the indicative mood guarantees that it can be used to express a proposition. What we need to ask ourselves, then, is whether there are good reasons for believing that the problem is a genuine cognitive issue, given the criterion the positivist employs for determining this—namely, the verification principle. We need to ask, in short, whether we can conceive of what it would be like to verify that we continue to exist as persons after the death of our body.

This is an issue about which there is no unanimity of opinion. However, it does seem that we can conceive of what it would take to verify this contention. But it also seems that, when we try to make clear what would be sufficient to do so, we come to see that the logic of the problem has interesting implications for the verification principle itself. And we also come to see that the conceivability of verifying that there is life after death requires that we make certain quite fundamental assumptions about what it is to be a person, assumptions that need further clarification and justification. If we can come to understand why this is so, we will have reached a not inappropriate place to end our initial inquiry into the problem of life after death.

Let us ask, then, whether we can conceive of what it would be like to verify that we continue to exist after the death of our bodies. Now, clearly, in order for this to be conceivable, we must be able to conceive of having certain experiences after our bodily death. For if we were to imagine that we had *no* experiences, then, of course, it would follow that we could not have any experiences that verified our continued existence. Thus, a prior question we must consider is whether we can conceive of having *any* experience after the death of our bodies. And the answer to this question does appear to be that we can.

True, without our bodies it does seem to be inconceivable that we might have, say, visual or auditory experiences. For how could we have experiences of these types if we had neither eyes nor ears? The very idea appears to be inconceivable, so that, in general, it seems, we should maintain that we cannot conceive of having experiences after the death of our body that, by their very nature, require that we have a body and that it be alive and functioning.

Granting this much, however, it still seems possible to conceive of having experiences after the death of our body. Consider, in particular, experiences of the kind discussed in the previous section—namely, telepathy and clairvoyance. Experiences of this type are said not to rely on the use of our physical senses. As such, it certainly appears to be *conceivable* that we might have experiences of these types even after the death of our body. And there are other types of experience that likewise seem to be possible for a disembodied being. Certain desires, such as our desire for knowledge and wisdom, for example, are not obviously dependent on our having a body, nor is our ability to remember what occurred in the past blatantly inconceivable without the body.

But still the question remains whether we also can conceive of what it would be like to verify that we *have* continued to live after our body's death. That is, what, in particular (if anything), would count as verifying that we have gone on living after the death of our body? Now, this question seems to be more difficult than the question of whether we can conceive of having experiences after our body dies. But at least certain things are clear here.

First, for us to know that we have survived the death of our bodies, there must be *some* way we could know that our bodies have *died*. Now, given that we cannot even conceive of having experiences after the death of our body that require the use of our physical organs of sense, how we could come to know this, if at all, would necessarily be by means of some extrasensory method—for example, telepathically. Thus, to say that we can conceive of verifying that we continue to go on living after the death of our body presupposes that we can conceive of what it would be like to know telepathically, say, that our body has died. And this means that we must be able to conceive of finding this out, not by making one or another physical observations, but rather by receiving the thoughts of another person's mind to the effect that we have died (physically). So the question we need to ask is whether this is conceivable? And the answer to this question, once again, seems to be that it is.

Assuming, that is, that telepathic communication here on earth represents a genuine way of coming to know various things, then there seems to be no reason to deny that it could conceivably continue to be a genuine way of coming to know various things in the furture, even in a disembodied world. And there also seems to be no reason to deny, a priori, that one of the things we might come to know, in this way, is that our body died. Now, assuming that this is the case, and assuming, further, that we can conceive of having other types of experience after the death of our body, then we have, it seems, justified the claim that we *can* conceive of verifying that we do go on living after our body dies. For one way in which we might verify this is by satisfying two conditions: (1) coming to know telepathically that our body has died, and (2) yet continuing to have experiences of various kinds. It seems reasonable to conclude, therefore, that we *can* conceive of verifying our continued existence after the death of our body, which, if true, implies that the problem of the survival of the person after death is not a pseudoproblem. And what this implies is that the thought that we and others have extended to this problem has been directed to a problem of genuine intellectual interest.

But one further point should be mentioned here. We have argued that we can conceive of verifying the proposition 'I will go on existing after the death of my body'. In doing so, however, we have not argued that we can conceive of verifying this proposition by means of our *physical* senses. On the contrary, we have denied that this method of verification is conceivable. Accordingly, we have observed the spirit but not the letter of the positivist's verification principle. For the positivist would have us believe that an issue is an empirical or factual issue if and only if it can be resolved, at least conceivably, by means of our physical senses. If, however, the argument just given is sound, we have a case where verification is conceivable *without* the use of the physical senses. And what this implies, if it is true, is that the positivist is mistaken when he contends that a sentence can be used to express an empirical proposition if and only if what it is used to assert can be verified by means of our physical senses. And once this point is made (assuming that it is made on reasonable grounds), we can see, once again, that positivism does not provide us with a completely satisfactory basis upon which to do our thinking about what is and what is not known, or about what is and what is not knowable.

IS MAN IMMORTAL?

If the preceding is sound, we may answer the question "Is man immortal?" as follows. First, we may say that the question poses a genuine question; that is, it is either true or it is false that the individual survives the death of his body. This we are entitled to maintain because we have argued that we can conceive of verifying the proposition 'I have continued to live despite the fact that my body has died'. And this should satisfy any reasonable criterion of what constitutes a genuine problem, in spite of the fact that it does involve a way of knowing—namely, extrasensory knowledge—that positivists may be expected to question. Moreover the question of the conceivability of personal survival has this important dimension: it is something that we can conceive of verifying, if it is true that we survive, but that we cannot conceive of falsifying, if it is false. For if it is *false* that we survive, then, of course, it also is false that we will continue to have experiences and be conscious after our bodies die, which means that we could not possibly have those experiences that would be necessary if we were to falsify the proposition 'I have continued to live despite the death of my body'. Thus, contrary to what we argued in Chapter 4, a proposition may be empirical and *not* be falsifiable. At least this is a possibility that deserves future consideration.

Still, is there any good reason to believe that we actually will continue to live after the death of our bodies? Our answer here, it seems, must be no. Those arguments we have examined that purport to show that it is true or reasonable to maintain that we survive have been found wanting. True, we have not examined all the possible or actual arguments that attempt to support the claim that we will survive. Nevertheless, those we have examined fail, and until we are presented with any argument that does not do so, it seems reasonable to maintain that we know of no good reason to believe we will survive.

But perhaps a stronger case than this can be made for denying the reasonableness of the belief in survival. To do so, recall, first, that the claim that we can conceive of our surviving the death of our body involves a very important assumption about what persons are—namely, that a person is his mind. For if it is the *person* who would have the nonsensory experiences that would verify his survival, then this person cannot in any way be identified with his body, which has died. Accordingly, the conceivability of personal survival after death does presuppose that a person is his mind.

But, though it seems *conceivable* that this is what a person is—that is, the proposition 'A person is his mind' is not a contradiction—serious difficulties still stand in the way of showing that this proposition is *actually* true. Some of these difficulties were mentioned above. For example, the problem of interaction must raise its ugly head in the course of any dualist's attempt to show that this proposition is true, and that problem appears to be rationally insurmountable, given dualism's presuppositions. Of course, if we were to maintain that our bodies do not *really* exist and that, indeed, the whole of the physical or material universe is unreal, then we would have no problem of interaction. But neither would we be dualists. Besides, to deny the reality of the physical universe is a great price to pay for making personal survival after death more plausible, and it clearly is not a price that dualists themselves have been prepared to pay. Short, then, of such a denial, and given the dualistic view of reality that has played such a vital role in the history of Western thought, it does seem to be more reasonable to deny, than it is to affirm, that persons survive the death of their bodies. It is to this conclusion that our argument seems to lead us, but it is also a conclusion that we should rethink again as future experience and interests allow. Certainly the last word has not been said here. Nor even thought.

FOR FURTHER READING

Flew, A.G.N., ed., *Body, Mind and Death.* New York: Macmillan, 1964, Best collection of essays on topics discussed above. Lucid, helpful introduction. Extensive bibliography that any serious student of the problems of personal survival after death will find most useful.

The Encyclopedia of Philosophy. "Immortality," by Flew, sketches same ideas as does his book. See also "Personal Identity," "Mind-Body," and "Substance."

Other particularly noteworthy books are as follows:

Broad, C. D., *The Mind and Its Place in Nature.* London: Routledge & Kegan Paul, 1925.

Ducasse, C. J., *Nature, Mind and Death.* La Salle, Ill. Open Court, 1951.

Flew, A. G. N., *A New Approach to Psychical Research.* London: Watts, 1953.

Hall, T. H., *The Spiritualist.* London: Duckworth, 1962.

James, William, *Human Immortality,* 2nd ed. Boston: Houghton Mifflin, 1917.

Rhine, J. B., *The Reach of the Mind.* New York: Sloane, 1947.

Ryle, Gilbert, *The Concept of Mind.* London: Hutchinson, 1949.

EXERCISES

1. Clarify what is meant by "the materialistic conception of man."
2. What is an astral body, and is it reasonable to believe that people have one?
3. Explain the two different views it is possible to take with respect to the idea of the resurrection of the body. In each case, is it reasonable to believe that our bodies will be resurrected?
4. What is meant by the idea of a substance? How do monistic theories of substance differ from pluralistic theories? How do idealism and dualism differ?

5. How does Descartes attempt to prove that he exists as a mind? How sound do you think his argument is?

6. Explain what is meant by "the problem of personal identity." Why is this problem an especially acute one for those who accept the view that a person is his mind?

7. Explain what is meant by "the problem of interaction." How do occasionalists attempt to avoid it? How do parallelists? How damaging do you think this problem is for dualism's claim to truth?

8. Explain what is meant by "the problem of other minds." How do you think this problem can be solved or avoided? In particular, how adequate do you think the so-called argument from analogy is?

9. Give a summary of Kant's moral argument for immortality. How sound do you think this argument is?

10. Give a brief summary of the so-called argument from psychic phenomena. How adequate do you think this argument is?

Afterword:
Retrospect and Prospect

It is time now to collect our thoughts and see what we have learned about philosophy. And it is also the occasion to look ahead and see what remains to be done.

LOOKING BACK

We began this book by asking for a definition of the discipline of philosophy, noting the difficulty in doing so, but defining it nonetheless. Enough has been said now to enable us to begin to appraise the adequacy of our definition. How adequate it is, is a question that needs to be reexamined in the light of our growth as philosophers. Later on in this section, in fact, we will sketch one way in which our understanding of the definition might be challenged.

However, even if we were to agree that philosophy is the search for good arguments to support claims to knowledge made in or about ethics, metaphysics, and so on, we would have at most a superficial characterization of the discipline, and we might want to ask ourselves here, after having worked our way through three of philosophy's traditional problems, whether we cannot add to our characterization of philosophy—whether we cannot mention further characteristics of philosophical inquiry that, even if they are not definitive, are helpful in depicting the main tendencies of the discipline.

FEATURES OF PHILOSOPHICAL INQUIRY

One thing we have noticed is that problems that present themselves to the reflective mind have a tendency to dovetail, so that we find that questions about free will, say, are at crucial points related to questions about God's existence and attributes. Or the question about whether we are free and morally responsible seems to depend on what we as persons are conceived to be. Indeed, once we recognize that how we answer one philosophical question often has immediate consequences for how we might answer certain others, we begin to sense why it is so difficult to bring philosophical inquiry to a close. The direct implications of any given philosophical question are not always immediately obvious. To determine them requires a good deal of thinking. Moreover, these direct implications have consequences of their own, and these, too, have further consequences. To trace these consequences, accordingly, is itself an absorbing and uncompromising task. In addition, we also need to ask whether what our answers imply is true or not. For if we should discover that a position of ours implies something false, then, of course, we could not rationally continue to believe that our position is true. So, in addition to articulating the implications of our answers to questions, we must also seek to justify our assumption that these implications are true.

This is why philosophical inquiry seems to be neverending. However, once we recognize these qualities, we see why Plato and Aristotle, Descartes and Leibnitz, Kant and Hume are the great thinkers they are. Unlike most of us, they have the capacity to put off bringing their thinking to an end until they have stretched it beyond the bounds that usually confine man's reflective capacities. When faced with the choice of being more or less arbitrary, they choose to be less so. They have the patience to think with care about the problems that philosophy brings to our attention.

Philosophy is also able to bring to our attention problems of whose existence we would otherwise be unaware. For example, the problem of how we know, if we do, that there is a physical world that exists external to us, or that there are other minds that exist in addition to our own, are problems of which most of us would have been unaware, had it not been for the disciplined inquiry of such a thinker as Descartes. It is in this, if in no other, respect that philosophy is a "mind-expanding" study. And lest it be thought, a priori, that such problems are stupid and a waste of time, it is worth noting that many thinkers, especially those of a mystical bent, would deny that there is a physical reality and that there are individual minds that exist. Thus, to dismiss these questions out of hand reflects a prejudice, which it is a goal of philosophy to remove.

It is important to emphasize that philosophy *is* a discipline. Those who practice it take on the responsibility of disciplined thinking, of thinking clearly and rationally—in a word, logically. They must come to that point of reflective maturity where they see that beliefs are not true just because they have been taught that they are or just because they make them feel psychologically secure. For example, when Leibnitz developed his theory of parallelism, he did not first ask what everybody believes about the mind and the body, and then go on to develop his theory. And part of the greatness of Descartes's thought consists in his willfully abandoning, at least for the sake of argument, the most psychologically stable and reassuring ideas—for example, that we have a body. These philosophers also show us that, despite the great emphasis on rigor and discipline, philosophy is not necessarily dry and unimaginative. What could be more inventive than Descartes's "malign genius" hypothesis or Leibnitz's "solution" to the mind-body problem? And yet, despite the beauty of the creative imagination, they never lose sight of the goal of disciplined inquiry. What is sought is not merely an idea, but the argumentative means to back it up. No philosopher would be content to be told that he had "a good idea." What he wants is a true one.

A final point is that philosophers are constantly reevaluating the soundness of the assumptions that gain a foothold in the discipline. For example, before the positivist introduced the verification theory of meaning, it was tacitly assumed that the use of any grammatically complete sentence in the indicative mood expressed a proposition. Thus, it was not thought necessary to show that the theist's use of "God exists" expresses a proposition; everyone thought he was entitled to assume it did. But the positivist made clear that this *was* an assumption and so stood in need of clarification and justification.

Another example is the concepts of analytic and synthetic propositions, which we introduced in Chapter 3 and then used to set forth the most general and important classification of knowledge claims—namely, synthetic a posteriori, synthetic a priori, and analytic a priori. But how adequate are these concepts? When pressed can we give a satisfactory explication of how they should be understood? Some recent thinkers have expressed doubts. For example, when we said that a proposition that is analytically true cannot be *conceived* to be false, we did not explain *why* this is so.

Now, if we ignore those propositions that are said to be analytically true because of their logical form, and concentrate instead on those that are said to be true because of their meaning, the difficulties become even more apparent. Suppose we say the proposition 'A spinster is an unmarried woman' is true because of its meaning. This statement seems to imply that the expressions "a spinster" and "an unmarried woman" are *synonymous;* that the two expressions *have the same meaning*. We are saying, in effect, that '*X* is *X*'. Then our problem becomes, how shall we give an explication of the concept of synonymy? For that we must give such an explication is clear from the fact that we rely upon this concept in giving an explication of the concept of analyticity. So our question is, when are two expressions synonymous?

Suppose we say that two expressions, 'X' and 'Y', are synonymous if and only if the proposition 'X is a Y' is analytically true. Thus, if 'X' is "a spinster" and 'Y' is "an unmarried woman," these two expressions are synonymous if and only if the proposition 'A spinster is an unmarried woman' is analytically true. Now, since this proposition is analytically true, it follows that these two expressions are synonymous.

How natural this line of reasoning is! Yet how inadequate, as a moment's reflection will show. For the concept of synonymy was introduced in the first place to serve as a basis for distinguishing between those propositions that are analytic and those that are not. Therefore, one cannot argue that a given proposition is analytic *because* it contains synonymous expressions. That the expressions are synonymous is a *consequence* of the fact that the proposition is analytic, *not* vice versa. Accordingly, this attempt to explicate the concept of synonymy fails. Indeed, many recent thinkers believe there is *no* satisfactory way of explicating this concept, which is why they also maintain that there is no satisfactory way of stating the distinctions between those propositions that are analytic and those said to be synthetic. A very basic assumption of philosophy since Kant, therefore, can be questioned, and it is uncertain even to the present day whether its credentials can be proven sound.

This debate shows that philosophers periodically are obligated to rethink the assumptions they make. The activity of philosophy, in short, is open at both ends—both at the end of examining the assumptions we might make and at the end of examining what follows, both directly and indirectly, from these same assumptions. And, needless to say, this disciplined reexamination of assumptions must at times be directed to the nature of philosophy itself. That is why the nature of the subject remains today, as it has been in the past, a controversial matter.

This also is why the definition we proposed of the subject should call for further reflection. For even if we were to agree that philosophy is the search for good arguments to support claims made in or about metaphysics, ethics, and so on, it still remains to be asked what constitutes a good argument. The model of a good argument we have used throughout this book is that of a formally and informally valid *deductive* argument containing premises known to be true. But is this the *only* model of a good argument that should find a place in philosophy? As might be expected, philosophers disagree on this point. But it is, nonetheless, for reasons too obvious to enumerate, one that needs to be addressed again and again throughout our growth as practitioners of the discipline we are trying to understand.

DOES PHILOSOPHY YIELD KNOWLEDGE?

Predictably, once we realize how open-ended philosophical inquiry is and have tasted the rich variety of answers philosophers give, we might begin to wonder whether philosophy can be anything more than intellectual gymnastics. Is it only a series of more or less difficult stunts (which some find exciting and others find dull) that fail to add to our storehouse of knowledge? After the dust of the debates over God, freedom, and immortality has settled, we still want to know whether philosophy does yield any knowledge.

This important question goes to the very heart of the discipline. But it also raises a question that is itself philosophical: "What is knowledge?" This question has been running between the lines of this book since its beginning. Yet it is not a question we have tried to conceal. As we stated at the end of our discussion of free will, the solution of that problem seems to depend on how adequate an account we can give of the concept of introspective knowledge. We have also challenged the positivist's account of knowledge on different occasions, and in other contexts have raised questions about the nature, variety, and extent of human knowledge. Still, we have not ventured to say what knowledge is, and even now, when we shall do so, we must express a cautionary word. The suggestion we are about to make is just that—a suggestion. We cannot come to a final conclusion about the nature of knowledge but only indicate a fruitful way in which it can be conceived.

One thing is clear: if a person knows that a proposition is true, then that proposition is true. This is a point we noted earlier in our discussion of free will, and, as we remarked there, this is one respect in which knowledge differs from belief. For we cannot validly infer from the fact that a person believes that a proposition is true that it *is* true, whereas we can validly infer the truth of a proposition from the fact that a person knows it is true. Knowledge and belief, therefore, differ from one another and never should be equated. But despite their differences, knowledge and belief seem to be related, and, in fact, we can define knowledge by making use of the concept of belief in the following way: *knowledge is justified true belief.* Let us reflect on the meaning of this contention before considering its relevance to the question of whether philosophy yields knowledge.

Notice, first, that the definition does not equate knowledge and belief, and, second, does not even equate knowledge with *true* belief. That this would be a mistake is easy enough to show. Suppose a boy believes that the Pirates will win the World Series next year, and it turns out they do win. We would not say that the boy *knew* that they would do so. At most we would say he had a true belief that they would. And this is in harmony with the definition of knowledge before us. For, according to this definition, we should not say that the boy knew who would win next year's World Series because, though he believes truly that the Pirates will, we have no reason to believe that his true belief is *justified*.

What does "justified" true belief mean? A belief is justified if we can present reasons that support its truth. These reasons will vary from case to case. For example, the reasons that are relevant to justifying the belief that it will rain tomorrow differ from those that are relevant to justifying where or when the first man lived or whether a monster lives in Loch Ness. Moreover, how the relevant reasons support the belief also will vary. For example, the supporting reasons may provide inductive support in some cases and deductive support in others. We must recognize, in short, that how a belief can be justified will depend on what kind of belief it is— for example, empirical or mathematical—and that the reasons and proce- dures appropriate for justifying a belief of one kind may not be appropriate for justifying a belief of some other kind.

In general, then, in order to know that a given proposition, *p*, is true, two conditions must be satisfied: (1) *p* must be true, and (2) we must have good reasons for believing that *p* is true. Neither condition by itself is a sufficient condition of knowledge, but each is necessary, and when taken together they are sufficient.

Given these general remarks about the concept of knowledge, how do they shed light on the question of whether philosophy yields knowledge? They do so by making it possible for us to reformulate this question in different terms. For, assuming that knowledge is justified true belief, what we want to know, when we ask this question about philosophy, is whether the practice of the discipline ever leads to the justification of true beliefs. And once the question is reformulated, its answer seems straightforward enough—yes!

For consider: Should we say that we only believe, but do not know, that, say, the design argument is unsound or that, in general, there can be no sound a posteriori proof of God's existence? Or should we say that we only believe, but do not know, that indeterminism cannot give an adequate account of moral responsibility? Or should we say that we only believe, but do not know, that Kant's moral argument for survival is unsound? To say that we only "believe" these things is surely to say considerably less than what we are entitled to say. On what grounds might it be argued that we do not know these things? Are not the beliefs in each case true, and have we not provided good reasons in each case for thinking so? And if we recognize that both these conditions have been fulfilled, how could it be reasonable to insist that we do not know, but only believe, these things?

The claims of philosophy as a source of knowledge can be made clearer still. Imagine that Jones has followed the criticisms we have raised against the design argument. And suppose he also has followed our discussion of personal survival after death. Suppose, finally, that he believes that the design argument is unsound, but that, despite the problems raised concerning life after death, he still believes that persons will survive the death of their bodies. Should we say that Jones's beliefs are just that—beliefs? This would not tend to clarity. His belief that the design argument is unsound is a true belief, and he has good reasons for believing what he does. But his belief in personal survival after bodily death may be true *or* it may be false, and he has no good reasons for believing that it is true. Given these important differences between the two beliefs, it would be misleading to say that Jones just believes what he does. It is, rather, given our hypothesis about what knowledge is, that Jones knows that the design argument is unsound but does not know—he only believes—that persons survive the death of their bodies.

It seems reasonable to maintain, then, with this hypothesis, that the discipline called philosophy can yield knowledge—that disciplined inquiry in and about the branches of philosophy does enable us to justify some true beliefs. This is a point Socrates never tired of making; inexhaustibly he drew the distinction between "right opinion" (true belief) and knowledge (justified true belief). And this point also ties in vitally with our remarks about prejudices in the introduction to the book. There we stated that our prejudices are not necessarily our false beliefs but are those beliefs that we have failed to examine critically or sought to justify. They are beliefs that we accept and act on without duly considering the reasonableness of doing so. Assuming that knowledge is justified true belief, then, we can see why no prejudice, even if it should happen to be true, can be construed as knowledge. This is because, as a prejudice, it must be an unjustified belief, which necessarily rules out the possibility that it is a source of knowledge. Thus, for example, someone who believes that God's existence cannot be proven but who has never considered attempts to prove it cannot reasonably claim to know that God's existence cannot be proven. More than likely, indeed, this belief is a prejudice—that is, a belief for which the person can provide no good reason. It is, then, not so much a question of *what* a person believes as *why* he or she believes it that is of vital importance and that represents the basis in terms of which knowledge and opinion, justified true belief and prejudice, can be distinguished. To say that philosophy can yield knowledge, therefore, is to imply what was said about the discipline at the outset—that by practicing the discipline we can reduce the extent to which prejudice colors our view of the world and influences our interaction with it.

Problems remain, to be sure. We have not confirmed the thesis that knowledge is justified true belief. We have not even clarified this thesis sufficiently. We have merely scratched the surface of a fundamental problem in philosophy—perhaps, indeed, the most fundamental problem. But whether or not we will have the opportunity and interest to explore this problem further, at least this much seems clear: Any account of knowledge that implied that we only believe, but do not know, that, say, the design argument is unsound, must surely strike us as an inadequate account of the nature of knowledge. For in understanding that the argument is formally and informally invalid, and that it contains premises that are not known to be true, we have seen all that any rational being could rationally be expected to see prior to claiming to know that the argument is unsound. Thus, rather than demand that philosophy make good its claims to knowledge, any analysis of knowledge that would make good its claim to correctness must allow that philosophy does yield knowledge.

LOOKING AHEAD

Because of the open-ended character of philosophical inquiry, it is impossible to state precisely what direction anyone's thought will take in the future. Perhaps we will want to reexamine certain key assumptions we make. Or perhaps we will look to the implications of what we believe. Or perhaps, which is more likely, we will consider both. What problems we will turn to next are likewise indeterminate. Perhaps we will consider new areas of thought such as the foundation of law or the nature of art. Or perhaps we will return and reconsider one or another of the problems we have discussed. Examples of questions of this latter kind are provided at the end of this afterword. Whichever it may be, our objective, and some of our techniques, will be the same as they have been here. We will seek a clearer understanding of various beliefs and we will examine how good the reasons are for accepting them as true. The only limit that can be placed upon how much and how seriously we will choose to pursue these objectives is the dedication with which we choose to pursue them.

Not all readers will choose to pursue them with dedication. Perhaps some will choose not to pursue them at all, and it is understandable why this is so. Not everyone is disposed toward the study of, say, mathematics or history, and there is no reason to suppose that philosophy should differ from other disciplines in this respect. Philosophy requires of those who would pursue it certain habits of thought and character that not everyone possesses to the same extent. And it also is clear that the rewards of studying philosophy are not directly marketable or "utilitarian."

But we might want to consider whether this is a sufficient justification for not thinking philosophically. We might want to ask whether, even if we do not yet possess those habits that are required to practice the discipline of philosophy, we should decide not to try to acquire these habits on the grounds that they will not, say, help us find a better paying job or a more respected place in society. Now, to answer this question, we need to ask whether only those things that lead to an increase in material values are worthwhile. And it seems that, as soon as we seriously consider this question, we are led to a negative answer. Love and justice, compassion and friendship, beauty and understanding, knowledge and courage commend themselves to us as valuable. And their value does not seem related to the material benefits they may or may not bring with them.

So there does seem to be a range of values that are not valuable *because* they can be used to bring us greater material comfort, or such things as public recognition. And it also seems the valuable things that philosophy can bring to us are values that fall into this class. In particular, the practice of this discipline promises to make us less prejudiced than we were before we began our inquiry. And what shall we say of the value of being unprejudiced? Does it guarantee us a better job? More money? A finer home? It guarantees none of these things. But anyone who reduces the amount and effects of his prejudice is, to that extent, a better human being. The more prejudice we remove, the closer we are to a certain ideal— the closer we are to becoming what we *can* be, and what, in view of the value we attach to being a person of this kind, we *ought* to strive to become.

Ultimately, therefore, as Socrates saw over two thousand years ago, the justification for the study of philosophy has to do with what the practice of it can help us to become. So, even if we do not now have the habits and interests necessary to do philosophy, it does not follow that we should forego all future study of it. What one needs to determine is what type of person he thinks he ought to become and how much the practice of philosophy contributes to realizing this ideal. To the extent that this ideal includes the removal of prejudice, to that extent philosophy must find a place within those disciplines we have an obligation to pursue, even if, in order to practice them, we must change our present interests and habits— even if we must change ourselves.

But that should come as no surprise. To suppose otherwise is to assume that we can achieve our ideals without changing! Of course, if we should not happen to include freeing ourselves from prejudice as part of our ideal, then, to that extent, philosophy will find no place in our future. But we must ask whether we would be satisfied with an ideal of human nature in which being prejudiced was included, or in which not striving to rid ourselves of prejudice was excluded. Once again, it seems, we need only seriously to ask ourselves this question in order to find our answer: Such an ideal would not be satisfactory. Such an ideal would include in it *less* than what a truly good person can be. In looking ahead to the place that philosophy might play in our lives, therefore, we need to ask ourselves what our ideals are, how reasonable they are, and whether philosophy can contribute to our realizing them.

No thoughtful person can be satisfied with asking anything less. And every thoughtful person will recognize that, in even attempting to answer these questions, we will find ourselves doing the very thing whose value is in question. We will find ourselves practicing the discipline called philosophy.

FOR FURTHER READING

Passmore, John, *Philosophical Argument*. (New York: Basic Books, 1969). Explores types of argument that find a place in philosophy.

Russell, Bertrand, *The Problems of Philosophy*. Oxford: Oxford University Press. 1959. An excellent book with which to begin disciplined reflection on the problems of knowledge.

EXERCISES

In our effort to develop a systematic and complete *Weltanschauung*, it is of cardinal importance to avoid internal inconsistencies. That is, we must be sure not to affirm two beliefs that cannot possibly be true at the same time. If we do, then, of course, we will have failed to present a possibly true view of the world. It is worthwhile thinking back on some of those views we have discussed, therefore, and asking whether they form consistent pairs. This is one way we can determine which views we can, and which ones we cannot, include in our developing *Weltanschauung*. Let us ask, then, whether each of the following pairs of beliefs is consistent, taking the time, in each case, (1) to clarify, briefly, the views in question; (2) to indicate those reasons we may have for thinking that the two views are (or are not) consistent; and (3) to evaluate how sound are the arguments for or against their consistency. Are the following pairs of beliefs consistent?

1. Belief in the Judeo-Christian God and belief in indeterminism.
2. Belief in the Judeo-Christian God and belief in soft determinism.
3. Belief in the Judeo-Christian God and belief in libertarianism.

4. Belief in the Judeo-Christian God and belief in parallelism.
5. Belief in the Judeo-Christian God and belief in idealism.
6. Belief in libertarianism and belief in occasionalism.
7. Belief in libertarianism and belief in dualism.
8. Belief in parallelism and belief in indeterminism.
9. Belief in indeterminism and belief in occasionalism.
10. Belief in positivism and belief in ESP.

Index